THREE QUESTIONS OF FORMATIVE JUDAISM

THREE QUESTIONS OF FORMATIVE JUDAISM

History, Literature, and Religion

BY

JACOB NEUSNER

BRILL ACADEMIC PUBLISHERS, INC.
BOSTON • LEIDEN
2002

Library of Congress Cataloging-in-Publication Data

Neusner, Jacob, 1932–
    The three questions of formative Judaism: history, literature
and religion / by Jacob Neusner.
        p. cm.
    ISBN 0–391–04138–X (hc)
        1. Rabbinical literature—History and criticism. 2. Judaism—History—
Talmudic period, 10–425. 3. Judaism—Historiography.
I. Title.

BM496.5.N48257 2002
296.1'206—dc21

2002010728

ISBN 0–391–04138–X
Paperback ISBN: 0–391–04177–0

PRINTED IN THE UNITED STATES OF AMERICA

THREE QUESTIONS OF FORMATIVE JUDAISM

CONTENTS

PREFACE

In sustained work over nearly a half century, I have taken the measure of formative Rabbinic Judaism in its initial canonical statement, from the Mishnah (200 C.E.) through the Bavli (600 C.E.). This inquiry has involved that Judaism's history, literature, religion, and theology. Here I ask what questions I deem settled and what questions demand attention. What concerns me are not the successes but the failures. These address matters of fundamental conception and imagination and logic. So I ask, seeing matters whole and in retrospect: at what points have we yet to face unknown, and perhaps unknowable, issues of description, analysis, and interpretation of the formation of what became the normative Judaism; and what logic have we yet to pursue beyond the elementary steps?

I

This book began in two conversations, both in the presence of death, that never ran their course. The one was with Erwin R. Goodenough, the other with Harry A. Wolfson, the two greatest scholarly personalities I have known well. When Goodenough lay dying, some thirty-five years ago, I called on him and asked him to spell out some of the problems he would take up if he were given more time and how he would solve them. I sought his perspective on learning. I was too young to understand why, under the circumstance, this is not what he wanted to discuss with me. A few years later, in a comparable circumstance, I tried to encourage Wolfson to speculate along the same lines: "What questions have you settled, what questions have you neglected?" At that moment the answers were not high on his agenda. In both instances I meant to elicit some guidance from experienced, accomplished scholars, some sense of how scholars see their results whole and in perspective. I was looking for models of imagination. Neither occasion proved opportune; I had asked too late. But at that time I put in my mind the notion that if and when I reached old age, while still able and vital, I would take a moment to stand

back and take stock of what is to be done. As I approach my seven-
tieth birthday, July 28, 2002, I wish to think about the future of learning in my chosen field of study.

I take as my model in this quest for perspective the final issue of
the *Journal of the American Academy of Religion* under the decade-long
(1985–1995) and remarkable editorship of William Scott Green. This
last corporate statement of his he devoted to discussions by specialists
concerning the settled questions and open questions in the academic
study of religion. Each wrote about his or her field, and I wrote on
the academic study of formative Judaism. Chapter One recapitulates,
with important deletions and revisions, my contribution to that sym-
posium. And the chapters that form the heart of the book address the
same program.

What are at stake here are the ways not yet taken, perhaps in some
instances not even imagined. These failures—problems not yet solved,
not even addressed at all!—entail not matters of detail nor familiar
theses still requiring refinement. Corrections of fact or reasoning
come about through the slow but exceedingly fine grinding of the
wheels of scholarship. These chapters point to failures not of perception but of conception, and here I mean to correct at least some of
them. I do so by asking the same questions in addressing studies of
formative Judaism, its history, literature, religion: what questions do
I think are settled, and which ones do I recommend for further
inquiry? At stake in the answers are new perspectives, a fresh range
of large problems awaiting attention.

II

The formative age of normative, Rabbinic Judaism is recorded in the
texts of that Judaism that have survived. There is no other source that
attests to that system in all its distinctiveness. Among the approaches
to Rabbinic Judaism in the first six centuries C.E., I have limited
myself to the four principal academic disciplines that serve in the
study of a religion accessible to us only in documents, principally
those composing its canon—that is, the history, literature, religion,
and theology that the study of the canon yields. The logical movement is from context and history to text and literature, to matrix and
religion, and finally to systematics and theology. In this book I deal
only with history, literature, and religion.

HISTORY: In the encounter with the canonical documents of formative Judaism, we begin with the recognition that our documents attest to a particular time and place and circumstance. They form events, each on its own, in an intellectual and social context. Situating the documents in history—that is, finding their secular context in intellect and society—then, forms the initial labor of learning.

LITERATURE: But this requires more than merely paraphrasing, in our narrative, historical language, what the documents say in their language of law, lore, exegesis, analysis, dialectics, or exhortation. It demands that we form an account for ourselves of the character of the literary evidence: how does the way things are said signal the meaning and purpose of what is said?

RELIGION: And given the program of those documents, devoted as they are to questions of religion, some notion of the religious world that produced and privileged those writings is required. The systems and structures of religious constructions of the social order (whether in theory, whether even in practice) require proportionate description, analysis, and interpretation.

THEOLOGY: Now, religion without theology remains inchoate, a mass of random information. Theology in context means thinking philosophically about religion: seeking to discern the inner structures of ideas and how they cohere, attempting to state the foundations, in deep structures of the mind, of the applied reason and practical logic that come to expression in the details of religious belief and behavior.

So, starting with an interest in history inclusive of culture, we proceed naturally to an analysis of the artifacts of historical culture, then to their messages, and finally to the composition and construction that those messages comprise.

As it happens, these three disciplines in their logical order—history, literature, religion—as well as the omitted one, theology, also recapitulate the story of my successive scholarly phases to date. These phases overlap. I began as a historian with a biography and then a systematic history, proceeded to work in the analysis of the literature of formative Judaism, moved on to the study of the religious system and structure that animated those documents, and then took up a set of theological constructions that impart coherence to those same documents.

I now plan to take up a massive new problem, so this retrospect marks the conclusion of sizable exercises in almost fifty years of active scholarship. What follows will make its presence known in due course.

III

A brief glimpse at how these phases—history, literature, religion, the-ology—have unfolded in my oeuvre may prove of interest, so let me briefly summarize the main lines of my scholarly life, matching the rubrics of the bibliography provided at the end of this book.

My work for the past five decades has pursued a single problem, which is to explain how Judaism as we know that religion came into being. I have wanted to account for its success when and where it succeeded in its social goals and to explain the conditions of its fail-ure when it did not. While a field theory of the history of Judaism, from beginning to present, has indeed emerged, my principal inter-est, from beginning to present, has been in the formative age, the first six centuries C.E., from the destruction of the Jerusalem Temple and Israelite polity in 70 to the Islamic reconstruction of the Near and Middle East in the seventh century. It was between those two axial events that the books came to closure. These together with Scripture ("the Old Testament") form the definitive canon of Judaism as we know it. The canon set forth in written form the Judaic way of life, worldview, and theory of the social entity that it called Israel.

The work of description, analysis, and interpretation has carried me across the four indicated academic disciplines within the study of religion, in an overlapping sequence—(1) history, (2) literature, (3) (history of) religion, and (4) theology, as I have now suggested. On what foundations have I done this quite secular work? I conceive reli-gion to be accessible to this-worldly study when it is viewed as an account of the social order and the statement of a cultural system, and the problem of studying religion, in my view, is to explain the relationship between the religious ideas that people hold and the social world that they create for themselves.

To do this literary-analytical work, I have translated Rabbinic Judaism's canonical books into English, many for the first time, some for the second: the Mishnah, Tosefta, Talmud of the Land of Israel, Talmud of Babylonia, and all of the score of compilations of scrip-tural exegesis, called Midrashim, that came to closure in late antiq-uity, down to the advent of Islam in the seventh century C.E. My translations have provided all of the documents with their first refer-ence system (equivalent to Scripture's chapter and verse), so that form-analytical studies of the way in which the documents make their statement could get under way. I have further read each document as a coherent statement of a theory of (its) Israel's social order (I called it "system") and asked about the worldview, way of life, and theory of the social entity that each writing set forth. Finally, I have provided a systematic account of the formative history of Judaism as a problem in the history of religions, specifically, the problem of how the religion that people practice together relates to the world in which they live.

After my three dutiful but intellectually undistinguished under-graduate years at Harvard College and a postbaccalaureate fourth year overseas at Oxford University, I discovered my métier and began my life's work in October 1954, when I returned to the United States from a year at Oxford and entered the Jewish Theological Seminary of America. There, in the beginning of that month, I met the most interesting piece of writing I have ever studied, the Talmud of Babylonia (Bavli), and was converted to its intellectual discipline. It is a strange kind of writing, compelling but elliptical, requiring active engagement in the reconstruction of its discourse out of its signs and signals. I decided I would spend my life trying to take it apart and put it together again so as to find out precisely how it worked. From then to now I have walked an absolutely unswerving path, each step forward the logical outcome of the step before.

Before that time, throughout my education, I had found everything easy, obvious, and boring. But one course at Harvard truly kept the promise to educate, and that made all the difference. It was Leonard Nash and Thomas S. Kuhn's general education course in the area of the history of experimental science, later on yielding Kuhn's classic, *The Structure of Scientific Revolutions*. From Kuhn and Nash I learned about the negotiability of learning, the possibilities of more than a sin-gle construction of data, more than the established system and struc-ture to impart coherence and consequence to facts. Those were just the lessons needed to decipher the Rabbinic literature of the forma-tive age of Judaism, particularly the Talmud. But at that time, in the fall of 1950, I had never heard of the Talmud, nor did I know much more Hebrew than the alphabet and some simple grammar. Then where, outside the laboratory, was I to find that realm of conflicts over applied reason and practical logic that matched my natural pref-erence for the concrete over the abstract, but also the consequential over the self-validating fact? Four year later I found my answer. The

Talmud of Babylonia and the documents leading up to it provided that mediating ideal, a realm where truth in concrete form embodied abstract principle, accessible through reasoned criticism.

So, meeting the Talmud and the other documents that it represented introduced me to my life's work. From kindergarten through Oxford, nothing much had ever challenged me, and most subjects seemed to me either obvious or trivial. In high school I loved algebra and geometry, but I never realized their possibilities and, faced with the choice of language or mathematics, chose to start another language. And like natural science in those days, it required memorizing formulas, not understanding processes. But the Talmud joined logic to process, its dialectics dazzled, its range of reason compelled concentration, even more than the algebra and geometry that I had so admired. From that month, October 1954, onward, I met my challenge, and soon afterward I was to be on my own, trying to understand the writing of great intellects engaged in the solution of massive, urgent problems of thought. I was never bored again. And from teachers I required only information and guidance, never motivation or inspiration.

Five periods over these nearly fifty years mark the divisions of this single project of mine. In the first, 1954–1964, I completed my formal education and postdoctoral studies in cognate subjects—besides the Judaic ones, in ancient history (Roman and Iranian), earliest Christianity, Zoroastrianism, Syriac, Armenian, and the like, a smattering of Oriental knowledge. In the second, overlapping period, 1960–1980, I thought of myself as a historian and wrote mainly history. During that time I called into question the validity of the utilization of the Judaic religious sources for answering the kinds of questions historians asked, and further came to the realization that the Judaic system behind the writings I studied answered questions different from historical ones.

Trying to find out precisely what questions the sources addressed, I moved from the study of history to the literary analysis of the forms and structures of the canonical documents of Rabbinic Judaism in its formative age. I invented form-analysis of Rabbinic literature and carried it out in my translations during this period, 1970–1980, and, further, produced the first of my explanations of those writings.

The third, also overlapping period, 1975–1990, marked the transition from historical and literary study to the study of the documents' religion. I turned to the history-of-religions study of Rabbinic Judaism in its formative writings, with emphasis upon its ideas. I had to devise a program of inquiry into religion and a means of accomplishing that program. For the program, I drew upon the reading of religion as a cultural system and adapted ideas in circulation with the conception of "a Judaism." By this I meant a religious system of the social order involving a way of life, worldview, and theory of the social entity that carried out the one and explained itself (who belongs, who does not belong) by appeal to the other.

But what sort of history of the religion at hand did I conceive plausible? As I grasped the literary structure and conceptual system of documents and began to see how one document related to others, I formed a theory of the character of the Judaism that the documents, each in its way, addressed or re-presented in context. I read the successive documents, from the Mishnah to the Bavli, within the interpretative model of a religious system, and then composed what I called "a documentary history of ideas" out of the results of systemic comparison and contrast. My work in the history of religion with special emphasis upon formative Judaism, moreover, required setting in historical context a multiplicity of Judaic systems besides the Rabbinic one that has predominated. That effort did yield the field theory of the history of Judaism that I had hoped to formulate.

But, by now predictably, the third period also contained within itself the beginnings of a fourth, the period devoted to hermeneutics and shading over, in due course, into the fifth, theology, which I have just now completed. From the later '80s to the late '90s, I shaped a set of inquiries into the hermeneutics of the two Talmuds in particular. I furthermore keep in view a broader, now systematic theological interest. What I wanted to know through the detailed examination of problems of structure and system—hermeneutics of a concrete order—is how the intellects whose writings I study made connections and drew conclusions, what theory of mind told them what they wished to know and how to find it out. In this quest for an explanation of the principles of self-evidence that govern in Judaism, I produced a commentary to both Talmuds, along the way also revising my prior translations, and to the large structures of the Midrash compilations of late antiquity. For a religious system works out, in vast detail, a few simple ideas. In the principles of selection and exegesis—the making of connections and drawing of conclusions that, in the case of Judaism, embody the faith's applied logic and practical reason—God lives.

The fifth period, 1994–2001, moved from the results of this rather sizable project in hermeneutics to take up, for systematic theological purposes, the results of this study of intellectual problems. I identified what I conceive to form the primary, cogent Rabbinic theological structure. I laid heavy emphasis upon its generative logic and its category formations, as these category formations sustained both law and lore, action and attitude, Halakhah and Aggadah. This is the work that has been completed. Coming to the end made urgent the question answered in these pages: where now? In these pages the logical answer becomes clear: a large problem of literature awaits systematic attention, bearing in its wake implications for historical and religious study of formative Judaism in its canonical representation. The question is, what of a non- or extradocumentary reading of the same canon? That is what I now take up.

IV

I benefited from conversations on this project with Professor William Scott Green, University of Rochester, for which I express to him my thanks.

Jacob Neusner
Bard College

CHAPTER ONE

SETTLED ISSUES, NEGLECTED QUESTIONS IN THE STUDY OF FORMATIVE JUDAISM

Here I exemplify both sides of the thought-problem taken up in this book: what do I think we now know, and what do I think is worth trying to find out? That is what I mean by the three questions—history, literature, religion—of formative Judaism. Here I begin with what I mean by a settled issue and a neglected question. I offer two examples of each. Two settled issues, in my judgment, are, first, that for antiquity we deal with data deriving from a number of distinct Judaic systems of the social order, or Judaisms, and, second, that the principal focus of learning is no longer history but religion (*Religionswissenschaft, Religionsgeschichte*). Two open questions are that the theory for the dating of documents remains to be debated and that the contemporary exegesis of the Bavli in an academic framework and in accord with the program of inquiry characteristic of the Western humanities has begun in only a primitive way.

The questions I deem settled today preoccupy some, but most scholarship acknowledges the diversity of the data concerning Judaism, and much learning concerns itself with religious ideas and institutions rather than with political events as in the past. So by "settled," I mean that the preponderance of learning has shifted, not that no one is doing what I think of limited interest and utility.

On the other hand, I too share in the neglect of the latter two, the neglected questions. These—dating documents, contemporary exegesis of principal documents—do not figure in the program I lay out in this book. I have concentrated on problems of Rabbinic religion and culture and have relied on the existing consensus for dates for documents, on the one side, and for detailed exegesis of words and phrases, on the other. While these therefore are not questions on which I have worked, they do show how one might ask and answer even the most fundamental, programmatic questions of learning.

In the substantive chapters that follow, I set forth further realizations of the same task with special reference to issues I find both urgent and congenial: questions I have begun to answer.

I. Settled Issues: 1. From Judaism to Judaisms

Academic learning no longer takes seriously the proposition that there is now, or ever in history has been, a single Judaism that defines the norm by which all allegations about what "Judaism" or "the Torah" teaches or imagines are measured. Books on Judaism in the formative age that posit a single, normative Judaism grow fewer, and those that analyze rather than synthesize Judaic data multiply. Moreover, dismissing as heretical or sectarian the bodies of evidence that do not conform to the law or theology of that official Judaism, in the manner of George F. Moore or Ephraim E. Urbach, no longer gains a serious hearing outside the Rabbinical schools and their secular national-ethnic counterparts overseas. And even there we find stirrings of doubt.

Furthermore, and more decisively still, textbooks that purport to describe such a single official Judaism rarely are adopted; they go out of print. But textbooks that differentiate among Judaisms go from printing to printing. So the coming generation is educated to deal with the complexities of the data. Dissertations on such a theoretical foundation as a single Judaism everywhere paramount rarely are written, and their authors seldom find secular positions. In all, the fabrication, for descriptive purposes, of "normative Judaism" or "Orthodox Judaism" for late antiquity nowadays meets with not so much incredulity as sheer indifference. Efforts to respond to the multiplicity of Judaisms take the place of a single Judaism, and whether these appeal to the lowest common denominator or allege what was essential to all Judaisms, they respond to the new episteme: not Judaism but Judaisms.

Until the recent past, that is not how matters have been. In standard usage in still-in-print monographs involving both Judaism and Christianity, the word "Judaism" served to signify pretty much whatever the user wants—and to stand for, impose itself upon, the entirety of the data produced by "the Jews" or the single religion, Judaism. This unclarity not only does not consign the word to desuetude; it secures for it wide usage. The religion contained in the holy books of

Israel, the holy people (a theological construct), from the nineteenth century in the West came to be called Judaism, the native category for most Judaisms being "the Torah." From the beginning of Christianity, it became important for Christians to define themselves in comparison with, and contrast to, the corpus of faith that rejected their claims, thus "Judaism" as against "Christianity." And to this day, "Judaism" serves as a critical analytical category for New Testament scholarship.

Accordingly, that religion, Judaism, was conceived to form an -*ism*, that is, a systematic and orderly construction of ideas about fundamental matters. If we wished to know what Judaism was, we had to open the holy books and find out. Where we found contradictions— for example, God is represented both anthropomorphically and not— the conflict was resolved in one of three ways. Either (very commonly) one text was normative, the other sectarian; or (rarely) the issue was dismissed as one on which Judaism took no position at all; or (also commonly) the contradiction was ignored, with the claim that the essential of Judaism was belief in one God, and trivial details concerning how God was supposed to be represented (thought about, known) were to be dismissed (often in the self-evidently spurious, self-serving claim "Judaism has no theology"—whatever that can ever have meant). This same Judaism, of course, had a history, beginning for the faithful at Sinai with God's revelation of the Torah to Moses, or beginning for the secular-minded with Ezra's writing up of the Torah book out of the received traditions (a much less common option); that history was single, harmonious, unitary, incremental, and traditional. We could therefore speak of one Judaism, with variations and exclusions, and at any given point determine what was old and what was new in that Judaism.

Books about that Judaism generated conflict; issues concerning the definition of the normative, the selection of canonical writings, the disposition of sources out of harmony with the main lines defined such debate as took place. In the context of contemporary theological debate between Judaisms, Reform accounts of Judaism contradicted Orthodox ones, of course, and the latter denied to the former the standing of authenticity, even while the former appealed to "history" to prove that change had precedents, reform was legitimate, and Reform Judaism came forth as a natural outcome of a "stream" or "current" in the unitary, harmonious, historical, therefore authoritative and authentic Judaism. The upshot was, polemics replaced probity. Politics overwhelmed learning. Thus, if you knew who paid a scholar, you also knew what he thought about anything of consequence, not to say what meetings he attended, where he published his books and articles (if any), and what he ate, or did not eat, for breakfast.

But the issue of a single Judaism involved a secular component as well: a single Jewish people (realized in due course in the founding of the Jewish state, the state of Israel). So in another arena altogether, Zionist historians wrote the history of "the Jewish people," meaning one, coherent social entity, with a single, linear, incremental, unitary history; periodizations, of course, distinguished the ancient, medieval, and modern, with the advent of the national movement, then the formation of the Jewish state, defining the contemporary and imposing perspective and order on all that had come before. Under religious and secular auspices, therefore, the study of Judaism and of the Jews rehearsed the category "Judaism" professed by the Jewish nation. In this iron consensus of unities, Christian scholarship was happy to concur: Judaism was an ethnic, national religion, in contrast to the universality and transnational character of Christianity. Or to put it differently: Christianity truly brought the God of (ancient) Israel to all humanity.

That is how matters stood until the final third of the last century. But now people realize diverse data attest to distinct Judaic systems. They are not to be forced into a single -*ism*, and no one tries to harmonize all the data, on the one side, or to pick and choose the theologically correct data, on the other. In the academic, not-theological, and not-ideological study of ancient Judaism, "Judaism" therefore has nearly everywhere given way to "Judaisms," a brief way of stating a complex category formation.

So it is now a settled question that, for antiquity, we can find no single Judaism practiced everywhere. We have diverse bodies of writings, which scarcely acknowledge anything in common beyond Scripture. We identify various social groups through archaeological evidence, asking about the interplay of religion and the social order, and then discover that correlating archaeological and literary evidence presents enormous difficulties for those who wish to harmonize everything into a single Judaism. The conception of a unitary, continuous, incremental "Jewish law," with a beginning, a middle, and a conclusion (for example, in the Talmud of Babylonia) scarcely correlates with the consequences of archaeological challenges to some of the laws of documents or with the literary evidence, for example, from Elephantine and from Qumran, harmonized only with difficulty with law found in later documents. Analytical questions addressed to diverse documents produce diverse and contradictory answers.

If, therefore, we ask the same question of any of the bodies of writing deemed to coalesce—apocalyptic, Rabbinic, that of Christians who identify themselves as Israel, that found in the Dead Sea library, Philo's, Josephus's, not to mention Jewish writing in Greek and Aramaic, the diverse translations of Scripture being only one, if enormous, body of evidence—what answers emerge? Each will give a well-formed answer that stands entirely on its own and excludes and contradicts all the others. Whether we ask about God, or Torah, or Israel—to identify the three generative categories generally thought to serve any Judaic religious system (standing for the system's ethos, ethics, and ethnos)—what we find is everything and its opposite. We address neither a uniform corpus of ethnic traits nor a coherent body of universally affirmed theological ideas. Indeed, the real question now demanding attention has shifted. If Rabbinic Judaism constitutes a single, coherent Judaism, as is presently broadly (and I think rightly) taken as fact, then can we find a set of premises that animate all of its canonical writings, and if so, where and how are we to locate them? The analytical program has now come to a problem of inductive synthesis.

Now in the world of sectarian learning, with its iron social rule that there is a "we" that is right and a "they" that is not so much wrong as undeserving of a hearing altogether, the conception of a single unitary Judaism forms an absolute. Since people know from everyday observation that they form a single, unitary, harmonious community of Judaism (or Jewishness), and since they can trace their beginnings in a linear and incremental development from some prior moment or point of origin, the facticity of a single Judaism—theirs in particular—accords with the givens of the social world. In the academy, by contrast, with its plurality of participants and diversity of perspectives, that given faces challenge. Explanations of why one set of writings is normative, another sectarian, find little hearing, such judgments being dismissed as "theological," not deriving from traits of the data themselves. Not only so, but as catholic and Protestant scholarship on the New Testament has found entirely plausible the conception of diverse communities of Christianity, each setting forth its encounter with Jesus, that same scholarly world has found entirely natural the notion that there was more than a single Judaism.

Consequently, efforts to explain away the diversity of data, or to define an "essence of Judaism," or to pick and choose among the data the writings that were normative—these efforts mount a holding action, a last-ditch defense of conceptions that have lost plausibility. The essentialist, lowest common denominators that have found a hearing—for example, any Judaism will believe this and practice that—never succeed in dealing with diversity; presenting the proposed essential Judaism to any corpus of writing yields only a simple judgment: necessary but not sufficient. That is to say, it is true that this Judaism did affirm these essential teachings, but it formed them into a statement of its own or it assigned to them far less consequence than the claim of essentiality leads us to expect. Above all, if we ask whether by appeal to the proposed essence we can explain what is distinctive, particular, and therefore characteristic of any one Judaism, the answer is always negative. The proposed essence or common denominator serves to distinguish any and all Judaisms from any and all other religious systems; that is the contribution of essences or lowest common denominators. But such is never sufficient to account for the social world that produced and valued a given body of writing, to describe and analyze and interpret its Judaic system. That explains the judgment of necessary but not sufficient, which is to say, the (proposed) common denominator is necessary to all Judaisms but insufficient to describe, analyze, or interpret any one of them.

A further trait of the academy's interest in the study of ancient Judaism requires attention. The academy takes shape, in the study of the social order, in not only humanistic but also social-scientific disciplines, and when religion is studied, interest focuses upon not only the beliefs people held—read philosophically (or theologically)—but also the social order that they aspired to make or actually made together. Religion forms a cogent statement of a social world, sets forth a cultural system, answers questions of social coherence and control. Religion is read therefore as not something personal, private, and merely intellectual but as a statement by a group of people concerning what they make together; it is public, communal, and subject to reasoned analysis as a this-worldly fact. Hence, in the academy, a principal interest in the study of any religion addresses the social ecology of that religion.

By the ecology of religion I mean the interplay between a religious system and the social world that gives to that system its shape and meaning. To me, when we understand a religious system in the context of the social order, we grasp whatever in this world we are likely to understand about religion in the shaping of the civilization of humanity. And no other generative force in civilization has exceeded in power and effect the formative force of religion. The social task of the academy—to explain the world that humanity has made for itself—requires close attention to how people formulate their conceptions of the social order. The study of ancient Judaism in the academy therefore is focused through the larger problem of how to relate the content of a religion to its context, social culture to religious conviction; and, above all, social change, which is public and general, to symbol change, which is particular and invariably distinctive to its setting. At stake in the study of the ecology of religion is whether and how religion forms an independent variable in the shaping of civilization.

In that context, the question—who in particular held what idea, how that idea fitted together with other ideas held by persons in that same social group, and in what way said ideas formulate a statement in response to the social world formed by those who held them—in its several parts simply sets aside as implausible the notion of a single Judaism, whether formulated in its essence or in its lowest common denominator or, all the more so, in its theological norms. Once we ask questions of a social character about the relationship of religion and society, constructs of a merely intellectual character no longer serve to sort out complex data, and they obstruct any sort of plausible inquiry. For, once people insist upon the social question, seeing religion not as a set of ideas in the abstract but as a statement of a community or a set of communities, the possibility of defining a single Judaism that can encompass all Judaic data or explain some and explain away others no longer proves compelling or even very important. True, Christian theologians find convenient the conception of a single Judaism as a foil to a single Christianity; but the unitary, incremental Judaism that they define for themselves rarely finds its way into other than theological discourse.

The upshot is simple. The issue, how we define Judaism, is now settled: we do not. We define Judaisms, and the first step in the work of definition requires identifying the particular Judaic community that stands behind a given set of writings or that values and lives by those writings. All analytical work in the academy proceeds from this premise, and books on Judaism that posit a single, unitary, incremental Judaism, deriving from Sinai through written and oral tradition, command slight attention these days. In this context, books that claim to define essential Judaism or common-denominator Judaism simply ratify the change that has taken place; in the sectarian world, people did not find urgent the problem that such books propose to solve. Consequently, we find ourselves asking theological questions concerning the coherence of discrete truths, but we propose to answer those questions not out of doctrine but, for literary study, out of hermeneutics. Precisely where the Jewish-sponsored centers of learning alleged to locate their greatest strengths—exegesis of texts, philology, even text criticism—the academy has now to carry its venture. For we cannot abdicate the gravest intellectual responsibility of all: the reading of the texts in the new, and sole right, way. That issue has been settled.

II. Settled Issues: 2. From History to Religion

The Israeli and secular-Jewish-sponsored centers of the study of Judaism, carrying forward the Teutonic tradition in which they originated, want to answer questions of hard historical fact, taking for granted that the texts sustain such questions. They further treat it as an axiom that history—"precisely what happened"—defines what matters about the Rabbinic documents, tells them what they wish to know. The secular academy, by contrast, commonly centering the study of ancient Judaism in departments of religious studies, brings to bear questions of religious study and interpretation. An apparent paradox, then, emerges. When the believers and ethnics read the text, they seek secular facts, and when outsiders read the text, they want to understand the realm of faith and imagination, the religious construction of an imagined social order, that forms the interiority of the text. But the paradox is readily resolved when we realize that, excluding the religious centers formed by Yeshivas in the Diaspora and in the state of Israel, all the Jewish-sponsored centers of the study of Judaism find their energy in an ethnic, not in a religious, episteme. They celebrate the ethnic group, the Jews, conceived to have a unitary, harmonious, linear, and coherent history. They appeal to (fabricated, imputed, often sentimental) unities of history and ethnicity to explain why, on the basis of history and culture, not religion, this ethnic group should continue to endure. And to that celebration and appeal, the facts of history bear self-evident, self-validating meanings.

The two principal theories that in the parochial setting define the Jews—both religious (Reform, Conservative, Reconstructionist) and nationalist (Israeli university) scholarship on Judaism—for different reasons concur on the primacy of historical knowledge, always meaning *precisely how things were*, in the study of the writings of formative Judaism. Facts bear imperatives, whether moral, whether ethnic and national. They validate, they justify, they resolve conflict. Child of post-Hegelian theology, Reform Judaism commenced with the claim that historical knowledge ("history") forms a reliable tool for the reformation of Judaism. Proposing to control and manipulate the corpus of precedents for change that would legitimate future reform as well, the Reformers maintained that change was all right because historical precedent proved that change was all right. It pays to dwell on this point, since only when we grasp why historical fact carried heavy theological weight shall we understand the character of Jewish learning in parochial auspices.

What provided the justification for the changes was the theory of the incremental history of a single, linear Judaism, and it played a powerful role in the creative age of Reform Judaism. The ones who made changes and founded Reform, then Conservative Judaism—and hence their Rabbinical schools—rested their case, first of all, on an appeal to the authoritative texts, read historically (as a collection of irrefutable facts). Change is legitimate, and these changes in particular are wholly consonant with the law, or the tradition, or the inner dynamics of the faith, or the dictates of history, or whatever out of the past worked that day. The justification of change always invoked precedent. People who made changes had to show that the principle that guided what they did was not new, even though the specific things they did were. So, to lay down a bridge between themselves and their past, they laid out beams resting on deep-set piles.

The foundation of change was formed of the bedrock of precedent.

And more still: change restores, reverts to an unchanging ideal. So the Reformers claimed not to change at all but only to regain the correct state of affairs, one that others, in the interval, themselves have changed. That forms the fundamental attitude of mind of the people who make changes and call the changes Reform. The appeal to history, a common mode of justification in the politics and theology of the nineteenth century, therefore defined the principal justification for the new Judaism: it was new because it renewed the old and enduring, the golden Judaism of a mythic age of perfection. Arguments on precedent drew the Reformers to the work of critical scholarship, as we shall see, as they settled all questions by appeal to the facts of history.

We cannot find surprising therefore the theory that Reform Judaism or Conservative Judaism or integrationist Orthodox Judaism (in the third case, via the figure of Maimonides) stood in a direct line with the prior history of Judaism. Each claimed to constitute the necessary, historically validated next step in the unfolding history of "Judaism," however defined. What we observed in considering the dogma of a single, unitary Judaism has now to register once more. Judaism is one. Judaism has a history, that history is single and unitary, and it was always leading to its present outcome: Reform Judaism. Others later on would challenge these convictions. Modern integrationist Orthodox Judaism insisted on the historicity of everything, producing precisely that natural outcome, the authentic, Torah-true, Orthodox Judaism; and other, self-segregationist Orthodox Judaisms would deny that Judaism ("the Torah") had a history at all. Conservative Judaism, calling itself "positive Historical Judaism," would discover a different goal for history from that embodied by Reform Judaism. But the mode of argument, appealing to issues of a historical and factual character, and the premises of argument, insisting that history proved, or disproved, matters of theological conviction, characterized all the Judaisms of the nineteenth century and therefore shaped the intellectual life of all Judaisms of the synagogue in the twentieth century as well.

The Judaisms of the age took shape in the intellectual world of Germany, with its profoundly philosophical and historical mode of thought and argument. Philology settled questions of theology and yielded historical fact, and principles of faith found definition in variant manuscript readings. So the challenge of political change carried with it its own modes of intellectual response: in the academic, scholarly framework. The method of the Judaism aborning as Reform exhibited a certain congruence to the locale. Whether Luther demanding reversion to the pure and primitive faith of the Gospels or the earliest generation of Reform leaders appealing to the Talmud as justification for rejecting what others thought was the contemporary embodiment of the Talmud's requirements, the principle remains the same. Reform renews, recovers the true condition of the faith, and selects, out of a diverse past, that age and that moment at which the faith attained its perfect definition and embodiment. Not change but restoration and renewal of the true modes, the recovery of the way things were in that perfect, paradigmatic time, that age that formed the model for all time—these deeply mythic modes of appeal formed the justification for change, transforming mere modification of this and that into Reform. And since all intellectual currents in Judaism in the West began with Reform Judaism, the powerful paradigm of historical research would deeply root itself in every place where, under Jewish auspices, the study of ancient Judaism flourished.

This observation brings us to the shift that now comes to conclusion. When the subject "Jewish studies," construed to transcend the study of Judaism, made its move into the academy, the one discipline that actively accorded it a welcome was the academic study of religion. History departments found slight interest in "Jewish history," not concurring with the Zionist and Judaic conviction that a single, unitary history written by the Jews everywhere and anywhere formed a historical episteme. Few history departments made appointments in Jewish history unless Jewish community funds paid for them; and then they focused on "the modern period" as a pretext to give Holocaust courses, which the donors wanted to foster. By contrast, many religion departments made appointments in Judaism without any outside support at all. As to the social sciences, they rarely make ethnic appointments, for example, Jewish economics, though area studies naturally accommodated the study of the state of Israel within the Middle East. In the humanities, where religion departments flourished, the academic study of Judaism found its home; where not, Jewish studies as a disciplinary potpourri defined the field. In religion departments, the secular historical program attracted slight interest, but the study of Judaism as a religion fit well into the study, along systematic lines, of a variety of other religions and especially their classical writings.

In place of the reforming program, which used philology and exegesis as instruments of change and had treated as secular—a matter of positive historical fact—writings with another focus altogether, the academic study of religion asked a different set of questions. These questions sidestepped and treated as null issues of whether a given rabbi said or did not say, did or did not do, what is attributed to him. The study of religion required reading the received writings as the canon, the coherent statement of a religious system, a Judaism comprising a worldview, way of life, and theory of the social entity Israel. To the description of Judaisms as statements of a social order grounded in a supernatural conviction, questions of historical fact, while not irrelevant, scarcely prove urgent. For what really happened on a given day and how a group of people formulated their shared life in response to, for example, the vocation of forming the Kingdom of God—these matters scarcely intersect.

But the issue never found its definition in whether things really happened, and the field did not redefine its agenda because people discovered in the 1960s and 1970s what mainstream scholarship in the New and Old Testaments had known from the time of Spinoza, which is, "It ain't necessarily so." The historical question had been asked too soon. But the historical-critical consideration formed a negative argument only. A positive one registered as well.

The field redefined the agenda away from history and toward religion because history massively missed the point of the documents on which everyone works. Interest shifted because people realized that once we have mined the sources for such historical information as they may contain, most of the sources and all of the truths they purpose to set forth form mountains of unassayed slag. History proved simply, monumentally irrelevant to the very sources that were supposed to contain history. History gave way to religion because of the recognition, a given in the study of religion, that the canonical writings of Judaism are fundamentally *religious* books, framing an account of a Judaic religious system.

A further factor in the decline of interest in history as the study of what really happened lay in the fact that the study of religion encompassed history within a different definition. The academy's insistence that a religious system deals in a fundamental way with an urgent and ineluctable question facing a social entity and that the system provides an answer deemed self-evidently valid to the question people confront—this redefined the study of history, as I shall argue in Chapter Two. The Judaisms of late antiquity, then, have come to form a laboratory case for the examination of religion and society: religion as something people do together to solve their problems.

Thus a different kind of history presents itself: the social and intellectual kind. In the canonical writings, as the academy reads them, authors speaking for communities have made statements about how they have worked out answers to critical and urgent problems that faced them. Read properly, these books tell us history of a different sort from the account of persons and events that earlier had been thought to emerge. In more general terms, conceiving that religion is the work of real people working together to solve pressing problems, the academy has worked out, as for other bodies of religious writings, a particular way of addressing the canonical writings. It reads them within the hermeneutics serviceable for religious writings that set forth the (to their authors) self-evidently valid answers that they have found to these problems. Read each on its own and then all together, the canonical writings form an account of the worldview, way of life, and theory of the social entity, the "Israel," that realizes the worldview in its everyday life and that we may call a Judaism. So the problem of the right reading of the canon is to discern the religion that the authors of documents meant to set forth for us. This is the framing of the matter that I claim to have innovated. The movement from history to religion as the focus of interest in the documents of formative Judaism took away the urgency of the question, whether it—a particular, one-time event—really happened.

This is not to suggest that all conventional history writing ceased— far from it. Some historians of the Jews, including historians of Judaisms, adopted the historical-critical program of historical study well established for Scripture in the academy. Many did not. Much paraphrase of Rabbinic stories, now converted into historical language, continued to serve. Indeed, in the Jewish seminaries and Israeli universities people still write articles on the personality of this rabbi and the events of such and such a time and place, and they write books using the Rabbinic writings to narrate the destruction of the Temple in 70, for instance, as though the Rabbinic narratives come to us from court reporters, accurately recording what was said, or from firsthand observers, or from journalists with a keen eye for accurate detail. The questions people think these sources reliably answer attest to those premises of gullibility and credulity on the veracity of the Judaic writings that, in biblical studies, are classified as "fundamentalist" and certainly as uncritical.

But outside sectarian institutions here at home and overseas, it is now a settled question that premises deemed unfounded in the study of Scripture (Old and New Testaments, for instance) have to be discarded also in the study of other Judaic writings. There is no longer any serious debate on why we should believe "our holy rabbis would not lie," and arguments for the historicity of attributions of sayings attract no considerable hearing and, where heard, are dismissed out of hand. What has shifted is the very program of inquiry deemed productive. Narrowly historical questions of politics, answered through paraphrases of Josephus or Rabbinic fables, no longer define academic inquiry. The times have changed, and two hundred years of the historical scholarship of the *Wissenschaft des Judentums* have concluded; the books and journals of that long age have become relics of a discarded past, mere curiosities of no interest for contemporary learning.

So the movement in the academy from history to religion also marks the end of the narrowly historical reading of religious writings for the formative age of Judaism. In the academy in North America and Europe, the old-style "history of the Jews in the time of the Mishnah and the Talmud," with its allegations as to facts supported merely by promiscuous citation, without analysis, of the line and page of a document's stories and sayings, limps along. But merely citing a story or saying as adequate evidence for what really was said and done hardly registers any longer in mainstream learning. The proof is simple. Most of that kind of credulous history is now published only in Hebrew, a mark of the disinterest of the writers in a hearing outside their setting and of their concession that outsiders to that setting will not likely take to heart the conclusions that are set forth. Talmudic history finds slight acceptance in the academy other than where Jewish theological or ethnic sponsorship pertains; everywhere else the study of the Rabbinic literature for the description, analysis, and interpretation of a principal Judaic system occupies the center of public discourse and debate.

III. Neglected Questions: 1. Dating Documents

Identifying neglected questions requires considerably less exposition than spelling out issues that have been settled, since, after all, fewer words suffice to say what we do not know than what we do. The governing generalization that characterizes all neglected questions is simple.

What the parochial setting takes as its own area of concentration remains in unsatisfactory condition, and the academy, with its distinct intellectual resources, has yet to ask questions beyond *its* conventional repertoire of religion and society.

That is because in the academy the study of religion is a generalizing science, as it should be, since religion so broadly characterizes the life of humanity. But in its interest in problems of theory and generalization, the study of formative Judaism has left to the sectarian scholars three problems that it has to address on its own. For, even in the areas of learning in which the parochial institutions are supposed to make their mark, the paucity of productive learning leaves enormous gaps in our knowledge. The Rabbinical schools and Israeli universities take pride in their mastery of texts, their ability to read any passage, whatever its origin, and their power of exegesis of them. But their areas of reputed and alleged strength—and the academy's areas of weakness—prove neglected, as a brief account shows.

First, no canonical document of Rabbinic Judaism bears the name, or the distinctive indicators, of individual authors or an identifiable group of authors. None bears anything like a date. And none comes to us in a manuscript tradition commencing near the time that, we think, the document was composed. Most come at the end of a long period of text transmission, for the character of which we have little or no manuscript evidence. We have yet to formulate a valid means for dating documents bearing no named author, coming to us in an indeterminate and sparse textual tradition. I cannot point to even a clear definition of what we might mean by assigning a date to a document. It is easier to explain what we do not now know than to define what we should want to find out.

The dates we do have depend upon the contents of a document and the attributions of sayings to named authorities within the document. These are notoriously unreliable criteria for dating documents, as the prevalence of pseudepigraphy in Scripture and other-than-scriptural

Judaic writings shows. The established protocol for dating a document rests on the premise that statements attributed to a given rabbi really were said by a historical figure, at a determinate time, and so permit us to date the document at the time of, or just after, that figure; if all the rabbis of a document occur in the Mishnah as well, then that document is assigned to the period of the Mishnah, called Tannaitic, and given a date of about 200. If the last-named rabbi of a document is assumed to have lived in about 500, then the document gets the date of 501. In general, documents presently are dated by reference to the names of the authorities who occur in them; for example, if the last-named authority is a rabbi who flourished in the Mishnah's period, the document as a whole is assigned to "Tannaitic times," that is, the first and second centuries, when, it is generally supposed, the Mishnah came to closure. But this mode of dating documents presupposes the reliability of attributions and does not take account of conventions of pseudepigraphy in the Rabbinic manner.

The same sayings may be assigned to two or more authorities; the Talmud of Babylonia, moreover, presents ample evidence that people played fast and loose with attributions, changing, by reason of the requirements of logic, what a given authority is alleged to have said, for instance. Since we have ample evidence that in later times people made up sayings and put them into the mouths of earlier authorities (the Zohar is only the best-known example!), we have no reason to assign a document solely by reference to the names of the authorities found therein. But no other basis for dating documents than gullibility about their contents has yet been devised, and since among the philologists and grammarians language usages are dated in accord with the dates of sages to whom sayings are attributed, philology provides no help whatsoever.

Second, dating presents other problems, some of which have been recognized forthrightly. Precisely *what* we date in dating a document proves less clear than once was supposed. Studies of the enormous variation in the text traditions and formulations of writings given the same title, for example, some of the so-called mystical texts, make us wonder what exactly we date when we assign a date to a document. Is it every word in the writing? Then what are we to make of the uncertain text tradition of every Rabbinic compilation, beginning, after all, with the Mishnah itself? But if the date does not situate at a determinate time (and place) the entirety of the document, then what in fact is alleged?

Third, a further problem arises in this context. If a document is assigned, for convenience' sake, to about 400 or about 600, people take for granted that the document accurately portrays the state of opinion not only at that specific time but for any time prior, the attributions of sayings to earlier authorities being taken at face value. It is commonly argued that merely because a saying occurs in a writing assigned the date of 200, this does not mean that the writing conveys no accurate information on opinions held prior to 200. If that view prevails, then we have to ask what else we know if we are supposed to know that the document was redacted (or reached closure) in 200. New Testament scholarship places a heavy burden on Rabbinic literature to portray the Judaism of the first century, the Judaism that Jesus and Paul knew. But nearly all New Testament scholars today rightly dismiss as uncritical the promiscuous citation, for that purpose, of Rabbinic writings dated many centuries after the first. Clearly, we have reached a negative consensus; it is time to frame a positive one, beginning with a clear formulation of what the dating of a document requires—and explains.

These and comparable problems on the dating of documents await rigorous reflection. Right now, we are working with the results of confused categories. The only fact now in hand is simple. We have a reasonably reliable order of writings, the Mishnah standing at the head of the line, the Talmud of Babylonia at the end, between 200 and 600. All histories of ideas formed on documentary lines tell us what came first and what then happened, but we have no clear knowledge of when the "first" or the "then" took place. When a well-grounded consensus on what we mean by a date for a document, as well as how we may determine the date of the document's contents, has taken shape, all historical work, including the histories of ideas that provide such academic history of the formation of Judaism as we now have, will be redone and, I think, even redefined.

IV. Neglected Questions: 2. Exegesis of the Talmud of Babylonia (the Bavli)

The *Wissenschaft des Judentums*, the academic study of Judaism, begins in the earliest decades of the nineteenth century. Now, two hundred years later, we still cannot point to the kind of systematic exegetical work that academic study promises and to why academic exegesis

yields insight and truth that the received exegetical tradition of the
Yeshiva world does not produce. Promising to produce "scientific"
texts and philology, the practitioners of the *Wissenschaft des Judentums*
have collected variant readings for a given document but rarely indicated the ones they prefer and why. They have conducted studies
of the meanings of words and phrases but produced, as modern dictionaries, works in English and in German that are now many decades, even a century, old. Alas, updated, systematic dictionaries
serving determinate documents are, though exemplary, still very few
and rare.

And as I shall try to explain, if the *Wissenschaft des Judentums* in its
contemporary realization has something compelling and systematic to
tell us about the principal Rabbinic documents, a way of approaching those documents with cogent hermeneutical thinking and systematic exegetical work based on that contemporary hermeneutics,
I cannot point to where it is to be found. Examples, yes, but encompassing and complete work, no. The great names in academic
Talmudic hermeneutics—for example, Emmanuel Lévinas—exemplify what has been done episodically but not in detail and completely, and the names of contemporary commentators, exemplified
by Adin Steinsaltz, stand for recapitulation and repetition and paraphrase of entirely familiar results of quite traditional methods. So far
as modern and contemporary scholarship of Judaism promised a new
reading of the received canon, it has yet to keep its promises.

The allegation that the systematic exegesis of the definitive statement of Rabbinic Judaism, the Talmud of Babylonia, awaits attention
will elicit surprise, and rightly so. How can anyone maintain that the
exegesis of the Talmud represents a neglected question when, after
all, the Yeshivas and some of the Rabbinical seminaries devote their
best energies to the study of that Talmud, its commentaries and codes
and the law based therein. They rightly maintain that the Talmud represents the law and theology of the entire Torah, oral and written,
which the world calls Judaism. They quite fairly point to an ancient
and complex hermeneutical tradition, to contending traditions at that,
in the exegesis of the Talmud. Not only so, but the American and
European Rabbinical seminaries as well as the Hebrew colleges
deservedly take pride in their studies of problems of philology and
exegesis. While, to be sure, they have yet to produce a complete dictionary for Rabbinic literature, a complete corpus of critical texts for

its main documents, and a reliable account of the meanings of words and phrases in context—the three tasks at which they claim to have excelled—still, the parochials have centered their best energies on problems of exegesis and philology. It is the simple fact that, in the past half century, marked by the growing prominence of the Talmud in public discourse, not a single sustained, ambitious, systematic exegetical enterprise has gotten under way; most of the work that has been done recapitulates received answers to conventional questions, forming a massive corpus of paraphrase, not an introduction in any provocative sense.

But exegesis of a text takes shape in response to the hermeneutics that defines how we wish to receive the document, and hermeneutics finds its definition in the intellectual framework of learning, whether theological, whether historical. Two bodies of received exegesis presently are deemed to suffice for elementary purposes.

The first exegesis is the paraphrastic and legal, given its definitive form in the Yeshiva world by the exegetical genius R. Solomon Isaac of Troyes ("Rashi"), 1040–1105. The simple meaning of words and phrases in context is conveyed by this exegetical mode, and the hermeneutics that comes to realization in this essential exegesis need not detain us; there is no reading of the Talmud without solutions to the problems of reconstruction into cogent statements of what are in fact notes on a conversation to be reconstituted by our own intellects. Rashi provides those solutions.

The second exegesis is the philological and text-critical, and this too conforms to the rule that exegesis is the child of hermeneutics. The critical program of the world of the Rabbinical seminaries and Israeli universities dictates the inquiry of philological and text-critical exegesis.

But it must follow that the new setting for the study of ancient Judaism and its texts has also to generate a third hermeneutics, and a consequent program of exegesis, the shape and structure of which are dictated by the intellectual forces in play where we are now working.

The exegesis that now is required takes shape in response to a simple fact: in the academy, we find our place within the same intellectual tradition that governed the intellectual lives of the framers of the Talmud itself. We understand the Talmud when it is properly mediated to us, because we are the children of the great tradition of intellect in which the Talmud too took shape. The Talmud is itself a philosophical document in the conventional sense in which "philosophy" refers specifically to the Graeco-Roman philosophical tradition. Formed in that same tradition, our minds therefore enter into the Talmud, requiring only a modest introduction to its particularities. That explains why we can join in the conversation, the spaces of silence leaving open to us a place even for our own active intellects.

This shared rationality explains the self-evidence of connections that are made, conclusions that are drawn. The matter of connection is prior. No document takes more for granted concerning relationships and connections, one thing to the next, than this one, and anyone reading this writing will find puzzling how one thing links to the last or the next. So a systematic exegesis in the setting of the academy must ask for an explanation of what was self-evident in the Yeshiva and seminary: *how do two matters (in the Talmud of Babylonia, meaning whole compositions set in sequence) relate, and what conclusions are we to draw from their deliberate juxtaposition by the Talmud itself?*

That is, the issue of cogency and coherence of Talmudic discourse demands systematic attention. Then the question about what the principal parts of a construction are and how they fit together comes to the fore. Large-scale issues of composition, traits of orderly discussion, now take priority. Also, because of the character of dialectical argument, with its tendency to strike out in new directions, it is easy to lose track of one's place in the large scheme of things. And, third, the implicit issues of a given, concrete problem require discovery and articulation. Abstract issues animate concrete discussions; they have to be identified. Finally, because Talmud study requires us to reconstruct much of the thought process and a fair part of the articulated arguments that are merely hinted at, signaled by the text before us, we have always to ask ourselves a harsh question: do we perhaps think we understand the text better than we do; have we not represented the text at hand more clearly than the words before us allow? This is the elastic clause, the open-ended egress, of all Talmudic study: an excess of certainty that we grasp what is before us.

But of the two questions above concerning exegesis in the academy, the second seems to me the most suggestive. Since the Talmud's discipline requires us to follow the shifts and turnings of a protracted analytical argument, the very dialectics of the document, to begin with, requires us to ask this question: what has this to do with that? And if we do not ask the question, we know for certain we are not following the argument at all. The program at hand demands that we examine the very character of the Talmud as a work of critical reflection, writing, and redaction: what does it say about a fundamental question, how does it make the successive parts of its statement, and in what manner do the components of the statement link together to form a whole that exceeds the sum of the parts?

The principles of exegesis may involve identifying these data in one passage after another:

(1) A Mishnaic rule is philosophical in its categorical structure:
(2) The Talmud examines that rule within the received Mishnaic categories:
(3) But there is a point at which the connection between one thing and something else requires elucidation, and this is the point at which, the Talmud (by definition) having fallen silent, we intervene.
(4) The work of exegesis then responds to the issue of connection when we explain the connections and draw the conclusions.

These principles point to the success of the Talmud's compilers and framers: they left space for generations to come to find a place for themselves in the discourse they precipitated. When the Talmud arouses our curiosity, it also leaves room for our own inquiry. Where a new point is not continuous with the other, the exegesis within the academy is going to ask why. Indeed, the connection between the exposition of the received categories of the Mishnah and the introduction of an entirely new consideration has to be established, that is, rationally explained. If we can draw a rational conclusion, a theological conclusion, from that odd juxtaposition, the adventitious intersection of two distinct compositions becomes a deliberate statement and imposes upon us the task of reasoned inquiry into the substance of that statement. It is at the specific point of discontinuity—the boundary marked by the conclusion of the Mishnah exposition by the Talmud, followed by the turning toward what is jarring and discontinuous—that our particular entry point opens up. Then we ask what this has to do with that. And we answer the question for ourselves. And this is the particular point at which we join the conversation; we do so by making a connection, or by explaining the

connection between what is merely juxtaposed but superficially discontinuous. Then we draw a conclusion from the connection we have
explained; the discord now has been resolved, harmony restored, a
single message formed out of two discrete statements.

The premise of all that has been said is that the Talmud is the way
its framers wanted it to be. The document conforms to its teleology;
we may seek out the connections between this and that and draw
rational conclusions from those connections. This we do by explaining how what is juxtaposed in fact interrelates. So, if the compilation
of the Talmud is deliberate and not simply the juxtaposition, without
purpose, of thematically congruent materials, then the Talmud makes
a powerful statement not only through the contents of its compositions (which really form the nouns of its sentences) or the context
defined by its composites (the verbs of the sentences) but also through
the selection, formulation, and presentation of the whole—which is
what we mean by hermeneutics, the explication of a received text and
the rules thereof.

Read from start to finish, from one Mishnah paragraph to the conclusion of its Talmud, the Talmud turns out to make a statement, not
merely collect relevant composites of compositions. So the hermeneutics of the Talmud consists in showing the connections between
things; the theology of Judaism as re-presented by the Talmud, the
formulation of the two Torahs, oral and written, as one, emerges
from drawing conclusions on the strength of making connections.
And, it is self-evident, these things being left implicit in the text for
us to discover, the hermeneutics dictates the asking of questions concerning what is not said or even suggested, meaning, in this case,
what one thing has to do with something else. I could not find a better way of saying what the academy takes as a principal intellectual
task than this—making connections, drawing conclusions from things
people have formerly thought unrelated.

The next important task in the study of formative Judaism calls for
the rereading of the definitive document of that Judaism, which is the
Talmud of Babylonia. In no publication in any language at this time
do we find a reading of the whole, or of any of its parts, that sees the
document in a coherent way, as a cogent statement. Talmudic exegesis goes forward with no articulated hermeneutics, and the meanings of words and phrases, on the one side, or the episodic and
unsystematic search for the original wording and meaning of passages

now in hand, on the other, define the current work of Talmud commentary. That work is ignored in the Yeshiva world because it answers no questions important to that world. And it also contributes nothing to the humanistic reading of the document, since the exegetes have no grasp whatsoever of the entirety of the document they purpose to explain, only its bits and pieces. We may now say with some certainty that the greatest authorities of the Talmud in the twentieth century really did not understand Rabbinic literature, since they saw only the twigs, never the branch, never the tree, never the forest. It follows that if the academy is to do its work, the next step leads to a rereading of, therefore a commentary to, the Talmud of Babylonia.

The title of the commentary I propose others do would then be *Making Connections and Drawing Conclusions: An American Academic Commentary to the Talmud.* Combining the categories "American," "academic," and "Talmud" forms the appropriate point of conclusion. For I can imagine no two things formerly thought so unrelated but now formed into such a close and constant union as the holy books of the Torah, on the one side, and the academy, on the other. What Athens has to do with Jerusalem is a question now rephrased by circumstance: what has the Talmud—which stands for Judaism in its formative age—to do with the university? The decade in the life of the *Journal of the American Academy of Religion,* 1985–1995, for which this essay was originally written, attests to the naturalization, into the academy, of a formerly alien tradition of learning. Quickly settled issues leave open the way for a long and leisurely encounter with neglected questions of considerable weight and acute relevance to the study of religion in the academic humanities.

We come now to the heart of the book: the three questions of formative Judaism that I recommend for attention, how I have responded to them, what I think is yet to be done. I thereby propose questions that carry us beyond the outer limits of the imagination realized to this time in acts of learning—a reasoned catalogue for the future curriculum of academic scholarship.

CHAPTER TWO

THE QUESTION OF HISTORY

I. Defining the Historical Question of Rabbinic Judaism

The character of the evidence predetermines the nature of an inquiry. We take up the historical question not in generic terms but in those particular to the Rabbinic canon: which kinds of historical questions pertain, and which do not, to the sort of writings that embody the religious system Rabbinic Judaism?

Let me start with the questions that the nature of the canon precludes, the ones that do not pertain. The study of the canon of formative Judaism only rarely produces answers to conventionally formulated historical questions of narrative: what happened that day, who said what to whom and why? More to the point, if we translate into historical paraphrase the stories we do find, they rarely yield the materials of great events, heroic deeds, dramatic passages—the stuff of historical literature comparable to the heritage of Herodotus, Thucydides, or even Josephus. The model of Joshua, Judges, Samuel, and Kings exercised no influence. Indeed, the canonical documents encompass no chronicles, let alone histories, for example, narratives comparable to Josephus's.

To ask for history about wars and politics, kings and heroes, and grand secular trends errs because the canonical documents do not pretend to produce history of a conventional order. It is not because of a different philosophy of history. It is because the canon does not encompass a philosophy of history at all. That is because no distinction functions between present and past, such as all history writing requires. In the canonical writings, the past is ever present, and the present takes place in synchrony with the past. Issues of history are lost when we invoke today's events to clarify yesterday's and when we treat yesterday's happenings as immediate, so that even a thousand years of yesterdays are never done.

That is what I mean when I say that the nature of the evidence predetermines the result. In the matter of history, when they speak of the past, the canonical documents set forth what is normative and exemplary, not what is singular, exceptional, and extraordinary. They contain no pretense at biography, for example, connected stories about principal figures, yielding lives such as the Gospels present. They do not ask questions of historical explanation that narratives of long-ago events answer. Nor is there a this-worldly theology of history to be derived from the canonical documents in the way in which such a theology emerges from the narratives of Genesis through Kings or the prophets. In that context it is trivial, finally, to note that critical study of the documents' sayings and stories yields little that conventionally serves as historical fact: "precisely how things were." We do not know much about exactly how things were and about the kinds of things subjected to narrative representation in the canon; for the most part we never shall.

So, if at issue is the history of the Jews in late antiquity, or even the history, in political and social context, of the religious system and structure of Rabbinic Judaism, the work, though done, is not done rightly. For the most part, it is not done at all. Further, addressing the historical question, concerning things said and done, to the legal and exegetical compilations that the canon does contain simply does not pertain. Rather, the Rabbinic writings represent cultural artifacts. So, with their little tales and precedents and exemplary stories of personal virtue, the canonical documents attest to the formative stages in the shaping of a religious system and structure. And by contemporary standards, the canonical documents therefore do sustain dense historical study—but of a sort. This history, specifically, takes up the historical-sequential and contextual unfolding of the Rabbinic culture, its design for Israel's social order, its engagement with competing conceptions of the same matter, and its response to cultural conventions of its own time and circumstance. Each document constitutes a massive, detailed corpus of information concerning a determinate circumstance in the past—time, place, condition. It is, moreover, information held to be true by, and therefore characteristic of, the authorities of said document. That corpus of solid facts affords a glimpse into how people thought and what they advocated as truth.

The documents, accordingly, transmit the abundant historical detritus of law and lore. They afford access to the intellect of their compilers and framers, offer entry into media and modes of thought and analysis. They portray even the cultural dynamics captured in the dialectical argument that imparts energy and movement to a religious system of the social order. This evidence, moreover, gives signals that it was formulated by generations directly linked intellectually and institutionally to those that framed the documents. So the canon attests to the views of particular classes of persons and types of institutions at specific times and places. The history of culture and the history of ideas turn therefore to the Rabbinic canon with coherent questions and legitimate expectations of finding compelling and reliable answers. A history of Judaic interiority in the formative age awaits.

But three questions forthwith present themselves to challenge the self-evidence of the very worth of seeking those answers. First, why should anyone care to know about the cultural context and historical unfolding of such a theoretical system of society? Second, what issues of general intelligibility do the data in hand, properly composed and interpreted, exemplify? Third, am I able to identify the urgent question, one of concern to us, to which the Rabbinic canon sets forth self-evidently valid answers, and am I able to show the relevance to later times and circumstances of that question, its urgency to others who are not presumed participants in the documentary culture or supposed continuators of ethnic continuity at all?

Affirmative answers are forthcoming. If we stand back from the details and contemplate the whole in its grand design, we can productively respond to these questions of general intelligibility. The records of Rabbinic Judaism show us what happens when a determinate group of intellectuals[1] of a society are required by crisis and disaster to deal with the politics of calamity. The literary sources of Rabbinic Judaism portray specifically the intellectuals' design for a social system engaged by two massive and urgent questions of culture and intellect: reestablishing continuity with an authoritative past and entering into reasoned confrontation with a distressful present, thus

---

[1] For "the Jews" in the aggregate, we have no random sample of opinion—or for the period in which the Rabbinic canon took shape, no competing corpus of writing—besides that of the Rabbinical sages. No other body of writing that addressed itself to an "Israel" has survived except for that preserved under Christian auspices. That the Rabbinical sages of the Mishnah, Talmuds, and Midrash speak only for themselves, while contemplating "all Israel" to be sure, is clear in the disjuncture between archaeological evidence and literary evidence on matters of synagogue decoration. But other archaeological evidence is congruent with the literary evidence.

situating themselves beyond calamity and reordering matters despite disaster.

Framed in these terms, the answers to the three questions of general intelligibility prove self-evident.

(1) The study of the Rabbinic canon in its existential context engages people who want to know how societies and cultures bring to intellectual expression and resolve through cultural media the political crisis of calamity and its implications for the social order. The canonical writings concluded between 70 and 600 C.E. articulately address the consequences of Israel's loss of Temple, Metropolis, and Land—not once but twice, the second time after a dramatic remission and restoration centuries earlier. The Israel imagined by the ancient Rabbinic sages of Mishnah, Talmuds, and Midrash presents only an example of how a defeated people endures the end of the old order—and of its prior restoration.[2]

(2) The issues of general intelligibility readily pass in review: the rationalization and internalization of defeat, the adaptation to despair, and, above all, the transformation of disaster into a source of social renewal and reform. Before us, in vast detail, is the outcome of just such a process, in documents that afford access to the workings of the process in detail.

(3) As to the urgent question to which the Rabbinic canon responds, here we see how the details of the everyday are reconstructed into a cogent account of the whole. We follow a path outward and upward, from masses of details to a few generalizations, from what the sages say to how their messages may be viewed as an exemplification of social policy. How did they make sense of the here and now? It was by appeal to an encompassing theory of the social order, recovered by us out of the patterns of cohering details. This shows us in acute, concrete contexts the unfolding of thought processes of rationalization, internalization, and adaptation. The process of transformation, laid out before us in rich detail and hard fact, of

---

[2] If I were required to choose a single case of intellectual confrontation with political disaster for comparison and contrast with that of the ancient Rabbinic sages, and if I could ignore considerations of context altogether, I would choose the response of the French artists, composers, poets and other writers, and philosophers to the fiasco of the Franco-Prussian War, their representation of exactly the values that reject militarism and nationalism. They simply redefined the issues altogether, just as did the Rabbinic sages.

fiercely held opinion captures the very essence of the intellectuals'
work of renewal and reconstruction, their ordering and proportioning
of the detritus of the ordinary life, the life of survivors.

So to the issue at hand: whence the dominant idea—the *idée fixe*
that dictates what matters and what does not—transforming details
into the components of a large and comprehensible scheme of things?
That scheme reestablished continuity with the certainties of past sages
selected for shaping the future. And it further engaged with the consequences of calamity, the grounds for despair, in a program of systematic reconstruction. This continuity and this confrontation were
effects of a governing idea of awesome power capable of provoking
disruptive expectations and remitting the consequent disappointment
when these were not met.

Specifically, this Judaism—the system for the Israelite social order
set forth in the Mishnah, Talmuds, and Midrash—took Scripture's
account of Israel's loss and recovery of the Land to account for
Israel's condition then *and now too*. Scripture provided a paradigm that
patterned contemporary events and rendered them meaningful. This
Judaism took the destruction of the Jerusalem Temple in 70, confirmed in the defeat of Bar Kokhba in 135 (not to mention the failure of the emperor Julian's plan to rebuild the Temple in 360–361),
to define the question that Israel's condition raised. Specifically,
Scripture had yielded the pattern of loss but recovery, exile but return
and restoration. The scriptural record had insisted that events express
God's intention for Israel and had further established the pattern, first
with Adam, then with Israel, of loss and recovery. Involved were
Eden and the Land respectively. Scripture further recorded, and
everyone knew, that Israel had recovered the Land. And Scripture
furthermore set forth that reliable recipe for restoration to the Land
and retention of it: what had worked would work once more. By no
means particular to Rabbinic Judaism was the insistence that keeping
the Torah defined the condition for Israel's retaining the Land. The
prophets had said no less. Then an urgent question of global proportions presented itself: how to account for the second loss, and—
more important—in light of the reason for the loss, how to provide
for Israel's ultimate and final recovery of the Land?

Scripture, the Torah, shaped the question and provided the
answer. Israel lost the Land for the same reason as before: sin, meaning rebellion against God's will set forth in the Torah. And Israel held

in its power the possibility of recovery, through the realization in Israelite society of the imperatives of the Torah. So no mysteries shrouded the future; everything was self-evident. And this knowledge empowered Israel to determine its own fate: "Today if you will it!" It defines the urgent question and self-evidently valid answer that the social system portrayed in the Rabbinic canon sets forth. But the documents form a huge corpus of historical facts, and the effort required to master their method and transform the facts into insight hardly finds its justification in these generalities. What specifically have we the right to expect to make the detailed effort worthwhile?

I see two engaging problems in the cultural analysis of ideas, each of them producing two issues worth sustained investigation. The first problem concerns cultural continuity; the second, the cultural context of reconstruction. Both pertain to coherent constructions of ideas for the design of the social order of a community in crisis. Let me explain the program of historical research that the Rabbinic canon sustains and that contemporary cultural inquiry can find consequential. It concerns establishing continuity and undertaking reform of the present in the model of the restored past. Each problem entails our taking up interior and exterior perspectives.

THE INTERIOR PERSPECTIVES: By "interior" I mean the history of ideas on their own, their sequential unfolding in their own framework and out of their particular temporal, social context. These ideas set forth the view from within, not refracted through the prism of history and politics. This interior perspective is both formal and logical. By "formal" I mean to ask how, in relationship to Scripture, the sages give signals that establish continuity and so reestablish order. At issue, then, is continuity with Scripture, received as God's view in God's own words. It involves answering this question: at what points and in what specific ways do the Rabbinic documents lay claim to foundations in Scripture? For, at the most superficial, formal level, that claim when satisfied embodies the continuity between present and past that sustained and validated the culture viewed whole. What the Rabbinic sages set forth defined the restoration of Israel to its original, intended condition: living beyond history in the Land.

But that account of the interiority of their system appeals to the results of reflection (*about what* to think)—not the modes of thought (*how* to think). And so we come to the interiority embodied in the perspective of applied logic and practical reason. By "logical" I mean a

simple thing: which ideas constitute primary and generative propositions, and which ones are secondary, derivative, and contingent? Are
there propositions that form the intellectual counterpart, in systemic
context, to independent variables, systemic building blocks? And having identified both the fundamental and the dependent, we ask our
question of generative logic: how did the primary, the former, generate the derivative, the latter; what logic made the connection self-
evident, the secondary development and extenuation obvious and
urgent? Stated in the simplest terms: what question had to find its
answer before a logically subordinated issue could be addressed in
sequence therefrom? Can we, in theory at least, trace a process of
thought through two or more steps in its unfolding? The answers, if
positive, show us not only the outcome but the process by which the
Rabbinic sages confronted the crisis precipitated by politics but fully
realized in the realm of culture and thought.

To make these matters concrete: specifically, on the formal side,
how do the Rabbinic documents systematically register their claim
authoritatively to guide the restoration of Israel's society in the model
set forth at Sinai? On the logical side, of intense interest is this question: what are the stages in the formulation of that grand design, the
sequences, whether formal or logical, of its unfolding? The interior
perspective, then, encompasses both what is articulated and what is
anticipated, taken for granted, always active. The upshot is, the
canonical documents are seen to constitute exercises in cultural continuity: how do people say they carry forward the received heritage,
and how in their thought processes do they work out the dynamics,
the continuities of thought and theory, spun out of a tight if simple
logic and its dialectics?

THE EXTERIOR PERSPECTIVES: By "exterior" I refer to the social setting in which ideas take shape, the point at which politics and power
intervene and impose their own kind of logic. Here exteriority is both
substantive and formal. The substantive question posed by considerations of setting asks the following: do the ideas give evidence of
responding to broadly held issues of the encompassing social order,
and if so, what response do the canonical documents suggest those
ideas elicit? We answer the question in a simple procedure. We view
the documents as compilations of answers to basic questions. From
their foci, points of generative tension and conflict (for example, with
the society beyond the text, as expressed by the framers of the text),

we reconstruct the questions provoked by the world beyond. Where are a document's foci, its points of emphasis and critical concerns? These we identify not by guesswork but by a systematic reading and outline of the whole: these topics, these considerations, these matters subject to vehement reiteration predominate. Then, if these are the answers, can we identify the questions? Of course we can; the Rabbinic sages never leave us in doubt about what preoccupies them. Whether or not their preoccupations reflect social actualities or inner fantasy presents another question, to which we shall attend in due course. But here exteriority forms a matter of perspective.

So at stake is the interplay between the ideas that people held and the world in which they conceived they lived.[3] The premise of that question is hardly controversial; it is that ideas do not take shape wholly within a vacuum, out of phase with the circumstances of those who think. And the setting that makes the premise self-evident is, once more, that of Scripture. The authoritative heritage of Sinai presents its imperatives for Israel's social order in terms not of abstract philosophy, like the systems of Aristotle and Plato, but of practical social construction and administration, like the system of Moses. The substantive question, then, asks about the specificities of doctrine, encompassing both law and theology, in relationship to the concrete realities of Israel's political condition and its cultural context.

The exterior perspective encompasses not only Israel at home— points of intersection between the Rabbinic sages and their master-disciple circles and other institutions, on the one side, and the rest of the Jewish community, viewed by them also as "Israel," on the other. It takes in also the document's compilers' conception of Israel's setting among other peoples in the Roman and Iranian empires of antiquity, on the one side, and also in relationship to other heirs of Scripture, in Christianity's various systems, on the other. Certainly a historical study of comparison and contrast will juxtapose Israel's response to its situation within Rome and Iran with that of other conquered peoples and (where accessible) with their unarticulated reactions and expressed responses, in doctrines and ideas, to a common circumstance of subjugation (inclusion in a world empire, Rome and Iran would have said). The most elementary issues require attention—for

---

[3] I know no way to move from their conception of the world in which they lived to the actuality of that world.

example, the very category formations "conquest" or "subordination" or "exile." Israel's circumstance exemplified a common condition in the two world empires. How other groups responded affords perspective on the Israelite system set forth by the Rabbinic sages.[4]

If the imperial condition of subordinated peoples defines one point of comparison, the shared circumstance defined by a common Scripture defines the other. The Israel portrayed in the Rabbinic canon represents only one systematic and sustained version of Scripture's imperatives for the age at hand. Other heirs of the same revealed Scripture, also calling themselves Israel, proposed to construct a social order and did so in comparable circumstances. The community represented by the library discovered at Qumran, on the one side, and competing Christianities, on the other, set forth the social implications of their readings of Scripture, their choices of what counted in Scripture and therefore also in the contemporary circumstance. These alternative constructions of Scripture's implications—for the present age and condition of the Israel to whom, in their view, Scripture addressed itself and also for the world—afford to each a depth of perspective upon the other. The conflicting modes of mediating Scripture to the social order establish contexts for comparison not accessible when the one is addressed wholly out of relationship with the other, with all others.

Let me now spell out outlines of what I consider plausible historical inquiries into cultural continuities. These outlines describe the effort to accomplish two scholarly goals. The first is to construct foundations in the received heritage of Scripture, stages in the sorting out of Scripture's authority. The second is to delineate confrontations between the canonical documents and the world beyond the texts, both

---

[4] This part of the question of history—the comparison of religions—does not preclude a corresponding part of the question of religion, also the comparison of religions. But the things that are compared are different. The comparison of religions in historical context, sketched here, concerns exterior traits, as will be clear in the detailed exposition. The comparison of religions in the context of religion, however, concerns itself with the interior structures of religious systems and how they contrast and correspond. In the present context I do not systematically spell out a systematic account of the comparison of religions in the setting of the question of religion. I do set forth elsewhere how I conceive such a comparative religions program is to be realized (in my "Augustine and Judaism," in *Encyclopaedia of Judaism* [Leiden: E. J. Brill, 2002], supplement 1). Adding a systematic chapter here on the subject would have made this programmatic statement still more prolix than it already is.

the interior Israelite world and the exterior realm of others, Christian and pagan. It is now my task to spell out the sorts of historical questions, both historical-cultural and historical-intellectual, that in the present context I think have not been, but ought now to be, systematically raised in the setting of the Rabbinic canon of formative Judaism.

We move from text (literature) to context (history) to matrix (religion) as the unfolding analysis dictates. The documents—texts—lay claim not only to an autonomous reading in their own terms but also to exegesis in context. But a further perspective exterior to the document also invites attention, and that is the larger world of discourse, a world of ideas shared by writings of the same time and place and intellectual program. In this matrix, which nourishes the text in context, we investigate points of congruence, shared traits of intellectual engagement, that characterize texts whose authors and sponsoring communities scarcely intersect: the exteriority of a common agenda. Thus we proceed from the interiorities of the text (sections II, III, IV, naturally more dense) to the contiguous exteriorities of the context (section V, necessary but not sufficient) and finally to the adventitious and more distant, but demonstrably pertinent, exteriorities of matrix (sections VI, VII, the most suggestive but least well grounded stage of the analysis).

II. An Interior Perspective: 1. The Scriptural Roots of Rabbinic Judaism

If asked how the system establishes its bona fides, anyone who has ever studied the formative age of Rabbinic Judaism must respond by exegetically linking to Scripture the system's own propositions of law and theology. No trait more characterizes the canonical documents than incessant citation of Scripture. Accordingly, we take for granted the scriptural roots of Rabbinic Judaism. No one can reasonably doubt that the constant appeal to scriptural foundations serves to establish continuity, to gain the authority of Sinai for the Rabbinic structure. No premise is so deeply grounded in learning as that Rabbinic Judaism carries forward the imperatives of Scripture. Nor is any so well founded in texts. Therefore people have quite reasonably taken as their field of inquiry the technology (for example,

exegetical techniques) for grounding Rabbinic law on scriptural formulations or for finding the bases for Rabbinic theology in scriptural
narratives. They have tended not to ask what is at stake in the Rabbinic sages' constant citation of proof texts in support of their rulings.

Let us take up an obvious answer to that question: proof texts
establish the authority, in God's legislation, for a given ruling of the
Rabbinic sages. But this answer begs the question, and for a simple
reason. If at stake is the exposition of Scripture's legislation in
Scripture's manner, then why—it is fair to ask—are Scripture's *category formations* not reproduced? And why does the Rabbinic canon not
suffice with the presentation of law through ad hoc exegesis of
Scripture's law? However we may explain and order Scripture's presentation of law, we produce systems of category formations—topics
that cohere into broad constructions of principles, yielding coherent
and proportionate details—that do not define those of the Rabbinic
canon.

If the systematic demonstration of the scriptural foundations of the
law defined the stakes, then Scripture ought to have defined the governing category formations of the law as set forth in the Mishnah-
Tosefta. Elsewhere I show what the result ought to have been. How
matters could have sorted themselves out is illustrated in Mishnah-
Tosefta tractates *Negaim* and *Parah*, which systematically construct
logical, coherent expositions of the laws of Leviticus 13 and 14 and
Numbers 19, respectively. These tractates show us how Scripture's
category formations could have governed the exposition of the Halakhah by the Rabbinic sages responsible for the Mishnah and the
Tosefta, hence also the Yerushalmi and the Bavli, in their category
formations. Readers may stipulate that this work is complete and
uncomplicated. Scripture's category formations define those of the
Mishnah and the Tosefta for the specified tractates.

But then where are their counterparts? Elsewhere in the Mishnah-
Tosefta we look in vain for the recapitulation of Scripture's category
formations, within Scripture's own theory of how data define a topic,
how facts should coalesce and be articulated into a cogent statement.
For Leviticus 1 through 11, for example, the exposition of the sacri-
ficial system, Scripture's category formations for sacrifices do not
dictate their Mishnah-Tosefta counterparts. Where Scripture differentiates among offerings, for example, the sin offering, the guilt offering, the whole offering, the Mishnah-Tosefta homogenizes offerings,

laying out the rules that govern all classifications of offering, in tractate *Zebahim*, for example. Matters are not limited to such global
shifts. What Scripture treats as unitary the Halakhic category formations differentiate. In Leviticus 15 Scripture combines the uncleanness
of the woman in her period with the uncleanness of the person who
suffers a flux, while in *Niddah* and *Zabim* the Mishnah-Tosefta treats
each category in response to its own generative problematics. And
that is all the more curious, since (as I have shown in some detail)
there simply is no understanding the category formations *niddah* and
zabim without treating the two kinds of uncleanness as a single problem. This is as Scripture insists; they are *not* differentiable foci of
exposition, as the Mishnah-Tosefta prefer. The upshot is simple.
Were Scripture to define the model for organizing the law and the
consequent category formations, the Mishnah-Tosefta would present
us with a construction considerably different from the one before us.

Finally, the very topicality of Halakhic category formations does
not correspond with Scripture's theory of what holds together a variety of diverse information in a single construction. Thus, where
Scripture combines a variety of topics under an overriding rubric
such as holiness, as in Leviticus 19, the Mishnah-Tosefta does not follow suit. Rather, it dismisses as null theological category formations—
holiness is a fine example—in favor of topical ones, so that Leviticus
19 contributes laws to no fewer than a dozen Mishnah tractate topical constructions, from *Kilayim* to *Baba Mesia*.

The point should not be missed. Superficially, the Rabbinic system
carries forward the exposition of scriptural law and theology. At a
profound, structural level, the Rabbinic system builds upon category formations that are asymmetrical with those of Scripture—sometimes replicating Scripture's topical program within Scripture's own
generative problematics, as in Leviticus 16/tractate *Yoma*; sometimes ignoring Scripture's category formations altogether; sometimes
acknowledging Scripture's category formations and adopting them
but infusing them with a corpus of concerns with no scriptural counterpart; and, finally, sometimes composing category formations with
little or no scriptural counterpart to begin with, as in *Makhshirin* or
even *Kelim*. So the questions present themselves: how do the Rabbinic
sages grasp the category formations of Scripture, and why do they
replicate some, amplify others, ignore many, and in not a few instances even invent their own, out of all relationship with those of

Scripture? Answering these questions requires specialists in Rabbinic Judaism to depend upon scholarship on Scripture for an account of the several constructions of category formations that Scripture puts forth—for example, in Leviticus, Exodus, and Deuteronomy, where we find not only details but large-scale composites, well crafted according to rules other than those that govern in the Mishnah-Tosefta.

We should not lose sight of what is at stake. It is, in my view, not the technicalities of exegesis but a fundamental issue of cultural continuity: how intellectuals composing a worldview in their own circumstance establish continuity with the inherited culture that they seek to preserve and to replicate, even to reform. This trait of the Judaic culture is so ingrained, its traditionalism so marked, that we take the matter for granted. And that is how the Rabbinic sages want us to see matters, for it forms a principal rationale and validation for their system: a secondary amplification of the revelation of Sinai. But this represents a decision and a claim, not an established fact everywhere characteristic.

We cannot take it for granted that the conservative impulse governs, that authority is vested in a myth of origins (at Sinai, for example) and transmitted to those who manipulate the myth and articulate its practical consequences. An obvious contrast presents itself. It is between the Rabbinic premise, expressed in exegesis, that the legal heritage of Scripture demands a critical place in the nascent system and the philosophical premise, expressed in the analytical processes of the Rabbinic writings, that naked reason, analytical dialectics, governs the articulation of the governing principles, for example, those of rationality and justice and good order. Much of the Mishnah's presentation of the law ignores the issue of origin in Scripture, a quality implicitly rejected every time the Tosefta and the Talmuds supply precisely the exegetical basis that the Mishnah ignores. So, articulately finding foundations in Scripture represents an active choice and preference, not an inert given.

The insistence on grounding in Scripture the message of a new voice in Israel—a nascent Judaic system with its own way of life, worldview, and theory of the social entity Israel—finds fine exemplification in the Gospel of Matthew, with its constant reference to scriptural narrative and prophecy in its presentation of the life and teachings of Jesus. But if we wish to see how that life and those teachings may come to authoritative exposition on their own, without the resort to proof texts supplied by scriptural narrative, we turn to the Gospel of John, which does not accord to scriptural proof texts of prophecy and narrative the same central position in the exposition as does the school of Matthew. The Gospel of John, then, comparable to the Mishnah, is as formally different from Matthew (with its exegetical focus and even mode of organization of its materials) as, for example, the Mishnah tractates *Zabim-Niddah*, *Negaim*, and *Makhshirin* are from *Sifra*. *Sifra* places the Mishnah's law into the context of verse-by-verse expositions of Scripture (scriptural laws are translated into cases, principles into rules); Matthew likewise places incidents in the life of Jesus in the context of expositions of Scripture (for example, prophecy translated into narrative). So Matthew is to John as *Negaim* is to *Makhshirin*, to take a homely case. Or to state more lucidly what is implied in these cases, some authorities of the Halakhah founded their category formations squarely on those of Scripture and stated in generalizations what was implicit in Scripture's particular laws, but others did not regard Scripture as the sole source of authority, validation, and continuity with the past.

The upshot for the large cultural issue is that those seeking cultural continuity in an age of upheaval confront a choice. On the one side, they may find a formal solution ready at hand. It is to interpret the received, authoritative tradition in light of new and unprecedented conditions. Thus, on formal grounds, we account for the quest for scriptural foundations for Rabbinic law and theology. By linking the new to the established and true, the abyss to the past is bridged, the continuity of culture established. But on the other side, those seeking cultural continuity may uncover a different principle of systemic construction, revealing contradictory tendencies. It is, specifically, the willingness formally (never substantively!) to ignore Scripture altogether in composing legal category formations and in articulating the laws thereof. Thus at stake is something other than mere secondary amplification of laws stated in primary form in Scripture. What is the difference? Two theories of the engagement with Scripture play themselves out, one asking for a constant presence, the other not. The second theory demands exposition.

The key to the approach linking present to past without explicit citation of Scripture lies in framing the question at hand so as to dictate its own answer. I do so in the following terms: what is continuous

with Scripture in category formations that do not commence with
Scripture's category formations, and how does the entire Rabbinic
system of law, constructed as it is in a completely freestanding composite of category formations, propose to establish continuity with a
past that is *not* replicated in categorical detail? Once the question is
asked in terms of wholes—the whole of Scripture, viewed in the perspective of its several sets of category formations, as against the whole
of the Rabbinic structure of the law, viewed in the perspective of its
category formations—the answer becomes obvious. It is in negative,
then positive forms.

The negative is simple. The Halakhic structure of category formations does not ignore Scripture in detail or in categorical construction.
Details of the law of the written Torah, however classified or cate-
gorized in that Torah, ordinarily find their way into the Rabbinic
recapitulation of the law. I cannot point to a single detail of the
Pentateuchal law codes, however trivial, that is wholly ignored in the
Mishnaic category formations as these are articulated. This recapitulation of the sages takes over some of Scripture's category formations
and replicates them, simply articulating detail. But it also transforms
other scriptural category formations into more elaborate composites
than Scripture's exposition of the same topical composites requires. It
even contributes entirely fresh category formations. When we view
the whole of Scripture in the perspective of its category formations as
against the Rabbinic structure, the two composites prove, if not symmetrical, then at least congruent in important dimensions. But the
congruence is not systematic, and it is not substantive.

Now comes the affirmative side: what does the Rabbinic system
contribute in the *other-than-scripturally-generated* category formations?
The cases of *Kelim*, on the one side, and *Besah*, on the other, neatly
serve to answer the theoretical question.

Besah takes up a simple fact that Scripture sets forth—cooking is
permitted on the festival but not on the Sabbath—and asks the question imbedded in the deep structure beneath that fact: how does the
sanctity of the Sabbath relate to, impinge upon, the sanctity of the
festival day, and more broadly, what hierarchy of sanctification is subject to differentiation? Scripture thus provides the case and the rule,
and the Mishnah's systematic category formation articulates details
that embody the implicit principles contained within Scripture's own

rule. Scripture provides a fact; the Rabbinic sages uncover the abstract principles that generate that fact and articulate, in cases of their own, the realization of those principles in concrete rules, in other legal facts. So, what looks like an autonomous category formation, taking over a scriptural given and making of it something elaborate and abstract, turns out upon reflection to investigate the profound layers of abstract principle contained in the concrete rule of Scripture (in context, one can scarcely call the scriptural basis of *Besah* a scriptural "category formation"!).

Kelim presents the simple facts about the capacity of utensils of various shapes, made out of various materials, to contain uncleanness. The details of the law instantiate such general principles as that what man deems useful is susceptible to uncleanness, what man deems useless is not. The cases then yield the rule: the topical category formations render feasible the presentation, in concrete form, of abstract theological principles concerning the interplay of the human will and the material world beyond. This yields a generalization: what the Rabbinic system contributes in the category formations that lack scriptural foundations altogether or that are not symmetrical with scriptural foundations is the concretization of principles of a theological or a philosophical order—their "topicalization." That is, the presentation, within a given topic, of the details of the Halakhah makes possible the exposition, in the preferred manner (from detail to abstract principle), of fundamental conceptual postulates of the entire Rabbinic system.

Through the selected topics—*Besah*, an egg born on a festival day; *Kelim*, utensils susceptible or not to uncleanness—profound abstractions of theology (issues of the hierarchical classification of types of sanctification) or philosophy (traits of materials, the effect of abstract human intentionality upon concrete qualities of objects and the classification of those objects by status) come to readily accessible expression through blatant instantiation.

What this other approach to cultural continuity proposes is simple. It concerns the very meaning of the conception of continuity. What is carried forward is not only the details and the forms, the concrete prescriptions of the received tradition. What is continuous is the principles that generate the rules, the abstractions of logical order (for example, hierarchical classification) that govern material and concrete

transactions (for example, the order of preference accorded to sanctification at various levels or to its counterpart and opposite, uncleanness at diverse removes).

I earlier referred to interior perspectives that are extrinsic and formal and those that are intrinsic and logical. The interplay of
Scripture and tradition with the contemporary representation of a
continuous culture provides an example. Linking matters by formal
exegesis takes an instrumental view of Scripture. Generating conceptions by reflection on deep principles implicit in Scripture shows the
logical view. The latter conceives of continuity as a given of truth:
Scripture in its details embodies the working of a logic. Recover the
logic, make it work wherever it serves, and Scripture's generative
principles endure, remaining in play.

How does this second approach to continuity work? If we may
penetrate from the detail to the generative logic that comes to expression in that detail, we may think the way Scripture thinks, not only
act the way Scripture's law decrees. And when we think the way
Scripture thinks, given the authorship to whom the Rabbinic sages
attribute Scripture (the Torah), we think like God. We see matters
from God's perspective. We recapitulate the modes of thought that
govern in God's mind. Scripture, then, conveys the result, and our
task is to decipher the cause; Scripture sets forth the conclusion, and
we reconstruct the reasoning that produced that conclusion; Scripture
lays out the imperatives, and from these we find our way to the rules
of analysis and criticism that dictate the course of reason.

To state matters simply: formal continuity establishes historical
authority based on precedent; logical continuity founds the social
order on philosophical rules of analysis and modes of thought that
rest on eternal truth. Made necessary by historical calamity, the
reconstruction of stability through establishing cultural continuity
requires bridging the abyss between past and present. Two kinds of
bridges accomplish the task: the exterior, formal and articulated; the
interior, logical and implicit. The Torah, in its details of law and their
exegesis, embodies the one. The inner dialectics implicit in the
Rabbinic system of law—in its category formations and their generative logic—engineers the other. Formative Judaism in its canonical
legal system insists on the match between form and logic, the accidents of culture and the organizing categories of culture. The genius
of Rabbinic Judaism comes to concrete expression in the union of the

two. So much for the scriptural roots of Rabbinic Judaism—a question of the history of culture embodied in the phenomenology of ideas. But this is not the only historical question that the Rabbinic canon permits us to ask, nor does cultural history form the only arena of inquiry.

III. An Interior Perspective: 2. The Documentary History of Ideas

The history of ideas traces the sequence and circumstance in which important propositions came to expression and began to influence thought. For the history of the ideas of its Judaism, the Rabbinic canon forms a massive source of data. These writings document the successive phases in the history of the shaping of that system. That is because each compilation in sequence makes a statement, so we have not only the end product, the canon as a whole, but the documentary phases in its unfolding. Hence we may follow how the ideas—propositions and principles and premises—of Rabbinic Judaism unfolded in time and in documentary sequence. No one imagines that the structure and system appeared all together and all at once. In fact, we are able systematically to trace the history of ideas as they move from one document to the next in sequence. That means, first in the Mishnah, then in the Tosefta, the Yerushalmi, the Bavli; and alongside, first in the so-called Tannaite Midrash compilations, *Sifra* and the two *Sifrés* and the *Mekhilta*, then in the Rabbah-Midrash compilations and *Pesiqta deRab Kahana*; first in *Abot*, then in *Abot deR. Natan*, and so throughout.

But the documents take for granted that they speak in one voice and impose a uniform statement, for that is precisely how the Rabbinic canon functions. The writings portray matters as a whole system and all at once, a fully articulated statement. Then how are ideas to be dated, presented in sequence, and placed into temporal context, and what evidence serves to answer conventional historical questions of this kind? Two sets of indicators of temporal venue and sequence present themselves, one uncertain, the other highly probable.

The uncertain indicators derive from attributions of sayings to named authorities of a determinate time and location and from stories about them. The probable indicators—as explained at the outset of this book—derive from the sequences of ideas that are signaled by appearance of a given proposition in a particular document and those following. The former yields conventional history, concerning things that really were said or actually happened. The latter sets forth the history of ideas in the order indicated by the sequence of completion of the documents that contain those ideas.

The former set of indicators has predominated to date. That is because, until the recent past, people took attributions of sayings to named Rabbinic sages as historical fact and recovered the history of Rabbinic Judaism by appeal to the assignment of sayings to named authorities. The history was very particular to determinate periods because the named sages were assumed to have lived at a particular time and place (the dates dictated by early medieval writers many centuries later than the times of the named sages). The stories told about those Rabbinic sages were ordinarily taken at face value. But all this has come to an end, and the old credulity and gullibility have given way to a critical view of matters.

Specifically, the critical program deriving from biblical scholarship—how do we know a sage really said what is assigned to him; how do we know things happened in the way in which the story says, or in some other way, or not at all?—has now called into question the viability of that assumption. People no longer concede the critical standing of the history, including the intellectual history, built on the results of simply paraphrasing as fact what are set forth as creative narratives. Once the generality of scholarship came to accept the critical premise that *what we cannot show, we do not know*, the reliability of attributions came into question, the dependability of stories into doubt.

For no means of falsifying, and therefore of validating, attributions and narratives present themselves. We have as evidence only documents that came to closure long after the lifetimes of those cited therein and decades, even centuries, after the events portrayed. It soon became clear to much of the scholarly world at work on Rabbinic Judaism that mere allegations of fact contained within the documents could not serve to establish the facts of what was said and done. History as an account of what really happened, not merely what given sources say happened, lost plausibility. Paraphrases of the sources in academic language, which were set forth as history and which for two hundred years passed as history, no longer served. A wholly fresh historical program demanded formulation; the old questions could no longer produce plausible answers. They turned out to be simply the wrong questions, given the character of the data. The character of the evidence predetermined the nature of the inquiry.

But the evidence supplies a rich corpus of facts once we recognize what they are. Specifically, the canonical documents themselves constituted facts of history: at a given point, a determinate group of compilers and redactors set forth as authoritative these sayings and stories. We are able to describe, analyze, and interpret the traits of documents, as spelled out in Chapter One. Documents come to closure in an accessible sequence in relationship to one another. Consequently, a different kind of history of ideas has come to the fore, the documentary history of the formation of Rabbinic Judaism. In this approach to the history of ideas, no claim alleges that we know what people really were thinking, what opinions characterized the generality of Israel or even the Rabbinic sages. In other words, we do not take the step from the document to the world beyond the document. Nor do we allege that we know what people in general were thinking. We restrict the history we set forth to the facts made available by the documents in hand. The sole facts taken to form the foundation of the history of ideas are the documents themselves. Then the sequences in the exposure of given ideas or principles—established by the order in which documents reached closure—can form the foundation of a history of ideas.

Order or sequence by appeal to the intellectual traits of the successive documents yields a limited intellectual history. It traces, in the sequence of documents, the passage of a principle or fundamental conception from stage to stage, the successive unfolding of sequences of ideas, and, more important, the successive compositions of ideas into coherent statements, systems. That is so because the documents reached closure not all at once but in sequence (a matter to which we shall return), with the Mishnah coming before, and being taken for granted by, the Tosefta; the Tosefta and the Mishnah by the Yerushalmi; and the like. We take as fact that when a document reached closure in the formulation documented by available manuscripts and first printed editions, within certain variables, the contents of the document are to be dated as well—if only by sequence. Along with closure of the document, all of the propositions contained therein were in circulation and attained canonical status. So we may assign to the point of documentary closure the last possible moment of temporal origin for everything in that document (again with the proviso that the manuscript evidence attests to the presence of a given item). And we may further posit that from the entry of the document into canonical status, subsequent documents are assumed to have had access to this document and its contents. These seem reasonable premises for the study of the history of the ideas that constitute the Rabbinic system; and within them, a documentary history of Rabbinic Judaism has been shown entirely feasible.

But what sort of history? It concerns not free-floating facts, convictions, or allegations, for example, concerning God, Torah, or Israel. No one claims to know the state of affairs beyond the outer limits of the successive documents—for instance, the state of opinion or the point at which, for the very first time ever, a given conception came to expression. This we cannot show, and we do not know. We simply do not know what people in general were thinking or what people made of given facts, whether of Scripture or of tradition, that they possessed in various forms and for diverse purposes. What documents attest are their own systems, where they can be shown to expose the interior architecture of systemic constructions. And documents that are read in order tell us the sequence in which sets of ideas unfolded within the documentary framework—a limited yield indeed, but not unenlightening.

Thus a document tells us how a given set of ideas was formed into a coherent and cogent statement, and a document establishes a systemic context for a variety of conceptions or ideas. The documentary history of ideas exposes, then, the various formulations of a range of conceptions as these fit together to make a systemic statement. Knowing that a given law or a given theological conception circulated in one context here, in another context there, bears no relevance to the documentary history of ideas, since at stake in this particular historical reconstruction is the composition of cogent wholes, not the circulation of bits and pieces, parts of we know not what. Once we recognize that not all sources deriving from Jewish authorships or redactors contribute, together with all other sources, to an account of a single, everywhere normative Judaism, then indeterminate, out-of-context histories of ideas held by Jews no longer provide plausible accounts of matters. Context is determined by system; systems are recapitulated by canonical compilations. The history of ideas records the unfolding of a given system, whether Rabbinic or other, of a Judaism.

IV. An Interior Perspective: 3. The Predocumentary History of Systems of Ideas

We come to the logical side of the interior perspective: the investigation, from the results of a process of thought, of steps of reasoning that yielded such results. In other words, I ask whether we can work backward from the known to the unknown, reconstructing processes of thought and their propositional outcomes, composing a hypothetical history of ideas by recapitulating a logical process of reflection that could have yielded these ideas in this sequence. Let me explain what I conceive to be possible and how I think it should be carried out.

Even within the humble limitations imposed by the documentary history of ideas—all we know is the unfolding of systemic ideas as indicated by the sequence of documents—a further question of the history of ideas demands attention. It asks for a hypothetical reconstruction of that history, based on the logical relationships and connections of propositions: which comes first and why? This predocumentary history of ideas concerns the theoretical, reconstructed order in which systems of ideas unfolded that are ultimately given final expression in a particular document.

What provokes the question of a predocumentary history of ideas is a simple postulate. No one can contend that a given idea or set of ideas originates only at its point of surfacing, that is, at the moment of its entry into a document and its system. On the contrary, documents draw upon a heritage of thousands of years of culture, both the particular Israelite legacy contained in Scripture and tradition and the general Near Eastern heritage of law and learning. The Rabbinic systems that come to concrete expression in canonical documents draw upon what everybody knew and took for granted, whether those data derive from Scripture or from the ambient culture. So the question is not whether the facts or ideas attested in a given document first surfaced in that document, lacking all prior history. The issue is a different one: on what basis, through what modes of reflection, are we to address the established fact that most of the important conceptions of the Rabbinic compilations derive from earlier times and other documents, beginning, after all, with Scripture itself?

What makes me so certain that the documentary attestation of a fact bears little consequence for the time of origin of said fact? A simple case serves. The random intersection of facts—for example, of the law set forth in the Mishnah or the Tosefta or a baraita, and of the law set forth in the library found at Qumran—forms a case in point. We may demonstrate that a given law was accepted as authoritative at Qumran and also, two hundred years later, in the Mishnah. No one may doubt that the law as set forth by the Mishnah circulated centuries before the Mishnah came to closure. But viewed on its own, this fact—that the same freestanding rule occurs both in the Mishnah-Tosefta and in a prior Judaic writing—produces no consequences for the history of ideas. It is a fact bearing no information beyond itself, imposing no conclusions of any compelling quality.

This judgment rests on a negative and a positive argument. The negative one is simple, deriving from the answer to a theoretical question: what conclusion would we reach if we knew that a given law surfaced in Scripture, the Elephantine papyri, the laws to which Philo makes reference, the Dead Sea law compilations, the Gospels' allusions to Judaic law, and a variety of Rabbinic sources? If we seek to know the sequence of occurrences of that same law, our account consists in the recitation of the pertinent facts: the law occurs here, the law occurs there. Since the law originates in Scripture, that is hardly surprising. But out of context, those facts yield no continuous history, no unfolding of the law of a single, harmonious, unitary Judaism. All we learn from the range of appearances of a given rule is that a variety of social systems, a range of Judaic law codes, has replicated Scripture's rule. A text out of systemic context bears no implications beyond itself; it has no answer to the question of what else I know if I know this.

And that carries us to the positive argument. A fact takes on meaning and produces consequences *only* in systemic context. That is where what is implicit comes to realization, where the fact bears meaning beyond itself. But for a history of the legal text in context, the inner history of a system is required. For a text out of context defies all questions of analysis, since there is no basis for comparing and contrasting that legal text with others of its classification; and it stymies all initiatives of interpretation, which demands textual affines.

The first step of interpretation, after all, aims at treating the fact as exemplary, at answering the question of what else I know if I know this. And to take that step, a path outward must lead from the text to its context, whether a path of comparison and contrast or one of secondary and tertiary extensions of its implications.

So external evidence of the antiquity of a given fact set forth in a Rabbinic document does not, on its own, dictate the shape of a pre-documentary history of a *documentary* fact. Then, does this mean that the road backward, to the system fully realized in the document before the closure of the document, is closed off? A reframing of the question shows what is at issue and what is at stake: do systems of ideas yield a history prior to the documentary presentation of those systems? In the context of the Halakhah of the Mishnah and the Tosefta, do we gain access to a predocumentary history of the system of law set forth in final form in the Mishnah?

To answer the question, let us consider what such a history of formative Judaism would encompass and what sort of evidence one might adduce in evidence for that history. I lay stress on the context of texts, on the determinative impact of the systemic context upon the standing of all facts—that is, particular laws contained and set into context by the system. Then one corpus of data proves determinative: the native category formations that make up the system of the Mishnah. Why deem the native category formations of the Mishnah the definitive statement of the Halakhic part of formative Judaism? Because, in quest of context, these category formations impart structure, order, meaning, a place to every fact contained in the document. They dictate the choice of facts and the use thereof within a document.

Then the question presses: do we have access to a generative model of the history of the categorical structure of the Mishnah's category formations? Of course we do—the *post-Mishnaic* history of the Mishnah's own category formations! The Tosefta, Yerushalmi, and Bavli are organized by the Halakhic category formations that dictate the structure of the Halakhah of the Mishnah—and they do not encompass the same category formations as function in the Mishnah at all. The Tosefta's category formations are marginally asymmetrical with those of the Mishnah. The Yerushalmi takes up only thirty-nine of the Mishnah's sixty-two Halakhic category formations (excluding the tractate *Abot*), and the Bavli takes up two fewer—thirty-seven, and not the same ones as the Yerushalmi. So people clearly made judgments about the category formations. They exercised taste and judgment and effected their philosophy through these choices. The upshot is simple. We do have access to a formal history of the Mishnah's Halakhic category formations, documented by the selections and omissions of the Tosefta (a few) and the Yerushalmi and the Bavli. Working forward from the Mishnah, history is possible.

That leads us from *after* to *before*: what about the prehistory of the Mishnah's category formations? Can we work backward from the Mishnah's category formations to the state of the Halakhic structure and system before its full exposure in the Mishnah? I have already stressed that an affirmative answer does *not* derive from evidence that a given law circulated decades or centuries before the closure of the Mishnah. Everyone understands that: Scripture suffices to make the point, with its massive contribution to the Halakhic corpus of the Mishnah. But what we noted earlier hardly requires articulation: the Mishnah's categorical construction only occasionally replicates that of Scripture and commonly does not.

How to proceed? By comparison and contrast. If I were to design a research project on the predocumentary history of the Mishnah's system of ideas, it would take up two questions, one of them external to the Mishnah, the other internal. The external question is this: how does the Mishnah's structure of category formations compare with the structure of other Judaic legal documents, for example, the system of Elephantine or of the Dead Sea library? This comparison—not of details out of context but of wholes, each in its autonomous context yet both in relationship to a common source of authoritative law in Scripture—will allow us to compare and contrast whole systems. And this process is three-dimensional: an account of Scripture's several categorical constructions, an account of the categorical construction of another Judaic legal system besides that of the Mishnah, and a comparison of these two with one another and with that of the Mishnah.

I cannot imagine a more suggestive arena for comparison and contrast than the one formed by two sets of category formations that respond to—and, as a matter of hypothesis, derive from—a third, prior construction common to them both. Such a comparison and contrast of the Mishnah's system with other Judaic systems in dialogue with Scripture's several systems yields not a temporal-historical but a phenomenological result. What emerges is an account of the several distinct logics of selection and organization realized in the systems that intersect in origin and in some data—logics shaped (in the present context) in response to a larger systemic purpose, for example, a tendency in the interpretation of Israel's tasks as Scripture defines those tasks.

The second question, the one internal to the Mishnah, carries us to the outer limits of the critical method that insists on tests of falsification and verification of propositions: how would I know if I were wrong? The question asks whether we can follow the unfolding of the category formations of the Halakhah of the Mishnah prior to the closure of the Mishnah. Are we able, hypothetically, to reconstruct a sequence of questions and answers that lead us from the current statement made by a category formation backward to the logically prior issues that had to be taken up before the formulation of matters as we now have them? In other words, what did someone have to know as settled fact before raising questions answered in the Halakhic category formations that we have before us?

A simple example shows the kind of thinking that can proceed. Tractate *Makhshirin* pursues a set of issues concerning the relationship between action and intentionality. Logically prior questions had to be settled before the issues that occupy the Halakhah of *Makhshirin* could be addressed. The Halakhah, to begin with, knows the fundamental fact, the given of the category formation, that produce that is dry is insusceptible to uncleanness and that produce that has been wet down is susceptible. Scripture, at Lev. 11:34, 37, is taken to lay down this fact. The Halakhah further knows, also as a matter of established fact, that what has been wet down unintentionally is unaffected by the liquid but what has been deliberately wet down is affected. So what is wet is not necessarily susceptible to uncleanness, only what is deliberately wet down.

Here we identify a layer of thought that interposes between Scripture and the Halakhic category formation *makhshirin*. This layer transforms the materiality of uncleanness as defined by Scripture into a matter of relativity, of status, changing what is palpable and tangible into what is intangible and taxonomic. The premise that forms the foundation of all else is an abstraction: uncleanness is a matter not of substance but of status. The absolute condition of uncleanness never takes over if two bodies of produce may be wet but only one of them—that deliberately wet down—is susceptible to uncleanness. Hence, just as the status of sanctification in the law of Scripture is material and palpable, so that merely touching the altar affects what has made contact with the altar, without regard to circumstance or intentionality, whereas in the law of the Mishnah the altar sanctifies what is appropriate to it but has no effect upon what is not appropriate to it, so the same principle—status, not substance—governs for uncleanness. Something is, then, not intrinsically unclean but only assigned to the status, the classification of uncleanness, by an intangible, impalpable act of intentionality. Between Scripture and the foundations of the Halakhic category formation lies a layer of reflection that has taken the physical, substantive definitions of sanctification and uncleanness alike and recast both into taxonomic categories, matters of intangible relationship out of phase with the material definitions of sanctification or uncleanness as forces that function *eo ipso*.

Now, as a matter of logic, the question of intentionality can be raised only after the reading of Lev. 11:34, 47 has established the generative fact on which all else rests. Intentionality had to intervene as a matter of taxic power at the second stage in the logical unfolding of the category formation at hand. These two stages represent sequential steps in the unfolding of the law prior to the ultimate, fully realized statement of the law in the Mishnah-Tosefta tractate *Makhshirin*. Both of them had to be taken before the issues of the tractate came into view. For these issues concern a refinement of step two, just now identified: intentionality to wet down the produce is required to effect susceptibility. This carries us to step three in the hypothetical reconstruction of the history of the Halakhic category formation *makhshirin*. It concerns the refinement of the matter of intentionality. Two such refinements may be represented by questions.

First, what about the division of a transaction in such wise that part of the act of wetting down the formerly dry produce effected one's wish and intentionality, and part did not? For example, if one at first affirmed the act of wetting down but in the end did not by, say, drying off what had been wet down, do we distinguish, in assessing the status of the produce, between the part wet down in accord with one's wishes and the part wet down despite one's intentionality?

Second, what about the relationship between intentionality and action? If one intended to wet down produce, does that classify the produce as susceptible to uncleanness even before one has actually applied water to the produce, on the theory that one will surely carry out what one has planned to do? Or do we insist that an act confirm the intentionality, so that if one has a plan, it produces no effect until actualized?

These two refinements of the matter of intentionality in relationship to actuality require considerable exposition in the category formation/tractate that is before us. Since the tractate does not articulate the initial matter—the reading of Lev. 11:34, 37—and also does not expound the relativities of intentionality in respect to deed as general principles but only in the tertiary refinements just now noted, a question presents itself: can we hypothetically reconstruct the prehistory of the Halakhah that is in our hands? I have now shown that, in theory at least, such a prehistory is entirely feasible as we work backward to Scripture and forward from Scripture through the logical steps that link Scripture to the fully realized, entirely articulated Halakhah in hand.

But there is a further hypothetical historical inquiry that awaits attention. It concerns the interplay of Halakhic category formations, and to instantiate here what is possible, I will remain within the framework of the category formation in hand, *makhshirin*. What strikes me as critical is the insistence upon intentionality as the decisive condition for assigning to dry produce the status of susceptibility to uncleanness. It means that as soon as one adds water to dry flour and yeast, one has to take heightened precautions to prevent a source of uncleanness, for example, a dead creeping thing, from falling into the mixture. But before that point, there is no change of status that comes about merely because a dead creeping thing falls willy-nilly into the mixture of dry flour (produce) and yeast. So the question presents itself: what does the addition of water—the wetting down of the flour—do to make necessary the heightened degree of precaution, such that one assumes responsibility for the cultic condition (unclean/clean) of the flour only if one has deliberately wet it down?

Asking the question in this way dictates the answer, which derives from the Halakhic category formation devoted to the setting aside of the dough offering required of all dough in its progress of preparation as bread. Dough offering may be separated from the dough at the point at which the flour and yeast are wet down. Why? That is the point at which the enzymes in the yeast come alive and the dough begins to leaven. The flour and yeast change from inert to living. Now, the Halakhah wants to know, under what conditions does a human being assume responsibility for the condition and status of the dough? And it answers that when someone has undertaken a deliberate course of action to bring the dough to life, then, but only then, is one also responsible to take precautions for the prevention of contamination of the rising dough by dead creeping things. One has brought the mixture to life, and one has to protect that life from sources of uncleanness, representing death.

What we see is that at the foundations of tractate *Makhshirin* is a conception that completes what generates the Halakhah of tractate *Hallah*. The tractates work together to explore the details of generative principles that work in the abstract, in order to realize a statement bearing broad implications of a metaphysical character. The system is generated by principles concerning the protection of life from the sources of uncleanness, which represent death, and these principles turn out to form an exercise, in this context, in a single conception: a particular class of human beings, here Israelites, are responsible to form a mature intentionality to forestall death through inadvertence, to take responsibility to protect what is holy from sources of uncleanness. And what governs in the entire transaction of contamination is a failure of intentionality, meaning here taking responsibility for what happens to what has to be kept separate from death and is therefore holy. With conceptions of such abstraction in hand, the Halakhah takes on the appearance of a third- and fourth-level exercise in the exposition of problems of detail and the refinement of principles established, in logical sequence, many steps before.

The predocumentary history of systems of ideas, granted, is only illustrated by the case of *Makhshirin*, both on its own and in relationship to *Hallah*. The Halakhic category formations yield a variety of further possibilities, so that monographs of considerable dimension present themselves, in imagination at any rate, as candidates for investigation. The Halakhic category formations fully exposed in the Mishnah-Tosefta (not to exclude what is fresh and not merely repetitive and paraphrastic and niggling in the Baraita corpus of the Yerushalmi and the Bavli) invite precisely this kind of exercise in the hypothetical reconstruction of levels of logical relationship of one stage in the law necessarily prior to another. What I mean to show is that the predocumentary history of systems of ideas—not only Halakhic but also Aggadic and theological—awaits reconstruction. And the results, while hypothetical as I have stressed time and again, are anything but speculative or arbitrary. They represent the working out of a dialectics that guides the logical unfolding of the Rabbinic system, and working backward from data to givens to premises, we are able to trace, from outcome to point of origin, the interior history of that system.

V. An Exterior Perspective: 1. The Relationship between the Ideas That People Hold and the Social World in Which They Live

But what of the context of the texts? Ought we not aspire to move from text to social context, to progress from what a text says to the world to which, and about which, its compilers and authors claim to speak? And if so, how are we to do so; what questions ought we to ask of documents of the sort we have in hand?

First, let us ask ourselves what is at stake and why we should wish to cross the border that separates the interiorities of a document from the world beyond its boundaries. Given the compelling possibilities of hypothetical reconstruction of logic, should we even care what lies beyond? One may make the case that the pure abstractions we find accessible through shared reason wholly satisfy, so that the interior history of ideas, the sequential stages of their unfolding, suffices for the cultural inquiry at hand. But the reason we should care is simply stated in a truism: even so pure and abstract an intellect as Aristotle is better understood when the system he put forth is placed against the background of the world from which he emerged and to which he spoke. The entirely interior perspectives just now outlined ignore the interplay of text and context—that is, of ideas and the social order to which ideas are intended to pertain. They require the pretense that people ignore interest and context in exploring the dialectics of logic.

Also, while admirable in its intellectual purity, the approach that deprives ideas of a place in the social order asks, in the end, too little of the sources. The texts speak of what is public and shared, situating Israel in relationship to the nations and treating the Torah as

the design for Israel's social order. Surely that claim cannot be
dismissed out of hand, its implications for social history ignored. The
foundation documents of formative Judaism, those of the written
Torah, concern themselves with the kingdom that God planned for
Israel to constitute. In that tradition the Rabbinic canon addresses the
social condition, the politics, the historical context of Israel. Surely,
given the acute practicality of the Halakhah, the Rabbinic sages
intended to speak not only to a social world of their own design but
to the social realities pertinent to realization of their vision. And the
social aspirations realized in the Halakhah, as much as the historical
conceptions adumbrated in the Aggadah, invite interpretation in the
context of the world onto which the Rabbinic sages projected that
vision.

So the exterior perspectives correct for an awry approach, one that
derives from a purely intellectual reading of a structure of ideas and
their logic. The error results from an excess of preoccupation with
textual interiorities, excluding attention to the other-than-logical
considerations, such as circumstance. A full understanding of the
Rabbinic canon entails asking questions of interest and bias, introducing considerations of values and social givens into the negotiation
that, for their part, the Rabbinic sages frame wholly in acontextual,
logical terms. So we are impelled to ask these questions: can the
Rabbinic writings be read in the setting of the Israel of which and to
which the Rabbis speak; can we move from what the text says to the
world about which it speaks; and does a picture of the world beyond
the text emerge?

Asking the Rabbinic narratives to tell us exactly what happened no
longer serves; and presenting the Rabbinic laws and stories with questions of social history and social description produces equally unlikely
results. When we can test the social description of the Rabbinic
writings against other evidence, we discover ample reason to desist
from asking these writings to serve as sources of social history and
description.

Were we to compose a social history of Israel based on what the
Rabbinic sages say or ignore, we would find ourselves misled. The
Rabbinic documents ignore important events, well documented in
other sources, that were critical to Israel's consciousness. On the basis
of Rabbinic statements, we would anticipate that at the time of the
first great war against Rome, 66–73, Israelite society in the environs

of Jerusalem was corrupt. Stories about a thieving judiciary and con-
niving social rulers suffice to make the point. In the model of prophecy, the Rabbinic sages explained Israel's defeat by Rome as the
result of social sins. But when we consider the course of events as portrayed elsewhere, we contemplate the spectacle of a society whose
purposes enjoyed broad public support, with dissent limited to none
other than circles of the sages themselves. By their own account, they
represented a suppressed minority of dissent, deeming the war policy
hopeless, not the heroic leaders of a broad political movement of
accommodation with Rome. Their reading of the social history of the
day does not compel credence. In addition, guided by the Rabbinic
documents, we would miss massive turnings. For example, Julian's
project of rebuilding the Temple in 360–361 never elicits explicit
response in the Rabbinic sources. So, for reconstructing social history
beyond the limits of the texts, the canonical documents turn out to
be remarkably limited. To ask the sources to tell us about Israel's
social order invites a theological viewpoint to translate itself into an
account of actualities.

What about social description? Here too, the imagination of the
writers and the internal, systemic considerations that motivated their
account of matters take over. We find little basis for translating allegations about the social order into critical social description. We find
ample basis for resisting the temptation to take at face value Rabbinic
accounts of points of tension or conflict between the Rabbinic sages
and the society round about. Stated simply: what the Rabbinic sages
say about the world beyond their circles portrays the Rabbinic system, not the social order constituted by the generality of Israel.

As with social history, so with social description: where we can cor-
relate the sages' allegations with facts established elsewhere, we find
little foundation in social fact for the sages' picture of Israel's social
order. To begin with, the Halakhic social order treats as constitutive
elements the householder who is a landholder, but the social category
formations make slight provision for trade and commercial classes in
the same context. Moreover, we cannot, without confronting the fan-
tastic character of their picture, consult the Rabbinic laws for an
account of the political institutions of the Israel of which they speak.
The Halakhah posits a government with three foci of power, king,
high priest, and sage. At no point in recorded time was Israel governed, either on its own or under imperial tutelage of Rome and Iran,

by institutions under the rule of kings, high priests, and sages. Again, the Rabbinic account of Israel's castes involves points of distinction and differentiation critical to the Rabbinic system (so *M. Qiddushin* 4:1: priests, Levites, Israelites, impaired priests, converts, freed slaves, Mamzers, Netins, "silenced ones" [*shetuqi*], and foundlings), but the actualities of social history portrayed by other-than-Rabbinic observers have yet to yield support for the maintenance of such a caste system in Israel's everyday life.

True, the Rabbinic documents portray tension between the Rabbinic sages and those outside their circles. So we ought to infer, from Rabbinic sages' points of tension and conflict with the world beyond their circles, the actualities of the society of ordinary Israel. But the sages' complaints about the ordinary folk, like the counterparts in ancient Israelite prophecy, reify doctrine, which posits conventional tensions between social critics (prophets, sages) and the community they propose to reform. These complaints hardly provide the basis for systematic social description, let alone social history. Nor do their exaggerated praises of all Israel—"if not prophets, then they are disciples of the prophets"—demand credence. Much that we find is conventional and apparently imaginary, and little compels credence. These represent cultural artifacts of documents of a particular classification. Whether they portray how things actually were remains to be demonstrated. The obstacles to moving from the text to the world beyond therefore prove formidable, since we have no way of situating the text in a particular time and place and since we have no corroborating evidence, for example, writing that stands outside a document and talks of the same social facts or political incidents.

What, then, of exteriority? How are we to move from the text outward, beyond the outer limits of the social world that produced and valued the text? The texts, in all their interiority, do speak of the world beyond their limits, and when they do, we are presented with two opportunities for assessing the plausibility of the message of the texts.

First, the texts set forth a broad range of laws bearing social consequences. Where material evidence permits, we find ourselves able to assess, in light of the facts of the matter, the extent to which the legal theory governs in actuality. Case reports in the Rabbinic codes, for example, serve as an indicator of areas of law that sages claimed to adjudicate in everyday life, as against those areas of law that remained, by sages' own words, of purely theoretical interest. Where the Rabbinic sages themselves differentiate, in their presentation of the law, between matters of theory and those of practice, I should be inclined to listen very closely to their testimony.

And that leads to a further possibility. For, second, the texts reveal tensions and points of conflict with the world beyond their limits. Archaeology produces data that intersect with topics on which the Rabbinic sages legislate. Once, in a given context, we are able to measure the law against the common practice as attested by archaeology, we may frame a theory of the interplay between how the Rabbinic sages design Israel's social order and how quotidian Israel composes its society. A single, blatant example suffices of how material and textual evidence intersect so as to place the text into the setting of the world. It concerns the effects of the commandment not to make graven images, generally understood to prohibit representational decoration for synagogues. Before the richly decorated synagogues of late antiquity were dug up, people generally assumed that (Rabbinic) Judaism produced no art. Then, when decorated synagogues did turn up, that art was not explained but explained away, in the assumption that the synagogues in question defied the norms of a single, unitary Judaism. Then the material evidence found itself subordinated to the literary imperatives of the Rabbinic Halakhah. Only when the possibility of more than a single Judaic religious system presented itself as a way of reading the data did the synagogue art, as actually dug up, begin to command a reading in its own terms and context, defined by the conventions of Graeco-Roman artistic convention. Once the Halakhic texts were no longer deemed a handbook for the reading of material evidence, the archaeological finds and the literary evidence were each accorded their own autonomy, and both were allowed to speak in turn.

What about economic history and other matters of material culture? These are data treated *en passant*, not in the framework of systemic analysis and advocacy, and I see no strong arguments of theory that call into question a broad range of commonplace facts set forth within the Rabbinic writings. To be specific: scholarship of a certain order has asked the Rabbinic documents questions of not only art and its interpretation but also economics, on the one side, and material culture, on the other. The documents allude to such matters of fact as the kinds of crops raised in diverse regions and the kinds of locks and keys people used. The texts speak of ordinary things of everyday use. These data, macrocosmic and microcosmic, rarely carry us to the heart of matters, nor are they designed to register a theological point. I cannot think of a reason to doubt that the documents could tell us about crops and locks if we knew that region or that object to which they make reference and if we could with some certainty situate the time and place of the crops and the venue of the locks.

But these data, subject to validation or falsification through intersecting references in non-Rabbinic documents or in the archaeological inquiry into material evidence of a culture, carry us far from the heart of matters, which is the description, analysis, and interpretation of formative Judaism the religion. I find limited utility in an exterior perspective that illuminates the documents only tangentially and in trivial details. Economic history and the phenomenology of material culture ask data of the Rabbinic canon that the canon supplies, even in abundance, without itself being clarified in any substantial, substantive way whatsoever. To be sure, knowing the shape of a given object clarifies the considerations that yield a Halakhic ruling of one sort rather than another—the object is or is not susceptible to uncleanness, for instance, by reason of containing or not containing a receptacle. But the focus, the point the Halakhah registers through its ruling, is not thereby clarified in ways otherwise left obscure. And this is so even though we appreciate the considerations beyond a given ruling better than before.

The result is simple. For a long time the same uncritical attitude of gullibility that defined how the texts would be read also accorded to the texts priority in the reading of exterior contexts, whether in narrative history and politics or in art and archaeology. Paraphrasing the texts yielded history. Looking up in the texts accounts of how things are would serve to place archaeological artifacts into their interpretative context as well. Now that the texts no longer are assumed without critical analysis to yield historical facts, the material evidence likewise makes an autonomous statement of its own. The exterior setting of the Rabbinic writing is not defined by material evidence, but it is at least adumbrated thereby. More to the point, archaeology only rarely helps us to move from the conceptions of the Rabbinic writings to the social world to which, by their own word, those writings addressed their message. The exterior context finds its definition in other sources altogether, outside the Rabbinic ones.

When the Rabbinic documents are interrogated for purposes extrinsic to their own interests, within narrow limits they yield useful facts. But I do not know how to address to the Rabbinic documents such questions of the social history of ideas as may illuminate the relationship of the ideas that people hold to the world in which they live. I cannot devise critical and analytical approaches for moving from text to social context.

Still, this does not conclude the shaping of an exterior perspective of critical interest to the history of ideas. The extradocumentary context of ideas carries us beyond the limits of ancient Israel altogether, and an account of promising fields of endeavor in the study of formative Judaism, for that reason, turns toward, first, the Roman-pagan, then the Christian counterparts to Rabbinic Judaism as a statement of the ordering of society and culture. That is why seeing the Rabbinic system and structure from without entails two perspectives, the contiguous one just now set forth, defined by points at which the Rabbinic writings intersect with the larger Israelite world in which they find their being, and yet another perspective.

VI. An Exterior Perspective: 2. The Extradocumentary Context of Ideas—Pagan

The contexts of cultural history are not bounded by contiguity but by synchronicity. Ages or periods bear their own characteristics, and cultural styles transcend ethnic boundaries. Systems for the social order, put forth in the same age and region by contemporary communities widely separated in origin and viewpoint, may be shown to address—indeed, to have to address—a common agenda of issues. They prove congruent in large shapes and structures even while the details scarcely correspond. These synchronic issues define an extradocumentary context of ideas that afford perspective on the Rabbinic documents read in the context of their age and location. I see two obvious synchronic settings: the worlds of pagan Rome and nascent Christianity. In the context of cultural and social history, Rabbinic Judaism intersects with (1) pagan Rome in the construction of law codes, the Mishnah coming into being in a great age of Roman legal codification, the second century, and with (2) Christianity in the formulation of a doctrine of the social order of the Israel conceived by the two systems' appeal to ancient Israelite Scripture—the Rabbinic Judaic and the orthodox, catholic Christian.

This exterior perspective therefore carries us away from the Israelite context altogether. It is the perspective afforded from a great distance, through comparison and contrast with other systems and their writings altogether—cultural systems of the same time and place that do not formally intersect with the Israelite ones. Here we stand at the outer limit of exteriority, and yet within common bounds of history and geography.[5] What in the present context makes the comparison of religions historical is the simple fact of historical synchronicity. The more distant comes first, paganism.

What do we learn about the history of Rabbinic Judaism when we take up the perspective afforded by pagan Rome? The answer is both general, involving systemic characterization, and particular, involving a principal cultural activity undertaken by both pagan Rome and Rabbinic Judaism in the same time period. The gain for historical study comes from comparison in general terms and contrast in particular ones.

Paganism affords a series of gross contrasts not only in theology but also in institutional expressions and structures. Viewed in the grossest cultural traits, paganism espoused a latitudinarian tolerance, and Rabbinic Judaism defined with great care what is required to live in God's Kingdom—and how one might lose his or her place in the world to come. For an account of the pagan counterpart to the Israelite social order, we follow what the great historian of pagan and Christian religion in late antiquity, Ramsay MacMullen, writes of paganism. He contrasts the tight, hierarchical organization of Christianity with the inchoate, uninstitutionalized character of paganism. Explaining the endurance of paganism long after the triumph of Christianity under Constantine, he says,

> This religion had no single center, spokesman, director, or definition of itself; therefore no one point of vulnerability. Everyone was free to

---

[5] Yet another, still more abstract perspective, that of comparable religious structures and systems of the social order put forth anywhere at any time—for example, early Islam of the seventh and eighth centuries C.E. compared with formative Judaism of the second through fifth, or classical Buddhism and classical Judaism—invites exploration, if not in the present context of historical study, then in the context defined by the comparative study of religions, treated later on.

choose his own credo; anyone who wished could consult a priest or ignore a priest, about how best to appeal to the divine. Appeal found expression in a great variety of words, acts, and arts, which . . . had been woven into the deepest levels of daily life and culture, the secular included. . . . Not only motifs but people circulated everywhere—meaning worshipers with their religious ideas. Over the course of many hundreds of years of peaceful stirring about, the mix became constantly more complex and intimate, at least in urban settings. Variety itself became a characteristic binding together the whole fabric of religion into one whole, across space, as on the other hand, the long peace of the pax Romana had bound communities also to their past.[6]

MacMullen underscores "the variety of words, acts, and arts." Paganism survived many centuries of the Christian challenge because it had no one point of vulnerability, he argues with great effect. And Judaism survived also. The tenacity of paganism gives us a standpoint from which to see Rabbinic Judaism, a foundation for comparison. The basis for Rabbinic Judaism's power to resist the Christian and later Islamic challenge is not that it had no one point of vulnerability. It is, rather, the intangible, if not at all inchoate, character of its sustaining power, which is its generative conviction. That is where Judaism differed from paganism and found its point of comparison with Christianity.

For, if we ask whether Rabbinic Judaism in its formative age possessed a single center, spokesman, director, or definition of itself, the answer is self-evident: of course it did. But it did not take institutional form, as with the Church, in a priesthood and a hierarchy. Rather, the single center located itself in the Torah as expounded by the consensus of the sages, especially in the Halakhah. The counterpart to Church, priesthood, and hierarchy was embodied not in a particular man or office but in a coherent body of ideas, represented by many men in many times and places. Rabbinic Judaism's was not a locative center: take that, and all else falls. It was utopian. And it was not a center formed by an institution: destroy that, and all else is lost.

Its center was its books, Scripture, and the oral tradition the sages themselves received from Sinai and handed on to their disciples in memorized sayings or notes or, in time, completed documents. That

---

[6] Ramsay MacMullen, *Christianity and Paganism in the Fourth to Eighth Centuries* (New Haven: Yale University Press, 1997), 32–33.

is where, if asked to point us to their center, the sages of any time and place would direct our attention. That too explains why, in medieval times, Christianity time and again burned the Talmud. True, this Judaism had as its spokesman Moses (called "our rabbi") and, for its definition, looked to his writings in Scripture and to the traditions held to commence with him. But Moses is represented as the starting point, the inner dynamics of the Torah's logic governing the articulation of the Torah. And as history would show, Rabbinic Judaism suffered no one point of vulnerability, for devastating a single center, silencing a single spokesman, would never accomplish the work of wiping out this Judaism, even in our own day and its singular disaster.

But unlike latitudinarian and tolerant paganism, Rabbinic Judaism, by its nature as the monotheist book-religion, found a ready definition of itself. On the one hand, permissible difference was clearly specified in the provision of contradictory opinion on both law and lore. On the other hand, no one was free to choose his or her own credo or ignore the sages' mediation in approaching the divine through the Torah. A simple expression of this fact dictates how one may lose his or her portion in the world to come—that is, by an act of unfaith:

Mishnah tractate *Sanhedrin* 11:1

A. All Israelites have a share in the world to come,
B. as it is said, "your people also shall be all righteous, they shall inherit the land forever; the branch of my planting, the work of my hands, that I may be glorified" [Is. 60:21].
C. And these are the ones who have no portion in the world to come:
D. He who says, the resurrection of the dead is a teaching which does not derive from the Torah, and the Torah does not come from Heaven; and an Epicurean.

No sanction more severe than losing one's portion in the world to come, which means giving up life eternal beyond the grave, is imaginable. This is ample proof that Rabbinic Judaism fundamentally differed from pagan tolerance, just as the Pentateuchal narrative and prophetic teaching insisted that God could not tolerate idolatry.

Stated more broadly: a particular set of words, acts, and arts certainly did define this Judaism, excluding a broad range of the other words, acts, and arts that Jews beyond the limits of the circle of the master and disciple valued. While, in centuries to come, these artifacts of religious culture would pervade the everyday life of all

Israel—Jews wherever they lived—in the formative age, the sources show, tension between sages and ordinary folk attested to the particularity of Rabbinic Judaism to its circles of masters and disciples. Its faith did not represent a common consensus, nor did its practices describe ordinary behavior. The way of life was learned, and the worldview was the product of particular knowledge and distinctive modes of thinking about and analyzing that knowledge. That is why, from the perspective of the sages and their disciples, no one was free to choose his or her own credo, and none could imagine ignoring the master of the Torah and his ruling.

If I had to choose the single most important trait of the Rabbinic system, it is its choice, for the medium of its authoritative statement, of the codification of law in the Mishnah and its continuator documents. Precisely in the same time, the second century, pagan Rome engaged in the same cultural enterprise. Hence synchronicity is unforced but compelling. The outermost context of comparison, then, brings the process of making the Mishnah into juxtaposition with Roman legal codification. This comparison exemplifies a variety of concrete possibilities of research, just as the contrast of the cultural policies of paganism and Rabbinic Judaism yields insight into the choices available to both and made by each party.

When it comes to the matter of legal codification, we find ourselves at the frontiers of established learning. On the one side, a great corpus of important research has compared Roman and Judaic law. A discipline of comparative law, Roman and Judaic, has produced a century of scholarship that, to this outsider, seems definitive in rich detail. But, for the history and comparison of particular legal documents and the processes that brought them into being and the characterization of each one of them, we have not many predecessors. So we venture into unfamiliar territory when we ask a simple question: is the Mishnah like, or unlike, its Roman counterparts?

The question demands attention because of the characterization of the Mishnah itself. On the one side, the question carries us back to the starting point: the history of Judaism in the formative age as a massive response to defeat and subjugation. Then we want to compare and contrast the process that produced the Mishnah, on the part of the defeated people and its legal authorities, with the counterpart process that produced law codes, on the part of the victors. What we are to make of the Mishnah in particular depends upon what we compare the document with, on the one side, and the context in which we address it, on the other. This will tell us what traits of the Mishnah register and what facts concerning the document make a difference. So the exterior perspective afforded by pagan-Roman law codification helps us to situate the first document of formative Judaism in its cultural-historical context.

The exterior perspective on the Mishnah does not originate here. It forms the foundation for ongoing scholarly debate. Indeed, some scholars advocate viewing the Mishnah as a second-century law code synchronous with other law codes of the time—and not as part of the Torah diachronic with Scripture, as Judaism sees it. I am party to the debate because I have viewed the Mishnah as sui generis and also as a statement of a closed system, complete in its own terms. To this view others have objected, invoking the genre of law code. So the issue figures prominently in contemporary debate. It also serves to illustrate historical research from the perspective of exteriority. That is why a brief and preliminary account of what is to be done warrants some attention. Does the Mishnah find its place within the framework of Roman legal codification of its time and place, and is it to be read as a law code like other law codes in the same time and place, *in the genre of law codes?* Or is the Mishnah to be taken in its own terms and encompassing framework? Since a genre is not defined by a single exemplar, the work of comparison and contrast is demanded. It also is quite feasible because the genre of law code is amply set forth by the Roman codification process of the second century.

Let me then frame the scholarly question of fact as I see it: is the Mishnah in general—process, premise, structure—sufficiently like Roman legal codification to sustain comparison, hence also contrast, as part of a single genre, or have the points of intersection and comparison been misconstrued or flagrantly misrepresented? Readers will answer for themselves. The questions, then, are these: is it true that the Mishnah fits into the context of Roman legal codification in the second century, and must or may we assign the Mishnah to the genre of law code as defined by Roman law codes of the same century?

To find out, I consulted a classicist, Stephen A. Stertz, for an account of Roman legal codification of the second century.[7] The

---

[7] Stephen Stertz, "Roman Legal Codification in the Second Century," in The

result is partial and one-sided. Stertz touches on a variety of issues that pertain directly to problems of legal codification but that scarcely intersect in character or in contents with the Mishnah. But at five points his account of Roman legal codification in the age in which the Mishnah took shape does afford perspective upon the Mishnah. Specifically, he treats five questions that may be addressed equally to the Mishnah and to the Roman process of codification. These points at which the Mishnah intersects with its Roman counterpart, not in detail but in large proportions, allow us to determine whether the Mishnah falls into the genre of legal code as defined in its time and place, the Roman Empire of the second century.

Concerning myself not with details of comparing a particular Roman law with a particular Mishnah law but rather with the large and fundamental questions of literary redaction, I will now systematically compare the Mishnah with the Roman counterpart as Stertz portrays matters. For each question, I italicize the main pertinent result of Stertz's account of Roman legal codification, then comment on the Mishnah's counterpart, if any. At only one point does the Mishnah intersect with its Roman counterpart: it deals with some of the same subjects. But the Mishnah also deals with a great many subjects that the Roman codes of its day ignore. In the aggregate, the points of intersection are few, the points of diversion many and important.

1. The Institutional Foundations of Legal Codification: Who Determines the Law and on What Foundations? Stertz: *By the second century—Hadrian's day—the emperor possessed the authority to make the law, hence to codify it.*

A law code derives from an institutional sponsor, finding its authority in the standing of the one who determines the law. Does the Mishnah qualify as a law code by defining its institutional foundations and by specifying the politics that sustain the code, whether in fact or in myth? So far as the genre, law code, includes a clear statement of sponsorship, the Mishnah does not fit. It rarely cites prior authoritative sources of the law, the Pentateuch, for example. If we relied on

Mishnah in Contemporary Study, ed. Jacob Neusner and Alan J. Avery-Peck (Leiden: Brill, 2002).

the Mishnah's internal evidence, we could not answer these questions for the document: who says, and why should anyone conform?

That is to say, unlike the Roman law codes, the Mishnah does not tell us who has determined the law and on what institutional basis he has done so. True, Judah the patriarch is credited in the continuator documents with promulgating the Mishnah. But not a single piece of evidence internal to the document itself supports that allegation. It is further taken for granted that the patriarchate, recognized as the Jewish ethnic government in the Land of Israel, formed the institutional basis for enforcing the law of the Mishnah.

The Mishnah does set forth a fantasy sponsorship, out of relationship with the politics that sustained the document itself. The Mishnah itself assumes that the king, high priest, and Sanhedrin (sages' court) took charge of law enforcement—so tractate *Sanhedrin*, for example, chapter 2 for high priest and king. But the Mishnah acknowledges that the Temple lies in ruins and knows no Israelite monarch. So the Mishnah contains no counterpart to the Roman emperor as sponsor of the system, and its authorities are fictive, perhaps eschatological.

What about the patriarch ("nasi")—is he not the sponsor of the Mishnah within the framework of the Mishnah? The evidence that the patriarch sponsored the Mishnah, employed sages educated in its law, and enforced their decisions is difficult to discern in the details of the Mishnah. To be sure, the Mishnah knows "the nasi," ordinarily assumed to refer to the patriarch. But by "nasi" is sometimes meant "head of the sages' court" (for example, *M. Hagigah* 2:2), sometimes "head of the local Jewish community" (for example, *M. Taanit* 2:1).

More to the point, there is a disjuncture between the representation of the nasi and his alleged position in sponsorship of the Mishnah or of the Halakhah in general. Where we do have a political power called patriarch (nasi), his alleged sponsorship of the Mishnah does not figure. The one context in which the ethnarch does figure is Mishnah tractate *Horayot*, where "nasi" clearly pertains to the principal authority of the community of Judaism in the Land of Israel. The context concerns errors of instruction or decision making made by the high priest or the nasi. None of this suggests that the Mishnah is credited to the Jewish ethnarch or patriarch. From the discussion in Mishnah and Tosefta tractate *Horayot*, we should have no reason to attribute the Mishnah as a law code to the sponsorship of the patriarch/nasi, in the way in which we have ample reason to attribute the

Roman law codes of the second century to the sponsorship of the emperor. A genre to encompass both the Mishnah and the Roman law codes would have to accommodate both a total fantasy system and a practical account of how a powerful government administers the civil order.

To sum up: the Mishnah does not explain itself or account for its institutional foundations. We do not know who determines the law and on what foundations. If we take for granted that the document speaks for the consensus of the sages who collected or made up its laws, our supposition is no more solidly grounded. In this aspect of matters, Stertz's account of Roman law codes in this aspect yields no common ground with the Mishnah.

2. OF WHAT DOES A CODE CONSIST? Stertz: *What occurred under Hadrian? The law was collected and fixed. Various documents were brought together and redacted, with some reorganization but minor changes in actual content.*

The Mishnah represents its contents not as a compilation of various documents that have been brought together and redacted but as a freestanding system, resting on its own foundations of applied reason and practical logic. The document only rarely preserves the indicators of a prior piece of writing. It ordinarily obscures the markings of origin in autonomous tradition. It rarely collects and sets forth opinions of a given school or authority or prior document. It homogenizes whatever language of individuality it has received and commonly lays out all opinion in a uniform rhetoric. Form analysis of the Mishnah is complete and detailed and leaves no doubt whatsoever as to these facts. So, while the Mishnah may have collected and fixed the laws of received documents, nothing in the document as we have it signals this fact, and the prevailing literary policy of the framers of the document contradicts it. So if the mark of the law code genre, as defined by the Roman laws, was to highlight the diverse origins of law now collected and reorganized with minor changes—a law code as the collection and arrangement of existing law—the Mishnah simply does not exhibit the indicative traits of a law code.

Let us then consider the facts of the matter, which those who assign the Mishnah to the law code genre do not address when they criticize the systemic reading of the Mishnah (and Tosefta). Is the

Mishnah composed of collections of laws, various documents brought together and redacted with some reorganization? It is difficult to answer with any certainty. But the general answer is that such occurs rarely and not as a paramount characteristic of the formal definition of the document. On the one hand, we can pick out anomalous compositions that clearly form a freestanding collection, for example, Mishnah tractate *Kelim* 24, representing a particular authority on a given set of closely related problems. There are, moreover, formal composites that cohere not on topic or problem, as is the norm for the Mishnah, but around formulations of language. These, uncommon in the Mishnah in general, are represented by Mishnah tractate *Megillah* 1:4ff. So they do exist. These anomalous compositions are organized not by topic, as is characteristic of the Mishnah, but by principle or by verbal pattern. The document does encompass selections from various legal documents. But these are anomalous, few, and unrepresentative. So if the case serves, then it underscores the uniformity of the bulk of the Mishnah, which is characterized by two traits. First, it is composed in highly disciplined language and adheres to a few uniform rules of rhetoric. Second, it is organized by topic, and it sets forth its topical program in accord with the dictates of the problematics of a given topic—the topic's specific issues that engage the framers of the law. The document is, overall, marked by recurrent formal traits, and these obscure the origin of law in prior compilations. It suffices to point out, for example, that the Mishnah forms its completed units of discourse in groups of threes or fives. The numerical patterns render inaccessible any supposed prior law collections that have now been formed into a single code.

So I maintain that Stertz's account of the second-century law codes gives us a kind of legal writing—the collection of prior documents—that does not characterize the Mishnah. If a genre is formed by common policies of rhetoric or topical programming—construction and organization and exposition—that characterize two distinct kinds of writing, then the Mishnah and the second-century Roman law codes simply do not belong together in a common genre. Those who categorize the Mishnah as a law code like Roman law codes have yet to do more than allege their reading of matters. They have not validated it. It follows that the Mishnah is mainly, though not exclusively, the work of its final redactors. Whatever laws they have collected, whatever opinions they have amassed, they have formalized and presented as a stylistically cogent whole. We cannot say that various documents have been brought together and cobbled into a single statement. If that is what Hadrian's lawyers did, then the Mishnah's counterparts engaged in an altogether different enterprise—no common genre here.

3. WHAT IS THE STANDING OF THE CODE? Stertz: *There was one uniform, permanent, unalterable edition from Hadrian's reign. What was done was to edit the received laws, forbidding alterations.*

If a law code is published in writing, then the Mishnah does not belong to the genre of law code because it was not published in writing. I invite the proponents of the view that the Mishnah is a law code like other Roman law codes of the time and place to explain how the Mishnah qualifies in this fundamental trait of the alleged genre: publication in conventional form. The Mishnah was not published in writing. True, there was a uniform text. But it was not generally accessible, as a law code in the Roman model was, to its constituency. In *Greek in Jewish Palestine*, on the publication of the Mishnah, Saul Lieberman maintains, "Since in the entire Talmudic literature we do not find that a book of the Mishnah was ever consulted in the case of controversies or doubt concerning a particular reading, we may safely conclude that the compilation was not published in writing, that a written *ekdosis* [edition] of the Mishnah did not exist."[8]

The Mishnah was published in a different way:

> A regular oral ekdosis, edition, of the Mishnah was in existence, a fixed text recited by the Tannaim of the college. The Tannaite authority ("repeater, reciter") committed to memory the text of certain portions of the Mishnah which he subsequently recited in the college in the presence of the great masters of the Law. Those Tannaim were pupils chosen for their extraordinary memory, although they were not always endowed with due intelligence. . . . When the Mishnah was committed to memory and the Tannaim recited it in the college, it was thereby published and possessed all the traits and features of a written ekdosis. . . . Once the Mishnah was accepted among the college Tannaim (reciters) it was difficult to cancel it.

---

[8] S. Lieberman, *Greek in Jewish Palestine* (New York: Jewish Theological Seminary, 1942).

Lieberman's evidence for these conclusions is drawn from two sources: first, sayings within the rabbinical corpus and stories about how diverse problems of transmission of materials were worked out, and, second, parallels, some of them germane but none of them probative, drawn from Graeco-Roman procedures of literary transmission.

Considerably more compelling evidence of the same proposition derives from the internal character of the Mishnah itself. But if stylization and formalization testify to a mnemonic program, then absence of the same traits must mean that some materials were not intended to be memorized. The Mishnah, and the Mishnah alone, was the corpus to be formulated for memorization and transmitted through "living books," Tannaim, to the coming generations. The Tosefta could not have been formulated along the same lines. Accordingly, the Mishnah is given a special place and role by those who stand behind it.

The Mishnah's publication represents a unique procedure, with no counterpart in the Roman practice of the second century as Stertz lays it out. If, as I say, the Roman codes belong to the genre of law code, then the Rabbinic one does not.

4. How Is the Code Organized? Stertz: *The codified praetor's edict is set forth topically. First come rules of procedure and jurisdiction, actions before the actual trial, then come legal remedies. The topics of the law encompass property of various classifications, for example, consecrated for religious purposes, belonging to wives (inclusive of divorce), stolen property, wills, guardianship, water rights, property destroyed in fires and shipwrecks, the execution of judgment, legal formulae, public property.*

The Mishnah also is organized topically, and this is an important point in common with the Roman code of its day. In this aspect the Mishnah certainly does compare to the Roman counterpart. But it also compares to the Pentateuchal codes that are organized topically, Leviticus 1–15, for example, and with the Qumran library's law code, with its (truncated) topical construction as well. Mishnah tractates *Niddah-Zabim* and *Negaim* exactly correspond with Leviticus 12–15, to take a blatant example, and *Parah* to Numbers 19, to take another. So the topical construction on its own does not establish a common genre, the law code, encompassing the Mishnah and the Roman codes—unless we assign to the same genre other law codes of other communities of Judaism. More to the point, the topics of the Mishnah intersect with those of the Roman codes only at some few points. If, for convenience' sake, we call "secular" the topics of the Roman code, then the Mishnah's topical program vastly transcends the secular, and the "sacred" ones vastly outweigh the secular. There is, then, no topical indicator that would tell us what belongs, and what does not belong, in the genre of law code. What is left is that any compilation of norms, whether or behavior or of belief, whether of a sacred or of a secular character, qualifies for the genre of law code.

But then the genre has no use; it tells us that any statement of how things should be done, whatever its formal traits, whatever its logical qualities, whatever its topical program, constitutes a law code. If it does not tell us what does not belong, it cannot tell us what does. The traits shared in common by the Roman codes of the second century and the Mishnah thus prove abstract, trivial, and unenlightening. Stated simply: the allegation that both the Mishnah and the Roman codes belong to the proposed genre makes no difference at all in our understanding of either code or both. What they have in common is nothing consequential, and we cannot then explain a trait of the one by appeal to a counterpart trait of the other. So the supposed common genre does not allow us to answer the question why this and not that. The upshot, in a word, is this: genre by topic—so what?

5. THE PURPOSE OF THE CODE: Stertz: *The code was meant to collect and organize the law, to order the received materials, annual accretions, repetitions, and ambiguities.*

The traits of the Roman codes permit us to state the purpose of those who made them. The Mishnah contains not a hint about what its authors conceive their work to be. Is it a law code? Is it a schoolbook? Since it makes statements describing what people should and should not do—or, rather, do and do not do—we might suppose it is a law code. Since it covers topics of both practical and theoretical interest, we might suppose it is a schoolbook. But the Mishnah never expresses a hint about its authors' intent. The reason is that the authors do what they must to efface all traces not only of individuality but even of their own participation in the formation of the document. So it is not only a letter from utopia to whom it may concern. It also is a letter written by no one person—but not by a committee, either. If the genre of law code serves to tell people what the law is, then the Mishnah certainly does not qualify. If the genre of law code provokes theorizing on the deeper philosophical issues embodied by practical cases, for example, issues of causation or of theology, then the Roman codes do not qualify within the genre, as exemplified by most of the Mishnah. For the Roman codes, the Mishnah encompasses too much within the genre it is supposed to embody; for the Mishnah, the Roman counterpart encompasses too little.

6. The Conclusion: Does the Mishnah Belong to the Genre of Law Code?

If the genre of law code is defined by the Roman codes as Stertz portrays them, then the Mishnah does not belong. A genre cannot be defined by a unique document, and in the contexts treated here, the Mishnah emerges without counterpart. No other document sufficiently compares to afford the occasion of defining a genre encompassing the Mishnah and some other compilation of social norms, including laws on topics treated in law codes—none.

Let me be clear. I recognize that comparative study of Roman law and the law of Judaism yields illuminating results. But here at issue are not details of the Halakhah contained in the Mishnah in comparison with details of Roman law contained in the codes. A vast and valuable corpus of detailed work has compared and contrasted the Halakhah (transcending that contained in the Mishnah, granted) and Roman law. But with what result for the categorization of the Mishnah? I see none whatsoever. For the Mishnah's Halakhah intersects with that of the Pentateuch, the Elephantine papyri, the Gospels, and the Dead Sea Scrolls—not to mention legal formulas and traditions of Sumer, Akkad, and Babylon! And no one has then insisted that we read the Halakhah of the Mishnah, let alone the Mishnah as a whole, in the context of ancient Israel, Elephantine, earliest Christian communities, Qumran, Sumer, Akkad, or Babylon. If the Mishnah is not sui generis, then by finding an appropriate generic companion, no one has yet established the genre to which, viewed whole and complete, the Mishnah belongs. In four of five definitive traits the Mishnah differs from the process and product of the contemporary Roman law codification. The burden of defining a genre encompassing the Mishnah and other sufficiently similar documents belongs on the shoulders of those who do not see the document, as I do, as sui generis—even in the context of Rabbinic Judaism of its time and for a thousand years afterward as well.

What is the upshot for answering historical questions out of the documents of formative Judaism? So far as the documents set forth a system of culture, they are to be juxtaposed, their system set side by side, with comparable artifacts of culture. This entails synchronous exercises on social policy and legal codification. Both exercises illuminate by forming a setting for comparison and contrast. And as I proposed at the outset, much is gained when we compare what the victors did with what the vanquished did. So, while we move only with great difficulty from the text to the social world beyond, and contiguous with, the text, when we take up a stance at some distance away but in the same time period, we see matters whole and in a fresh way. So much for the documents of formative Judaism in the setting of cultural history. What about considerations of social policy? How does an exterior perspective illuminate historical processes? For one answer, we turn from pagan to Christian Rome, and from law to doctrines of the social order.

VII. An Exterior Perspective: 3. The Extradocumentary Context of Ideas—Christian

The program of historical study of formative Judaism encompasses not only exterior perspectives on the legal documents and system but those concerning social policy put forth in those legal documents. And here, as the basis of a program of future inquiry, Christianity takes the place of paganism. Let me explain.

The study of history advances through the comparison and contrast of systems of the social order: how did people propose to organize society in determinate times and places? And answers to this question derive not only from secular philosophy but also from theology and religion. Accordingly, the study of history encompasses the history of religions when religions propose policies for the shaping of society.[9] Since formative Judaism certainly offers a detailed design for

---

[9] Those same religions self-evidently provide a focus for the study of religion in its

Israel's social order, an exterior perspective invites raising questions
on the social teachings of Rabbinic Judaism; and to realize this perspective, comparison and contrast with a competing corpus of social
teachings promise insight. The exterior perspective afforded by comparison and contrast yields points of intersection. Out of the entirety
of Scripture, each system chooses, both in general terms and in detail,
those issues of acute interest and those passages of Scripture that
speak to these issues.

Here the principal Christianity of the same time and region presents itself as a source of comparison and contrast because that Christianity, for comparison, responds to the same corpus of Scripture and,
for contrast, sets forth a competing view of public policy on an agenda common with that of formative Judaism. When, as in the case of
orthodox, Catholic Christianity and Rabbinic Judaism, these systems
address the same age and draw upon a common heritage of authoritative writings to rule on the same topics, by their contrasts each
illuminates the other, showing choices made out of a common selection and highlighting ways not taken.

If, then, we treat Rabbinic Judaism as the norm and Christianity
of the same age, the first six centuries, as the variable and allow three
principal Rabbinic teachings of the social order to define the topics
for comparison and contrast, we produce three main issues.

First, how does the social teaching of early Catholicism, as portrayed by one standard account of matters, compare with that of
Rabbinic Judaism?

Second, do we find a systematic account of the relationship between the counterpart to corporate Israel—which ought to be the
social order of the Church—and the individual Christian? How does
the Church propose to regulate relationships of a civil character
between Christians?

And third, how does the Christian social order prepare itself to
accord an abode to God in the society and culture of Christians?

The basic questions that illuminate formative Judaism come down
to these: (1) Does Christianity in its orthodox, catholic statement put
forth a social vision for itself that categorically corresponds to that of
Rabbinic Judaism? (2) Do we find not simply episodic doctrines on

_____

own terms, as I shall propose in Chapter Four. There the two religious traditions will
be shown to address comparable issues, each in its own idiom.

particular questions but a general theory of the social entity formed by Christians that resembles in its basic structure the general theory of Israel embodied in the Halakhah?

Within the program of the present book—to assess possibilities of new directions in the study of the formation of Judaism—it suffices to answer these questions in a very preliminary way. For this purpose, I turn to a standard work on the subject. That work inspired my life-long interest, beginning with *A History of the Mishnaic Law*,[10] in the social description of Rabbinic Judaism out of the category formations of the Halakhah. It is Ernst Troeltsch, *The Social Teaching of the Christian Churches*.[11] What I seek there is a routine, reliable represen-tation of the normative, orthodox, Catholic Christian conception of the social order. It is, specifically, the one constituted by orthodox, Catholic Christians, also known as "the Church." A founding figure in the study of religion and society, Troeltsch presents the formative Christian conception of social realities, and for the preliminary ini-tiative undertaken here, that presentation will serve.[12] Troeltsch's account is at the center of matters. To a section of his *Social Teaching*,[13] I ask the elementary questions and require only basic facts. Here are

---

[10] Jacob Neusner, *A History of the Mishnaic Law of Purities, Holy Things, Women, Appointed Times, and Damages*, 43 vols. (Leiden: E. J. Brill, 1974–1986; reprint, Classics in Judaic Studies, Binghamton: Global Publications, 2002).

[11] Ernst Troeltsch, *The Social Teaching of the Christian Churches*, trans. Olive Wyon, 2 vols. (New York and Evanston: Harper & Row, 1956), with an introduction by H. Richard Niebuhr.

[12] The scholarly literature on Troeltsch, all the more so on the problems he addresses, refines matters considerably. But I know of no more systematic and orderly account of matters, and the points important to this comparison are of such an ele-mentary character that I deem Troeltsch on his own quite sufficient to the task.

[13] Vol. 1, ch. 1, part iii. The chapter, "The Foundations in the Early Church," deals with three topics: the Gospel, Paul, and early Catholicism. The nature of our comparison of conceptions of the social order requires a focus on the third of the three, since at interest here is not ethical theories bearing social consequences, atti-tudes toward the state, economics, family, or society, such as Troeltsch describes for Jesus and Paul, but a different matter altogether. It is how Christians thought of themselves as a social entity and how they integrated attitudes toward the state, eco-nomics, family, and society into that encompassing social theory of who, and what, they were all together and all at once: the counterpart to Israel at Sinai, for exam-ple. I chose the survey of early Catholicism because there we deal not with individ-ual opinions, however authoritative and influential, but the collective doctrine and consciousness of the community viewed whole: "the Church." Troeltsch signals that difference. In reference to Jesus, the focus is on Jesus' main ethical idea and its socio-logical significance. Concerning Paul, he speaks of religious community, but at issue is theological doctrine, signaled by, among other instances, language such as the

my questions: (1) How does Troeltsch treat the categorical program
that has seemed to me native to Rabbinic Judaism and its design for
Israel's social order? (2) What perspective do we gain on the Rabbinic
sages' system from the Christian alternative and the contrast it
affords?

My answer is, in line with Troeltsch's account, that the Rabbinic
social teachings contemplate a social order that is not congruent, in
its basic components, to that of early Catholic Christianity. The external perspective highlights contrasts. The differences are so fundamental that, as we shall see, Christianity yields no teachings pertinent
to the generative issues that are critical to Rabbinic Judaism and vice
versa. And that is so, even though we could readily find pertinent
doctrines in the corpus of Catholic Christianity and Rabbinic Judaism
for a common agenda, questions of a domestic and economic character, for example.

Then how did the Torah figure in, and where did the Torah's
narrative make its impact upon, the social order of the Christian
Church? What is astonishing is how the model of ancient Israel's
Kingdom of God, valued by orthodox, Catholic Christianity as much
as by Rabbinic Judaism, served not at all for the former but governed all social thought of the latter. At later times and under other
circumstances, the vision of Israel conveyed by Moses in the Pentateuch would challenge important communities of Christianity and
move them to mighty efforts—the founding of my native Connecticut
within New England is a prime example of a Christian society mod-
eled on Israel of old. But in the formative age of the Christianity and
the Judaism subject to discussion here, that was not the case for
Christianity.

Put simply: to make sense of Christianity's social teaching, we
require Scripture only very rarely. Indeed, we could understand the

---

following: "Through its faith in Jesus as the Risen Lord, through the identification
of Jesus with the Messiah and . . . with the universal redeeming Divine principle,
through the new worship of Christ and its mystical idea of Redemption, through
Baptism and the Lord's Supper as the means of becoming one with the present
Exalted Christ, it has become an independent religious community, which, in ideal
at least, is strictly exclusive and bound together in unity." These and comparable passages do not serve our purpose. The institutional focus of his unit on early
Catholicism, by contrast, addresses issues of "Church," "state," and "society" that
correspond to those we have taken up in the Halakhic framework.

main lines of Christian social thinking in its formative age without the map supplied by Israelite Scripture at all. But—by contrast—scarcely a line of the Rabbinic account of its Israel's social order, let alone the vision of the whole, makes sense outside the framework of Moses' Torah. The Church, as portrayed by Troeltsch out of the resources of orthodox Christianity, simply does not form the counterpart to the Israel of which the Rabbinic sages speak. Presently I shall show in a concrete example precisely how disparate the two entities—Church and Israel—are. Language natural for the one proves egregious—indeed, beyond all comprehending—for the other.

Let us, then, turn to the compatibility of discrete category formations, the starting point for any comparative exercise. Troeltsch outlines, as topics of social teaching, such themes as "possessions, work, callings and classes, trade, the family, slavery, charity"—all topics on which Rabbinic Halakhah sets forth considerable bodies of rulings, even entire category formations, as this study as shown.[14] So, on the surface, the constituents of the structures to be compared do match. And yet the basic context is so different that the details, however comparable, do not sustain comparison. Two of Troeltsch's category formations tell the story: "the ethic of the Church which was developed out of this opposition between the Church and the world and how it bridged the gulf," and "settlement of the social problems within the Church and by the Church as a state within the state."

The former of the two categories underscores the sense of separateness that characterized Christian society vis-à-vis the world beyond. The counterpart would be the Rabbinic doctrine of Israel and the gentiles. But there is this difference: Israel regarded itself (in the Rabbinic design) as a fully articulated society, not separate from the world but constitutive of the social world it occupied and utterly autonomous of any other. Its doctrine was one of separation of a working community from the inchoate world beyond. The Halakhah afforded no recognition to the legitimacy of any entity like itself, for example, "a state within a state." Indeed, it only grudgingly and on

---

[14] And see also Jacob Neusner, *The Economics of the Mishnah* (Chicago: University of Chicago Press, 1989; reprint, South Florida Studies in the History of Judaism, Atlanta: Scholars Press, 1998); and also *Rabbinic Political Theory: Religion and Politics in the Mishnah* (Chicago: University of Chicago Press, 1991).

an ad hoc basis accorded recognition to the power of the gentiles and their empires, for example, in tractates *Abodah Zarah* and *Tohorot*.

Everything else was something else. Israel was sui generis, unique, out of phase with all other social entities, none of which the Rabbinic sages knew as legitimate counterparts to Israel. That is because Israel served God and inchoate humanity served idols. And more to the point, Israel was meant to realize the Kingdom of God, to form an abode for God's presence on earth. It was deemed unique on that account. There was no bridging the gulf between Israel and the realm of idolatry. The Halakhah leaves no doubt whatsoever on that score. And along these same lines, the Israel of Rabbinic Judaism did not regard itself as "a state within the state," but as the sole *state*, the state of Israel, pure and simple.[15] That is to say, it accorded recognition, legitimacy, rights of bona fide negotiation to no other entity.

The Halakhah, moreover, legislates for Israel as though the Halakhah were the sole authority over Israel. The social teachings of Christianity in the formative age take account of two authorities with whom Christians engaged, Church and state. Learning from its three centuries of persecution, Christianity could differentiate the sacred from the secular, the Church from the state. Such a conception lay wholly outside the imaginative power—or the historical, social experience that was formed in consequence—of Rabbinic Judaism. I assume this is because, in its conception of Israel's past, Rabbinic Judaism found in the Scripture no picture of a subordinated or marginalized Israel, at the fringes of the nations. Rather, the Pentateuch told the story of an Israel in command of its own destiny, responsible for its fate by reason of its adherence to, or divergence from, the covenant of Sinai. Leviticus 26 and Deuteronomy 33–34 tell the story not of an excluded and persecuted community but of a self-governing, morally responsible nation—unique in humanity. Rabbinic Judaism was guided by Scripture's narrative to explain defeat by Rome, a natural enemy because it was pagan, but not persecution of the kind Christians endured from Rome. Israel was never the victim of Rome, only of its own failure.

---

[15] This is the Halakhic view. The Aggadic view differentiated among the nations Rome, Greece, Media, and Babylonia and knew also Egypt, Canaan, and the like. All of these attain significance only in relationship to Israel; for example, Rome and Israel were deemed counterparts and opposites.

The Rabbinic Judaic system of the social order therefore, in its imaginative reconstruction of social reality, designed the society of not a minority settled among an encompassing majority, a state within the state, a people within a people (like Israel in Egypt), but as an autonomous social order, equivalent in standing to Rome, Greece, Media, and Persia (as the standard list of the empires in reverse order has it). That is why Rabbinic Judaism could in no way distinguish the realm of the sacred from the realm of the secular, the city of God from the city of man, to allude to a famous point of differentiation. It could not form a doctrine of the relationship of Israel to the state because, as I said, there was, from the Torah's perspective, no legitimate, lawful state other than the state of Israel, lawfully constituted by the Torah to govern.[16]

Before proceeding, let us consider principal parts of Troeltsch's "social teaching" for "early Catholicism" in the age of the Rabbinic sages: the social organizations of the state, the family, and economics, within the fundamental theory that religious ideas shape those organizations. As with the exteriority at issue here, Troeltsch's argument is also outward-facing, interested as he is in "the effect *on* civilization of Christian-sociological principles" (p. 12). But he states flatly,

> It is an actual fact of history that from the beginning all the social doctrines of Christianity have been likewise doctrines both of the State and of Society. At the same time, owing to the emphasis of Christian thought upon personality, the family is always regarded as the basis both of the State and of Society and is thus bound up with all Christian social doctrine. Once more, therefore, the conception of the "social" widens out, since in the development of a religious doctrine of fellowship the Family, the State, and the economic order of Society are combined as closely related sociological formations. . . . The ultimate problem may be stated thus: How can the Church harmonize with these main forces in such a way that together they will form a unity of civilization? Thus the question of the attitude of the churches toward the social problem also includes their attitude towards the State. (p. 32)

---

[16] But as everyone knows, Rabbinic Judaism also accorded recognition to the validity of the law of the gentile kingdoms in which Jews resided; thus "the law of the kingdom is law." But here we speak of the Torah and its categorical effects in the Halakhah, and that is another realm of being altogether.

Here we have the model for the systemic analysis of theories of the social order. "How can the Church harmonize with these main forces . . . [so that] they will form a unity of civilization" is another way of asking my question: how do the details fit together and work together to form a social system? Christianity ("the Church"), however, does not form the ground of being of the social order but only one component thereof. For in Troeltsch's language there is a single word that marks a major difference. It is "harmonize with" as against "harmonize." "Harmonize" can be used intransitively, as in "harmonize with," or transitively, as in "harmonize" plus a direct object.

To be clear: the language for Judaism must be, "How does the Halakhah harmonize these main forces so that they will form a unity?" That would have been my way of putting matters for Rabbinic Judaism. Here, in the distinction between preferred formulations, lies a profound difference. "Harmonize with" conceives the Church as an entity apart from family, state, and the economic order of society—all of them autonomous of the Church. Thus the concept of Church-state relations would follow. But natural to Rabbinic Judaism is this language: "How does the Torah harmonize—*impose harmony upon*—family, state, and the economic order of society to form a unity?" The Torah, as set forth by Moses in the Pentateuch, conceives each component of the Israelite social order to cohere with all others in a cogent whole, each part harmonizing with all others to form the unity of society that Israel is to embody.

Accordingly, we find a question that the sages would not have framed for Rabbinic Judaism: how can the Church harmonize *with* those main forces—family, state, economy—in such a way as to form a unity of civilization? That is because the sages could not imagine a state other than the one that they contemplated, for example, in tractates *Sanhedrin-Makkot* and *Horayot*—the state of, the state embodied by, Israel, whether in the Land of Israel, whether not.[17] Nothing in

---

[17] The Rabbinic theory of Israelite politics took it for granted that Israel would form an empowered political entity, capable of self-government (perhaps within an imperial system) wherever it was located. In that sense, the state of Israel as a political entity was not enlandised or localized. And as a matter of fact, the Rabbinic documents represent the Jews of Babylonia as self-governing in a wide variety of transactions, backed up by the threat of legitimate violence. The "Israel" of Babylonia was no voluntary community of coreligionists of faith but an empowered

the doctrine of the family conceived of the Israelite family outside the framework of the Israelite society that the sages designed, so that asking the family to form a unity with the state would have been incomprehensible. As noted elsewhere, the family by definition formed an integral component of Israel. As the economic order of society was subject to the ordering of the state and related to the family, it too is integral to the Israelite system as a whole: an economy conducted with God as landlord and overseer.

So much for the signals supplied by the diverse uses of common language. But what are we, then, to compare? Troeltsch asks about "the intrinsic sociological idea of Christianity and its structure and organization." He moves from sociology to Christianity: "What is the relation between this sociological structure and the 'Social'? That is the state, the economic order with its division of labor, and the family" (p. 34). Troeltsch follows a practical program, following "the actual influence of the churches upon social phenomena." Rabbinic Judaism sustains an interest, by contrast, in the theory of things, the analysis of a system of thought concerning those same phenomena. Here questions of historical method—how we know about the past, what we know about the past—intervene. On the basis of the Rabbinic documents, I do not know much about the actualities of Israelite life in the time and place in which the Rabbinic sages formed their system. I do know that the Rabbinic documents do not claim that people did things the way the rabbis said they should; rather, in general, they did things in their own way, sometimes in conformity with Rabbinic doctrine, sometimes not.[18] But insofar as Troeltsch describes the theory, not only the reality, he proves a suitable guide for so preliminary an exercise in comparison as this one. For, to make the matter explicit, all we wish to know are Judaic and Christian ideas about the social order, with special reference to the role of Scripture in shaping those ideas.

---

political entity, subject to superior power, granted, but with the right to inflict sanctions of property and person.

[18] My *History of the Jews in Babylonia*, 5 vols. (Leiden: Brill, 1965–1970), contains systematic presentations of the Rabbinic sages' accounts of their relationships with the ordinary Israelites in their communities. These show that in some areas Rabbinic authority governed but in others the population was recalcitrant, doing things as it, not the rabbis, wished.

What sort of historical inquiry do I conceive worthwhile? We could compare part to part, but out of context, the comparison yields little perspective and no insight. So we turn to the largest components of the social order, the principal aggregates. For Troeltsch, it is the Church, and for Rabbinic Judaism, Israel. The perspective of the Church upon itself and the perspective of the Rabbinic sages upon Israel yield two distinct angles of vision. The Church sees itself as a minority, not a freestanding, autonomous sector of humanity, not a political entity corresponding to other, comparable entities; as a minority; as different from the generality of humanity. The Rabbinic sages see Israel as an autonomous community, formed by God's intervention to constitute a component of humanity, a politically empowered society, a state unto itself, sui generis among states as Israel is also sui generis among nations or peoples. Ultimately, following the prophets, the rabbis conceive that all humanity will worship the one God and so form part of the same Israel that those who eschew idolatry and worship God now constitute. That is how Scripture portrayed God's people. And that is how the Rabbinic sages viewed the Israel of whom they spoke, that corporate community so fully articulated as to yield orderly relationships governing the state and individual Israelites.

So, to double back, the key to the social order, the source of coherence for the social teaching of the Christian Churches, is, for Troeltsch and surely for the Christian social order described by him, "the Church." And it is to be differentiated from "the state." There is no Israelite counterpart to "the Church," there is no distinguishing "Church" from legitimate "state"; there is only—once more—the unique state of Israel. That is because Israel, God's portion of humanity, encompasses both the political and the religious order corresponding to state and Church in the Christian context. Were "Israel" counterpart to "Church," we should find a comparison plausible. But it is not, so we cannot. The basic social category formation, "Church," as distinct from "state," simply has no match in Rabbinic social categories. And though the rest—work, trade, family, slavery, possessions—may correspond to Rabbinic category formations or sizable components thereof, there is no foundation for other than episodic and casuistic comparison and contrast.

A brief account of the details therefore suffices. Troeltsch opens with the Gospels, then Paul. Only with early Catholicism (p. 89) does he reach the counterpart to the Rabbinic statement: a large, coherent religious system speaking on fundamental issues of social organization. Troeltsch explains the formation of the Church in this language:

> The sociological idea of the Gospel was based on that faith in God which arose out of the Jewish Bible and the Jewish national life, intensified and illuminated by the proclamation of the Kingdom of God, and on the incarnation of this idea in the personality of Jesus himself. When, however, . . . this new faith had severed its connection with Judaism and Jesus was no longer with his disciples, it then felt the need for something to take the place of this outward relationship; it needed an independent center of organization which would incarnate the idea at any given point of time with reference to its relation to the actual setting in which it found itself. Both aspects of the Christian faith—its individualism and its universalism—needed this independent organization in order that they might find fresh and vital forms of expression. (pp. 89–90)

Here, in this theory of the whole, we find the key point of departure: the Kingdom of God. The Halakhic structure and system provide a detailed account of how Israel lives in God's presence and in God's Kingdom, accepting upon itself the yoke of God's dominion and the yoke of God's commandments. What is the Christian counterpart to the entire social order formed into God's Kingdom? It is—in Troeltsch's own words!—the incarnation of the Kingdom of God in the person of Jesus. The counterpart Rabbinic conception is self-evident: the embodiment of the Kingdom of God in the society of Israel. The metaphor invoked by Christianity to account for the social entity constituted by Christians, then, is personal; that invoked by Rabbinic Judaism for the social entity constituted by Jews is public, corporate, collective.

Whatever Christianity understood by the language to which Troeltsch refers, it is not what Judaism understood by the laws of the Torah. When, in the Torah, God addressed Israel as a kingdom of priests and a holy people, when he assigned to Israel the task of serving as his witnesses, when he asked for an abode on earth for himself within Israel, God spoke of corporate Israel, beyond individual Israelites or any one of them. God's Kingdom involved the acceptance of God's rule, detailed in the laws of the Torah, and the acceptance of the yoke of the commandments, set forth in those laws. None of this has any counterpart in any incarnate being but solely in the entirety of the Israelite social order. Insofar as the Church was conceived as "the mystical body of Christ" (as Troeltsch's language implies even here), Israel does not compare. Insofar as Israel forms God's abode within humanity, the Church does not compare. Troeltsch describes the formation of a social teaching for a community formed in relationship to an individual and shaped by life first in his presence and then not, in a palpable way, in his presence. What we have seen in the Halakhah, particularly in this part of the study, is that Israel always found itself in God's immediate presence, acting on that fact in countless transactions. And yet, from a certain perspective, God's abode (Israel) and Christ's body (the Church) prove remarkably congruent in conception—if not in execution.

But the conception is everything. The Church portrayed by Troeltsch emerges as a response to a circumstance, to the passage of time, to the change in the society formed by Christians. Its institutionalization is described as a matter of historical sequence. Israel, by contrast, is presented by the Rabbinic sages as eternal, atemporal, unrestricted by time, place, or circumstance. This is underscored by the execution of the governing metaphor. The Torah made little provision for the kinds of authority that the new age required; the rabbis themselves form no authorized clergy, comparable to the Christian priesthood; the politics of the community of Israel yielded no counterpart to the Church's order of priests and bishops and onward. What emerged in time was "the Christian priesthood," with emphasis on a genuine tradition, secured by the bishops, and the development of the sacramental idea, which "constitutes the development of early Catholicism."

Troeltsch sees the formation of the episcopate of sacrament and tradition as a "limitation of the original sociological idea of absolute religious individualism and universalism." He says, "The religious community is now no longer bound merely to the worship of Christ, to baptism, and the Supper of the Lord, but to the Church, to tradition, to the bishop, and to the use of the sacramental means of grace through the legally appointed bishop" (p. 93). The Rabbinic sages, by contrast, never differentiate between religious imperatives (*misvot*) (worship of Christ, baptism) and other-than-religious institutions, traditions, and authority (Church, tradition, bishop). Their own authority is implicit, institutional only in the loosest framework. They do not differentiate between Scripture and tradition, the whole constituting the Torah of Moses. The hierarchy of learning sufficed; there was no counterpart to a bishop among the Rabbinic sages, even though some figures are represented as broadly accepted authorities; the whole was governed by consensus.

So the Church and Israel do not correspond at all. They form contrasts, not comparisons. The Church was organized as an independent body, which formed its own "juridical constitution." "She gradually founded her own system of law, the law of the Church, in which, from her own standpoint, without any consideration for the State (which until then had been the only possible source of law), she evolved her own peculiar conception of the legal relation between society and the individual, between the Church and the world" (p. 96).

> The legal subjectivity of the whole body and of the individual congregation, the sphere of authority of the bishops . . . the representation of this legal subjectivity, the rights of individuals over against this objective law, the ecclesiastical possession of property, religious institutions of charity, the ecclesiastical control of sections of life which could be reached (above all, in the law of marriage), decisions affecting disputes of Christians amongst themselves and the care of morals—all this became increasingly the subject of an ecclesiastical-juridical system of thought. (p. 96)

The Rabbinic sages' Israel emerged out of centuries of Jewish political entities; the sages could not think socially except through politics. That is why there was no counterpart to an ecclesiastical body, no distinction between state and church authority, for the sages. True, they made decisions affecting disputes of Israelites among themselves, but resolving conflict was accomplished by appeal to governing principles, rules of mediation, and only rarely by force majeure—and then, in the form of the oath, it was God's.

In a word, the Rabbinic Israel formed not a state within a state, or an institution requiring state recognition, but a political entity, pure and simple—an entity of a political character that also constituted a religious body (in the ordinary sense), a state that was also a church, a society governed by rules of sanctification and so also a kind of monastic community. This Israel did not seek recognition by the Roman Empire, beyond the matter of political legitimacy, because this Israel saw itself as the sole legitimate public body to begin with. Rome could confer nothing; Iran could keep its distance.

By contrast, out of the ecclesiastical juridical system of thought developed a system that craved recognition, that was finally recognized by the state, and that in due course had to make its peace with the state. But in the early Church this system was limited, within its own borders, and did not affect the larger social world.

For Christianity, "the world" meant "all those social institutions of life outside the Church," and the world was "denied or depreciated" (p. 110). The Christian moral law

> consists in directing all activity toward the ultimate goal of union with God and then expresses itself in contemplative purity of heart and in active brotherly love. . . . In obedience to the Church and in sacrifice for the unity of the Church . . . the destruction of the ego and self-sacrifice for others is exercised, good works are acquired, and future salvation is assured. . . . That which a man renounces he gives to the Church and by means of services of this kind . . . he secures salvation in the other world, and this again is mediated by the Church. (pp. 110–11)

For Rabbinic Judaism, this entire program would have proved exceptionally difficult to follow. That is not because Rabbinic Judaism differed, for example, on destroying the ego and on self-sacrifice for others. On the contrary, in so many words, the *Sayings of the Fathers* affirm both moral virtues:

> He would say, "Make his wishes into your own wishes, so that he will make your wishes into his wishes. Put aside your wishes on account of his wishes, so that he will put aside the wishes of other people in favor of your wishes." Tractate *Abot* 2:4

A program of self-sacrifice for others, good works, and future salvation would thus not have surprised the Rabbinic sages, and renunciation in favor of service to others would have formed a commonplace of Rabbinic teaching on virtue. Wherein lies the difference, then?

What is the counterpart, for Judaism, to the Church? If we substitute "Israel" for Troeltsch's "Church," we get gibberish. To recapitulate Troeltsch's language, now with reference to "Israel":

> The Judaic moral law . . . consists in obedience to *Israel* and in sacrifice for the unity of *Israel* . . . the destruction of the ego and self-sacrifice for others is exercised, good works are acquired, and future salvation is assured. . . . That which a man renounces he gives to *Israel* and by means of services of this kind . . . he secures salvation in the other world, and this again is mediated by *Israel*.

How grotesque! I cannot imagine anything so incomprehensible as the notion of Israel as a focus of obedience, of sacrifice for the unity of Israel, of renouncing something and giving it to Israel, or of securing salvation mediated by Israel. None of these statements makes any sense whatsoever in the language of Rabbinic Judaism. But there is language that does work. What if we substitute "God" for "Israel"? Then the Judaic moral law

> consists in obedience to *God* and in sacrifice for the unity of *God* . . . the destruction of the ego and self-sacrifice for others is exercised, good works are acquired, and future salvation is assured. . . . That which a man renounces he gives to *God* and by means of services of this kind . . . he secures salvation in the other world, and this again is mediated by *God*.

Thus, whereas Troeltsch speaks of the Church, Rabbinic Judaism invokes God for the same declarations. I cannot imagine a more perfect statement of the Judaic moral law than this formulation, which is natural to the native category formations of Rabbinic Judaism. Israel forms a this-worldly social entity, sui generis in humanity, bearing supernatural tasks. It is God's abode. But in the drama of humanity en route to salvation in the world to come, Israel constitutes no principal player, is not the subject of obedience or the recipient of sacrifice for its unity, and no one renounces anything to Israel; God is at the center of the social order, and the social order is contingent upon God's wishes and God's word.

The exterior perspective places everything in a new light. For now we realize that in the Rabbinic vocabulary it is impossible to find a category formation that would function as does "Church" in Christianity. "Israel" does not work. "God" does not work either. But to turn to an obvious candidate, what of "synagogue"—is it not the counterpart to "Church"? Since Christians go to church for prayer, and Israelites to synagogue, the two institutions appear to function in the same way. But a moment of consideration shows us that "synagogue" certainly does not work in that way.

A synagogue in fact does not function like a church; it is not a place where, uniquely, Israel meets God or conducts rites particular to that location, except for one. The Halakhah knows two principal venues for Israel's meeting with God: Temple and the enlandised household, that is, the household that possesses real property in the

Land of Israel. The Temple forms the center of service, and the offerings for the Day of Atonement, Tabernacles, and Passover define a principal interest of the Halakhah in these occasions. The enlandised household defines the matching locus for the celebration of Passover and of Tabernacles. The Halakhah of *Shabbat-Erubin* explicitly takes shape around the binary opposites Temple and household; what on the Sabbath (and, except for cooking, on festivals) one may do in the former location one may not do in the latter.

What of the synagogue—is that not a space for meeting God? The answer emerges when we ask what Israelites do in the synagogue, vis-à-vis God, that they do not ordinarily do elsewhere, and what defines a synagogue in time or in space. The one point at which Israel finds God in the synagogue in particular (if not uniquely) is the declamation of the Torah. It is specifically in reference to the synagogue that the Halakhah provides its category formation accommodating the rules for declaiming the Torah, and—more to the point—it is in that context, and there alone, that the Halakhah further specifies *other* rules that govern the sanctity of the locus of the synagogue. So the synagogue finds its definition in its function; it is not a place to which Israelites go to meet God, as—the Torah indicates—the Temple is. Rather, it is utopian in the simplest sense: *anywhere where ten Israelite males conduct a specified activity, the public declamation of the Torah, the function of the synagogue is carried out.* This is without regard to the location of the Israelites or the character of the dedicated space, if any, that contains them. In this context, the church and the synagogue have nothing in common; they constitute different institutions, serving different functions, in different contexts, and for different purposes.

To conclude: the pre-Constantine Church did not see itself as integral to the state or vice versa. The post-Constantine Church "was still too much concerned with the next world, still too much agitated by the heat of conflict and victory, still inwardly too detached to be able to weave ideas of that king into the inner structure of the State" (p. 145). State and Church were two

> essentially separate magnitudes: the State and the social order in general actually constitute the "world." The conception of a sinful lost world over against a Church which alone can offer redemption became more and more the governing idea in the State and the social order. (p. 146)

The Rabbinic sages did not find in Scripture and tradition the notion of the alien state as legitimate and also distinct from Israel; the world they contemplated was God's, and Israel's task was to make of it God's Kingdom, as God planned from the beginning. This is the lesson Scripture taught them. The world was divided, for them, between idolators and those who know and worship the one true God. This is the lesson that Scripture taught them, and they took as their task the realization of this lesson in the actualities of Israel's social order. The three social teachings of Rabbinic Judaism represent the lessons that the Rabbinic sages learned from their profound reading of the Torah, both Scripture and tradition.

Here, then, we encounter God's Kingdom, not as against the world but as the fulfillment of God's plan in making the world. How did Christianity propose its counterpart? Here is Troeltsch's account:

> Christianity described herself as a *basileia* [Kingdom], and therefore her counterpart, the world, was also conceived as a *basileia*, which is plainly manifested in the Emperor, in the Imperial Law, and in the worship of the Emperor. The world becomes a "Kingdom" and it is thus the summa of the existing laws and ordinances. For a Kingdom is the support of law and order; and law and order covers the whole order of Society. The world is . . . that period in history which precedes the Return of Christ. . . . The doctrine of the Old Testament was retained—that the Creation was good, but that the "world" is the result of the Fall, of the corruption of the will, and a Satanic delusion. The state also sprang from this source, and thus it comes under the uniform and essentially unchangeable principle of the "world," together with all the institutions of marriage, labor, property, slavery, law, and war. (p. 147)

So we have come to the center of the matter, the understanding of "Kingdom." The two heirs of Israelite Scripture part company at the notion of a kingdom of God. That meant for Christianity the contrast between two kingdoms, God's and Rome's, the emperor's. It entailed for Rabbinic Judaism the single, unique Kingdom of God realized by Israel in the here and now. Here the social teaching of the Christian churches and that of Rabbinic Judaism diverge and present irreconcilable differences. If among them I had to identify the critical difference, it would be in the Christian language as formulated by Troeltsch, "that the Creation was good, but that the 'world' is the result of the Fall, of the corruption of the will, and a Satanic delusion." On that language Rabbinic Judaism concurs: creation was good, and the age that followed the fall represented the result of Man's corrupt use of free will. But Rabbinic Judaism adds a sentence that Christianity omits. It concerns the Torah: the event of Sinai.

Reading from Genesis through Kings along with the Prophets as a single, unfolding and coherent narrative, the Rabbinic sages formed their social teaching in response to the Torah's account of the repair of the world under God's sovereignty through Israel's regeneration in the Torah. They took as their task the realization of God's Kingdom, as God had designed that Kingdom and as humanity in the end of days would join itself to that Kingdom, acknowledging God's rule and accepting his dominion (as do all those called Israel even now). Rabbinic Judaism designed the social order in response to God's plan set forth in the Torah, and orthodox, Catholic Christianity in the same age did not. Rabbinic Judaism tells and retells the story of ancient Israel's Scripture—the Torah's story. Orthodox, Catholic Christianity tells the story of Jesus Christ. Each narrative follows its own lines of development. They do not coincide. In a profound sense, they scarcely intersect. But the differences based on Scriptures in common afford an illuminating perspective on the choices made by each.

VIII. THE QUESTION OF HISTORY: WHAT IS NOW AT STAKE?

What historical questions await investigation, and how should I define future inquiries? The range and complexity of the questions adumbrated here leave no doubt that history remains a principal issue in the study of the canonical documents, in two ways.

First, if scholarship of a literary, religious-historical, and theological character does not rest on sound historical foundations, by definition it lacks temporal perspective and ignores social context. It is an exercise in formalism, whether the literary traits of the canonical documents are set forth, or the religious ideas are identified, or the theological structures (native category formations) are defined. All constitute details, dependent variables, secondary expressions of a primary and generative conception of things, to which history, *and history of the indicated classifications alone*, affords access.

Second, history—in particular, cultural history, history of ideas, social and institutional history—defines the material context in which the literature, religion, and theology find their being. There, in the approaches broadly encompassed in the German *Geisteswissenschaft*, they make sense, integrate with one another to form a large and coherent, whole statement. And, it is clear, by "history" I mean not merely anything that happened the day before yesterday, and by "the study of history," I intend not the generality, the study of anything before this morning.

By history in the present context, therefore, I mean the purposive, focused study of the unfolding social culture that is embodied in the canonical evidence and that sustains and nourishes and imparts cogency to those sources of formative Judaism. In this definition I recapitulate the definition of theology—the philosophical study of religion—that will serve in due course. I stress that the work of the historian of culture and society, of ideas and the lives of those who held them, is to integrate, make sense of data. It is to identify the coherence of details, show the whole that is formed by the parts—and that may exceed their sum. It is this grand design that the disciplines of literature, history of religion, and theology help form but do not themselves, on their own, convey; only history, broadly defined, does.

At the outset I offered a general theory of the formative history of Rabbinic Judaism: the story of the reconstruction of a society that has suffered not merely defeat but cultural disaster in the collapse of the received formation of the social order. The interior perspectives, then, concerned themselves with establishing continuities in the face of massive disruption, bridging the abyss between a long-continuous past and a present lacking all precedent. These interiorities involved the inner logic of documents, the sources of continuity in reason and in textual exegesis alike. The exterior perspectives then focused upon the context in which that logic worked itself out: the relationship between the ideas people held and the social crisis that they faced, and, further out still from the innermost precincts of culture, the contexts—both pagan and Christian, in the Roman codification of law and in Christianity's social policy—in which the Rabbinic system carried out its reconstruction of law and social policy.

When we turn from the historical to the religious study of the religion Judaism in Chapter Four, I shall have to distinguish the historical study of religion from the history-of-religions study of religion.

Let me conclude where I began, with an unrealized conversation with the late Erwin R. Goodenough and Harry A. Wolfson, models and mentors of mine. I did not succeed in interrogating them successfully to find guidance on where to direct my scholarly energies after coming to the end of the preliminary phase of my academic career and completing my first major projects. Where to go now, within the range of learning—all things being possible? So to return to the Preface.

If in an appropriate circumstance a beginning scholar, doctorate in hand, dissertation in print, were to interview me, then, about work I think worth doing, what should I suggest? Clearly at issue is a program of study that is not derivative of work already done and a mere improvement in detail but is imaginative and essentially fresh: huge holes in the structure of our knowledge and understanding of the formative age and stage of Rabbinic Judaism. In the Preface I defined the task: to try to reckon with what to this point has eluded my imagination.

In response, for historical study, I have laid out six areas awaiting systematic inquiry, all of them, at best, now in their elementary stages and each of them awaiting sustained attention. The scriptural foundations of Rabbinic Judaism, to take one obvious example, await analytical study of the types, purposes, and contexts in which those foundations are identified and defined or are omitted altogether. Scriptural authority, both in law and in theology, awaits sorting out. To date the work has been mostly formal; types of data have been differentiated, and the media of connection (exegesis, for example) have been constructed through the collection and arrangement of data, but the large-scale analytical work awaits, and questions of systemic comparison and contrast—Philo's use of Scripture, the authority of Scripture in the Dead Sea library, the role of Scripture in the Elephantine papyri, for instance—are yet to be asked. Each of the five other sections, III–VII, implicitly responds to the question of what next. Yet that is not what I would prefer to suggest to someone looking for direction and perspective, possessed of a completed degree and a published dissertation and a proper academic employment for his or her work, yet seeking purpose and direction on long-term problems for sustained, detailed research.

Rather, I would say, for the kind of sustained, coherent, narrative, problem-solving history that I advocate—cultural history, history of ideas, social and institutional history—go in search of the large ideas, the generative problematic that everywhere engages, the whole that comes to expression in the parts and that imparts coherence to the details. And then engorge yourself in details. That is, undertake that question, search and sift those smallest whole parts—artifacts of culture, documentary expositions of ideas—to see how in context they fit together. The great histories are those that yield an increment of understanding, not only a sediment of knowledge. They are those that ask large questions and answer them, that project a vision of the whole, to be discerned in all of the parts—and that find consequence in the details. But this is not the first and most important question that awaits. In Chapter Three, we shall encounter what I regard as the ineluctable and urgent question that stands athwart all further progress in the analytical study of formative Judaism.

THE QUESTION OF LITERATURE

I. Defining the Literary Question of Rabbinic Judaism

The character of the evidence predetermines the nature of an inquiry. We take up the literary question not in generic terms but in those particular to the Rabbinic canon. In this singular context, which kinds of literary questions pertain, and which ones do not? Questions that in this context do not register are generated by those broad and general issues of aesthetics or hermeneutics, philology or exegesis, that cannot be settled within the limits of Rabbinic documents at all, or even within the boundaries of the Judaic documents all together.

Concerned with the religion, Judaism, I have never asked the Rabbinic documents merely to illustrate problems of broad literary or philosophical concern, for instance, "narrativity" or "poetics" or "the parable." I do not doubt that the Rabbinic canon contributes a rich store of suggestive examples pertinent to questions of general intelligibility in literature (literary criticism), as much as to those in religion. I point, for instance, to the efforts, not wholly successful to be sure, to turn Rabbinic Midrash into a source of insight for hermeneutics and the consequent exegetics, and to the self-evidently more successful efforts that have transformed the Bavli into an arena of philosophical construction. To the study of Rabbinic Judaism, the religious system and structure, however, generalities of literary theory contribute only marginally.

The literary study of the Rabbinic canon as evidence of a religious system and structure of the social order asks a limited question: what do we learn about Rabbinic Judaism—the religion—in its formative age from the *formal* traits of the corpus of documents it deems authoritative? These traits involve (1) patterns of rhetoric, the rules of correct formalization of language; (2) the logic of coherent discourse, the laws that join two discrete propositions into a cogent statement and that decree intelligibility for the consequent composition; and (3) the governing topic, the determinate program that dictates what belongs and what does not in a given compilation, whether of law or of lore. So the question is this: can we move from the tripartite medium— rhetoric, logic of coherent discourse, and topic—to the substantive message of that same writing?

The premise of the question is that *how* people express their thoughts, not only *what* they say, conveys the message of their religious system. Questions that pertain therefore look to evidence that the religious system has found for itself appropriate media of discourse. What we want to know is how, document by document, traits of rhetoric, topic, and logic of coherent discourse are shaped by the framers to make the distinctive statement intended for that particular venue. So, in more general terms, by "the literary question of Rabbinic Judaism" I mean to ask what the medium conveys about the message. This affects how we are to describe, analyze, and interpret, *for the study of Rabbinic Judaism,* the documents that alone constitute the testimony to that religious system and structure.

The task of answering the literary question therefore requires the systematic characterization of these documents, a determinate project of description, analysis, and interpretation. It is carried out in two stages. First, we determine the documents' indicative traits of rhetoric, topic, and logic of coherent discourse. Once we establish the documentary program of a given compilation, we are able to identify all compositions and composites thereof that conform to the documentary program. Then, second, we take up the rest, the nonconforming compositions and composites. Here we characterize the documents' constitutive components that do not exhibit the documents' distinctive traits.

Because of their formalization in the terms just now defined, the documents permit us to identify a corpus of non- or extra- and (I claim) possibly predocumentary writing. This nonconforming writing has been preserved in compilations by authorships that valued these other-than-documentary compositions but have not imposed their program upon all compositions included in the compilation. The predocumentary and nondocumentary sources upon which the final framers have drawn have then to be examined on their own as evidence of an approach different from that of the documents and their compilers, to setting forth the Rabbinic statement. These classes of components we recognize, then, on entirely formal grounds. That is because they do not conform in their indicative traits to the traits that

define the documents in which they appear. So the composite character of documentary evidence predetermines the nature of literary
inquiry.

I have already alluded to my generative conception, in the language of Chapter Two, that context is determined by system and systems are recapitulated by canonical compilations. This approach
dictates the theory of matters laid out here in formal terms. So first
come the religious system and structure that animated the framers'
work in the composition of the documents in hand. Second, we turn
to evidences of a distinct system that are contained within other-than-
documentary-dictated forms. Thus we take up the traits of form and
program of writing that did not originate in the work of composing
the documents in which the other-than-documentary compositions
and composites ultimately find their place. The literary form analysis
in the present context thus serves the inquiry, in particular, into the
religion, its history and dynamics.

Much of the analytical work is in hand, but fresh questions await
attention. I have already shown, in a variety of works now in print,
how the documents, as we have them, represent the outcome of the
framers' writing *for those documents in particular*. But I also have signaled
the result of the compilers' taste and judgment in selecting, from
available compositions and even composites, what they used for the
document. Three important projects, however, await, specified below
in sections IV, VI, and VII.

II. The Documentary Starting Point:
The Distinctive, Indicative Traits of Documents

Since the form-analytical program attends to manifest traits of the
documents, one must find surprising that, like the critical program
involved in asking the historical question, so here also the initial
inquiries have met a fair amount of resistance. Why ignore the indicative traits characteristic of, and in diverse combinations distinctive to,
the respective documents when these are formal and therefore blatant? Yet differentiating one document from some other—and from
all others—represents a much mooted approach to literary study,
which for many remains focused on the literary atoms, the smallest
whole units of thought, to the exclusion of the molecules, the compositions and still larger composites formed by them.

As with the question of history, so here also theological conviction has impeded matters. But it is a different theological issue. The view that everything in all documents is part of one and the same Torah of Sinai conflicts with the analytical approach. This approach, as I have made clear, requires the recognition that canonical documents may bear distinctive indicative traits and that these traits bear exegetical implications for the documents that exhibit them. According to the contrary, synthetic approach, which ignores documentary boundaries altogether, every document forms part of the Torah, and this Torah, lacking all differentiating traits, occurs everywhere and anywhere. It sets forth a coherent, uniform truth, not differentiated by circumstance but everywhere and always the same truth. So point of origin, place or time, is irrelevant. Consequently, within the theology of revelation encompassing the Torah of Sinai, written and oral, that has now come to transcription in the Rabbinic canon, we have no reason to read by itself any document. The analytical project just now laid out violates the theological context and character of what is analyzed, since all documents equally participate in a common system and structure (to use our language).

With all compilations thus held as equally authoritative and formally interchangeable, the task in studying formative Judaism is only constructive, never analytical. It is to collect whatever all documents say on a determinate subject—for example, sayings of a particular authority, yielding biography, or sayings on a given topic, yielding a composite of a theological theme or legal category—and so define the Judaic position on said subject. Hence all sayings on a given topic, without regard to the document(s) in which they occur, join together to give "the Rabbinic view" of that topic. The Judaic equivalent of "the harmony of the Gospels"—"The Talmudic and Midrashic View of . . ."—defines a nondocumentary hermeneutics. This yields the labor-saving device of concordance scholarship: hunting and gathering, collecting and arranging topical sayings. This is the result of a hermeneutics that commences with the unity, historical and theological, of all canonical writings.

Differentiation within that approach takes place not by documents but by names of authorities cited in those documents. For the paramount trait of all documents—their constant attribution of sayings to named authorities—affords a distinct point of differentiation. Whatever is given to a specific name, whether in a document that reached closure (only) two hundred years after he flourished or in one

sealed as long as five hundred or a thousand years later, serves
equally well to tell us what the named authority really thought and
said in the time in which he lived. Lives of Talmudic masters, along
with histories of Talmudic times, have therefore brought together,
collected, and arranged in intelligible order the attributed sayings
without a shred of interest in the time or place or circumstance of the
documents that preserved them. The result, once more, is simple.
Considerations of time and circumstance do not register. Every writing is equally useful. All may be assumed to wish to make the same
factual contribution to "the Torah." History, like theology, consists in
opening a document, pointing to a sentence, paraphrasing the sense
of that sentence, and speculating on its meaning: a labor of paraphrase and pure fabrication.

These theological and secular-historical premises represent welcome labor-saving devices, since people have taken for granted that
it is not necessary to examine documents one by one, whole, complete, and in their own contexts. Indifference to documentary venues
has affected not only historical, biographical, and theological studies
but literary ones as well. These take up a given trait or form, for
example, the parable, and examine all evidences of the same without
the slightest concern for comparing and contrasting the form of the
phenomenon as diverse compilations portray it.

Entire careers have thus been devoted to expounding the Rabbinic,
the Talmudic, or the Talmudic-Midrashic view of one thing after
another, or a biography of a named authority. Such literary criticism
as has taken place has concerned itself with the literary traits of a formal or exegetical sort common to the entire canon or, better still, to
"Judaism" pure and simple. Synthetic inquiries have yielded an entire
library of monographs resting on the simple presuppositions now generally dismissed: (1) a single Judaism, (2) revealed in a unitary tradition of completely reliable historical veracity, (3) comes down to us in
a variety of undifferentiated writings—a single book with many freestanding sentences and few coherent expository chapters, certainly
not a library made up of many freestanding, but cogently selected,
volumes. This set of coherent premises explains the character of
translations of the Rabbinic documents before my own. They spell
out why people before me translated the documents in long columns
of undifferentiated words, rendering impossible any sort of form-

analytical work on the character, composition, and construction of documents, each viewed on its own.

But this has been and can be done if we identify chapter and verse, on the one side, or compose a still more serviceable reference system, on the other. What are the analytical category formations I offer as an alternative, and what is at stake in the documentary reading of the Rabbinic canon? These questions I answer in succession. The costs of homogenizing everything into one thing are best measured by the gains of differentiating time, circumstance, and literary venue. What we see when we differentiate—to which we are blind when we homogenize—defines the costs of the one and the benefits of the other: a clearer understanding of the Judaic religious system that took shape in the age at hand and that is recapitulated, in its historical and theological nuance, by the canon in its sequential unfolding.

III. THE DOCUMENTARY CONTEXT: AUTONOMY, CONNECTION, CONTINUITY

The literary question of Rabbinic Judaism takes shape when the respective documents are viewed as freestanding and autonomous of one another (except where a document later in sequence explicitly cites one that came to closure earlier). Each requires its systematic description, analysis, and interpretation. For all exhibit their own respective, differentiating traits. The Mishnah viewed whole, in line with recurrent formal traits of rhetoric, topic, and logic of coherent discourse, is different in its indicative traits from *Leviticus Rabbah*, which, by indicative traits defined by a program pertinent to all documents, is different from the Talmud of Babylonia—and so throughout. To show that this is self-evident, I venture to claim that a random sample of completed units of exposition, for example, five-hundred- or thousand-word coherent statements, from one document can seldom be confused with a random sample of completed units of exposition of the same order from some other documents. Once we have deciphered the key to the formal rules of composition of all documents, we can use this key to assign one piece of writing to one compilation and another to its right and proper venue.

That is commonly the case, with an important qualification. Some compositions and composites in a given document do not conform to the documentary protocol that pertains. Other compositions and composites circulate in two or more documents and therefore by definition are non- and extradocumentary. Thus I say "seldom" rather than "never." But these peripatetic passages form a very small portion of any one document and therefore of the canon as a whole. And as a brief sample will show in due course, they do not play a critical role in delivering the documentary messages of the respective documents in which they occur—for example, they are subordinated and clearly secondary in their function (and formal position). It is very rare for a peripatetic composition or composite to take a primary task in the exposition of the two or more documents in which it occurs. These matters will return to our discussion in due course.

In fact, each of the canonical documents sets forth its own program in its own way. How do we know? Systematic analyses of distinguishing traits of rhetoric, logic(s) of coherent discourse, and topical programs of the various documents leave no ambiguity. Each writing exhibits its own formal traits, and each document sets forth its own message. Viewed as a whole, no document is readily confused with any other. Many, though not all, also exhibit a cogency of program, working on the same few questions time and again. Documents are therefore to be perceived in three relationships: first, as autonomous writings; second, as writings connected with others of the same class; and, finally, as parts of a complete corpus deemed unitary and coherent. Autonomy, connection, and continuity are the key words. The labor is one of description, analysis, and interpretation, and it involves study of the text, its literary context, and its intellectual matrix. A brief recapitulation of these matters will suffice.

A. *Autonomy: Description of the Text on Its Own*

A document is viewed first in its own terms, with examination of the text in particular and in its full particularity and immediacy. The text is described in accord with the three distinct, differentiating traits of rhetoric, logic, and topic: the formal traits of the writing, the principles of cogency that dictate how one sentence links up with another, and the topical, and even propositional, program that the entire document addresses.

B. *Connection: Analysis of the Text in Context through Comparison and Contrast with Intersecting Affines*

A document connects with others in two ways—first and less important, through shared sayings or stories, and, second and far more
important, through recurrent points of emphasis found in a number
of documents. A set of documents may address a single prior writing,
Scripture or the Mishnah; they may pursue a single exegetical program or take up a common question, deemed urgent in two or more
compilations. They may intersect in other ways. Groups of documents may take shape out of an inductive examination of points of
differentiation and aggregation.

C. *Continuity: Interpretation of the Matrix That Forms of the Canonical Texts a Coherent Statement*

The examination of the entire corpus of Rabbinic writings (or the
writings found in the library at Qumran, or other groups of writings
deemed by common consensus to form a textual community), finally,
leads outward toward the shared matrix in which a variety of texts
find their place. Here description moves from the interior world of
intellectuals and their logic to the exterior world they proposed to
shape and create. The inquiry defines as its generative question how
the social world formed by the texts as a whole proposes to define
and respond to a powerful and urgent question; that is, I read the
canonical writings as responses to critical and urgent questions. A set
of questions concerning the formation of the social order—its ethics,
ethos, and ethnos—for example, will turn out to produce a single set
of answers from a variety of writings. If that is the case, then we may
describe not only documentary cogency and the coherence of two or
more writings but the matrix in an intellectual system that the continuity among many documents permits us to outline. These represent
intellectually ambitious problems. They constitute a complex agenda.
Solving them involves a dense corpus of data.

D. *Imagining the Rabbinic Canon: Toward a General Theory*

How, in light of these findings, should we imagine the canonical writings and their life situations as data of the Rabbinic culture? As

stated, the Rabbinic canon is composed of a community of texts
related in three dimensions: autonomy, connection, and continuity.
The documents stand on their own. They intersect at specific points
with other documents. And they form a continuity with all other documents, constituting a canon. To clarify this perspective, let us consider the analogy of a library. Books brought together form a library.
Each title addresses its own program and makes its own points. But
books produced by a cogent community constitute not merely a
library but a canon: a set of compositions, each of which embodies a
common norm and each of which contributes to a statement that
transcends its own pages. The books exhibit intrinsic traits that make
of them all *a community of texts*. We would know, on the basis of these
characteristics, that the texts form a community even if we knew
nothing more than the texts themselves. In the Judaic writings, moreover, the documents at hand are held by Judaism to form a canon.

Seeing the whole as continuous, which is quite natural, later theology maintains that all of the documents of Rabbinic literature find a
place in the Torah. But that is an imputed, and post facto, theological determination, not an inductive and intrinsic fact. It is something
we know only on the basis of information—theological convictions
about the one whole Torah God gave to Moses in two media—deriving from sources other than the texts at hand, which, on their own,
do not link each to all and all to every line of each. Extrinsic traits,
that is, imputed ones, make of the discrete writings a single and continuous uniform statement: one whole Torah, in the mythic language
of Judaism. The community of Judaism imputes those traits, sees com-
monalities, uniformities, deep harmonies: one Torah of one God. In
secular language, that community expresses its system—its worldview,
its way of life, its sense of itself as a society—by these choices and finds
its definition in them. Hence, in the nature of things, the community
of Judaism forms a *textual community*. A cogent community that forms
a canon out of a selection of books therefore participates in the process
of authorship, just as the books exist in at least two dimensions.

Let us turn to the problem of the *community of texts*, utilizing the
relationships defined in our description of the canon. We take the
measure of two of the three relationships, autonomy and connection.
Continuity among all documents introduces theological, not literary, problems for analysis. That is to say, a book enjoys its own
autonomous standing, but it also situates itself in relationship to other

books of the same classification. Each book bears its own statement and purpose, and each relates to others of the same classification. The community of texts therefore encompasses individuals who (singly or collectively) comprise (for the authorships: compose) books. But there is a set of facts that indicates how a book does not stand in isolation. These facts fall into several categories. Books may go over the same ground or make use, in some measure, of the same materials. The linkages between and among them therefore connect them. Traits of rhetoric, logic, and topic may place into a single classification a number of diverse writings. Then there is the larger consensus of community members who see relationships between one book and another and so join them together on a list of authoritative writings. So a book exists in the dimensions formed of its own contents and covers, but it also takes its place in two other dimensions of relationship to other books.

The relationships in which a given document stands may be expressed in the prepositions "between" and "among." That is, in its intellectual traits, a document bears relationship, to begin with, to some other; hence we describe relationships between two documents. These constitute formal and intrinsic matters: traits of grammar, arrangements of words and resonances as to their local meaning, structures of syntax of expression and thought. But in its social setting, a document finds bonds among three or more documents, with all of which it is joined in the imagination and mind of a community. These range widely and freely, bound by limits not of form and language but of public policy in behavior and belief. Documents, because of their traits of rhetoric, logic, and topic, form a community of texts. And documents, because of their audience and authority, express the intellect of a textual community.

The principal issue worked out in establishing a community of texts is hermeneutical, the chief outcome of defining a textual community, exegetical, social, and cultural. What is at stake, as I shall spell out in section IV, is how to make of a document its own best commentary, how to turn the authors' and authorship's signals into guidance on how to intuit their deepest meanings.

The hermeneutics teaches us how to read the texts on their own. The exegetics tells us how to interpret texts in context. When we define and classify the relationships between texts, we learn how to read the components—words, cogent thoughts formed of phrases, sentences, paragraphs—of those texts in the broader context defined by shared conventions of intellect: rhetoric, logic, topic. More concretely, hermeneutical principles tell how, in light of like documents that we have seen many times, to approach a document we have never before seen. Hermeneutics teaches the grammar and syntax of thought. Memorizing a passage of a complex text will teach the rhythms of expression and thought that make of the sounds of some other document an intelligible music. Also, documents joined into a common classification may share specific contents, not only definitive traits of expression—meaning and not solely method. In the context of the debate on intertextuality, this represents the results of my inquiry into the status of the Rabbinic canonical writings, a status captured in the single word "document."

One theory is that a document serves solely as a convenient repository of ready-made sayings and stories, available materials that would have served equally well (or poorly) wherever they took up their final location. In accord with this theory, it is quite proper, in ignorance of all questions of circumstance and documentary or canonical context, to compare the exegesis of a verse of Scripture in one document with the exegesis of that verse of Scripture found in some other document. Documentary boundaries demarcate nothing. Their lines of structure and order are null.

The other theory is that a composition exhibits a viewpoint, a purpose of authorship distinctive to its framers or collectors and arrangers. Such a characteristic literary purpose—by this theory—is so powerfully particular to one authorship that much of the writing at hand can be shown to have been (re)shaped for the ultimate purpose of the authorship at hand, that is, collectors and arrangers who demand the title of authors. According to this theory, context and circumstance form the prior condition of inquiry. The result forms, in exegetical terms, the contingent one. But the documentary hypothesis readily recognizes in any given document a component of other-than-documentary writing—writing that does not conform to the program of the document before us, even writing that does not conform to any documentary program at all. So the documentary hypothesis recognizes the complexity of the Rabbinic documents, made up, as they are, of writing undertaken for a given document in particular and of writing utterly unresponsive to the conventions and protocol of a documentary venue of any known kind.

To resort to a less-than-felicitous neologism, I thus ask what signifies or defines the "document-ness" of a document and what makes a book a book. I therefore wonder whether there are specific texts in the canonical context of Judaism or whether all texts are merely contextual. We have to confront a single Rabbinic composition and ask about its definitive traits and viewpoint. When we investigate the textuality of a document, we therefore raise these questions: is it a composition or a scrapbook; is it a cogent proposition made up of coherent parts, or is it a collage?

The answers help us to determine the appropriate foundations for comparison, the correct classifications for comparative study. Once we know what is unique to a document, we can investigate the traits that characterize all the document's unique, and so definitive, materials. We ask about whether the materials unique to a document also cohere or whether they prove merely miscellaneous. If they do cohere, we may conclude that the framers of the document have followed a single plan and a program. This would, in my view, justify the claim that the framers carried out a labor not only of conglomeration, arrangement, and selection but also of genuine authorship or composition in the narrow and strict sense of the word. If so, the document emerges from authors, not merely arrangers and compositors. For the same purpose, therefore, we also take up and analyze the items shared between this document and some other or among several documents. We ask about the traits of these items, one by one and all in the aggregate. In these stages we may solve, for the case at hand, the problem of the Rabbinic document: do we deal with a scrapbook or a collage or a cogent composition; a text or merely a literary expression, random and essentially promiscuous, of a larger theological context? That is the choice at hand and defines what is at stake.

IV. THE QUESTION OF LITERATURE: A. WHAT IS AT STAKE IN ESTABLISHING THE DOCUMENTARY CONTEXT? LEARNING HOW THE DOCUMENT SUPPLIES ITS OWN BEST COMMENTARY

What is at stake in recognizing the acute formalization of the canonical writings? The answer forms a program for future literary study of the Rabbinic canon. It is that the documents contain signals of their own exegesis, internal evidence on the anticipated hermeneutics of their compilers. In simple language: the Rabbinic documents, in their distinctive indicative traits, signal how they are to be read, forming out of the internal evidence their own first and best commentary. When we understand their formal traits of rhetoric, topic, and logic of coherent discourse, we not only can differentiate one compilation from all others; we also can identify the principal parts of the writing and how these parts hold together: the large composites and their main point, the compositions that make up composites and their contribution. In this way, knowing the rules of composition, we are guided, in the coherent reading of their compilations, by the internal evidence supplied by the writers and compilers.

If we turn to the contents of a given document, the external evidence does not help us much in determining the place of origination, the purpose of its formation, the reasons for its anonymous and collective plane of discourse and monotonous tone of voice. A document's authorship never tells us why one topic is introduced and another is omitted or what the agglutination of these particular topics is meant to accomplish in the formation of a system or imaginative construction. And yet abundant signals guide us in our reading of the text. Let me show how this is so with the Mishnah, stipulating that corresponding data are available for less opaque documents.

A. *The Case of the Mishnah*

First, take, in the case of the Mishnah, the problem of differentiating one completed unit of exposition from some other, which we accomplish by paragraphing, heads, sub-heads, and the like, not to mention tables of contents, book titles, and so on. In antiquity paragraphing and punctuation were not commonly used. Long columns of words would contain a text, and the student of the text had the task of breaking up those columns into tractates, chapters, sentences, large and small sense units. Hence we have to find out how an author or authorship told us beginnings, middles, and endings of units of completed thought ("paragraphs"), units of completed argument, proposition, or other sustained discourse ("chapters"), and whole books. For this purpose, with the Mishnah, we start with the entire document and work our way back to the paragraphs in three rapid mental experiments. This exercise shows how form analysis of the interior traits of the document, as defined just now, opens up the document as a source not only of exegetical problems but also of solutions to those problems.

B. *The Topical Construction of the Mishnah as a Whole*

If we had the entire Mishnah in a single immense scroll and spread the scroll out on the ground—perhaps the length of a football field!— we would have no difficulty at all discovering the point, on the five-yard line, at which the first tractate ends and the second begins, and so on down the field to the opposite goal. For, from *Berakhot* at the beginning to *Uqsin* at the end, the breaking points practically jump up from the ground like white lines of lime: change of principal topic. So, the criterion of division, internal to the document and not merely imposed by copyists and printers, is thematic. That is, the tractates are readily distinguishable from one another, since each treats a distinct topic. So, if Mishnah were to be copied out in a long scroll without the significance of lines of demarcation among the several tractates, the opening pericope of each tractate would leave no doubt that one topic had been completed and a new one undertaken.

C. *The Division of Topics into Their Logical, Constituent Components*

The same is so within the tractates. Intermediate divisions of these same principal divisions (we might call them chapters of parts of books) are to be discerned on the basis of internal evidence. This is accomplished through the confluence of theme or subject matter and form or patterning of language. That is to say, a given intermediate division of a principal one (a chapter of a tractate) will be marked by a particular, recurrent, formal pattern, in accord with which sentences are constructed, and also by a particular and distinct theme, to which these sentences are addressed. When a new theme commences, a fresh formal pattern will be used.

D. *The Division of Paragraphs into Sentences*

Within the intermediate divisions, we are able to recognize the components, or smallest whole units of thought (cognitive units, defined at greater length presently), because there will be a recurrent pattern of sentence structure repeated time and again within the unit and a shifting at the commencement of the next theme. Each point at which the recurrent pattern commences marks the beginning of a new cognitive unit. In general, an intermediate division will contain a carefully enumerated sequence of exempla of cognitive units, in the established formal pattern, commonly in groups of three or five or multiples of three or five (pairs for the first division). A single rhetorical pattern will govern the whole set of topical instances of a logical proposition. When the logical-topical program changes, the rhetorical pattern will change too.

Accordingly, the Mishnah's authorship gives exegetical signals that are not to be missed, once we realize their presence. The document presents its discourses as thematic expositions, with beginnings, middles, and endings, principles and secondary developments thereof. Throughout the Mishnah the preferred mode of layout is themes, spelled out along the lines of the logic imbedded in those themes. The Mishnah's authorship conveys its message through aesthetic, as much as philosophical, expression: how things are said matters as much as what is said.

E. *The Logic of Coherent Discourse: How Form Analysis Points to the Construction of Syllogisms, Yielding Cases Producing Rules*

To learn how to read the Mishnah, we have once more to turn back to an inductive inquiry. Our task is to find out, first, how the language works and, second, how through its formalization the language is made to produce intelligible exchange of thought. The Mishnah's authorship took as its mode of expression not the statement of generalization but the implicit communication of generalization only through *grouped examples of a common rule*, which rule would rarely be articulated. Then, how do we know the examples that belong to a group and yield a rule? It is through matched sentences. When the formal pattern of a sentence shifts from what is established, we know that a new topic has come up, the old one has closed off, and the governing examples are now differentiated and yield their generalization.

These fundamental traits tell us two important facts about our authorship. These concern the logic of coherent discourse and the appeal to highly formalized rhetoric. As to the former, the framers proposed to make an autonomous, freestanding statement, which did not appeal to some other writing for order, proportion, and, above all, coherence. Rather, they treated the topics of their choice within an autonomous logic dictated by the requirements of those topics. Specifically, they exhibit the sense that a given topic has its own inner tension and generates its own program of thought and exposition.

As to the latter, their freestanding statement was set forth in a highly systematic and rhetorically careful way. Since the exposition bore the burden of clarifying itself, unable to appeal to some other document for structure and cogency, the formulation of this exposition would have to exhibit signals of sense—beginnings, middles, endings—that instructed the reader (or hearer) on how to follow the whole. These traits will strike us as consequential only when we take up other writings of the same set, in which discourse is not propositional and in which the formalization of language is not critical to the exposition at all.

Let me summarize the criteria of formalization and organization of the Mishnah, criteria that apply throughout and that characterize the Mishnah, and only the Mishnah, in all of Rabbinic canonical documents. The first of the two criteria derives from the nature of the principal divisions themselves: theme. That is, it is along thematic lines that the redactors organized vast corpora of materials into principal divisions, tractates. These fundamental themes themselves were subdivided into smaller conceptual units. The principal divisions treat their themes in units indicated by the sequential unfolding of their inner logical structure. Accordingly, one established criterion for delineating one aggregate of materials from some other will be a shift in the theme or predominant concern of a sequence of materials. The second fundamental criterion is the literary character, the syntactical and grammatical pattern, which differentiates and characterizes a sequence of primitive (that is, undifferentiable, indivisible) units of thought. Normally, when the subject changes, the mode of expression, the formal or formulary character, the patterning of language will change as well.

The patterns of language, for example, syntactic structures, of the apodosis and protasis of the Mishnah's smallest whole units of discourse are framed in formal, mnemonic patterns. They follow a few simple rules. These rules, once known, apply nearly everywhere and form stunning evidence for the document's cogency. They permit anyone to reconstruct, out of a few key phrases, an entire cognitive unit and even complete intermediate units of discourse. Working downward from the surface, therefore, anyone can penetrate into the deeper layers of meaning of the Mishnah. Then, while discovering the principle behind the cases, one can easily memorize the whole by mastering the recurrent rhetorical pattern dictating the expression of the cogent set of cases. For it is easy to note the shift from one rhetorical pattern to another and to follow the repeated cases articulated in the new pattern downward to its logical substrate. So, syllogistic propositions, in the Mishnah's authors' hands, come to full expression not only in what people wish to state but also in how they choose to say it. The limits of rhetoric define the arena of topical articulation. Once we ask what three or five joined topical propositions have in common, we state the logic and can therefore propose the syllogism that is shared among them all. The analysis of the Mishnah's linguistic formalization requires brief attention to the forms not only of cognitive units ("paragraphs") but also of sentences ("smallest whole units of thought"). The smallest whole unit of discourse is made up of fixed, recurrent formulas, clichés, patterns, or little phrases, out of which whole pericopes, or large elements in pericopes, for example, complete sayings, are constructed.

The proposition illustrated by the Mishnah—that the formal traits of rhetoric, logic of coherent discourse, and topic provide each Rabbinic canonical document with its own best commentary—pertains throughout. The details change radically, but the result is the same. A variety of messages come forth from the media of formalization. This has now been systematically demonstrated for the canon of late antiquity and prepares the way for inquiries that have yet to get under way. So much for the solution of exegetical problems by appeal to the internal evidence signaled in the form-analytical program realized in the regularities and order of the several canonical writings.

F. *How the Document Produces Its Own Best Commentary*

What is at stake in these recondite problems of literary description and analysis? The ultimate issue is this: can we speak of Judaism as a coherent religious construction, a system and structure of cogency, or is there only a mass—a mess, really—of discrete, chaotic facts, insusceptible of rational composition? The testimony of history favors the documentary construction of the Rabbinic canon and challenges the nihilism of the effort to bring about the literary deconstruction and then the historical demolition of this ancient, enduring religious tradition: Judaism, the coherent religious structure and system that are set forth in the dual Torah at Sinai. We will now turn to the non-documentary context and its promise of access to the predocumentary venue of some compositions.

V. Nondocumentary Writing: Compositions and Composites of an Other-than-Documentary Venue

Having established the traits of documentary writing, we carry forward the literary question of Rabbinic Judaism to focus upon anomalous compositions and composites. These do not conform to the distinctive, formal traits of rhetoric, topic, and logic of coherent discourse characteristic of the document(s) in which they occur. How are we to identify such literary remnants of the redactional process that produced the canonical documents in all their formal elegance, and what interpretation for the religious system and structure of Rabbinic Judaism are we to propose in that context?

Once we define the indicative traits of a document, we follow up on two facts. First, documents dictate the forms of their components, and we can define the documentary writing. Second, Rabbinic documents draw upon a fund of completed compositions of thought that have taken shape without attention to documentary conventions of the compilation in which they occur or of any other extant compilation in the canon. Within the distinction between writing that serves a redactional purpose and writing that does not, we see four types of completed compositions of thought. Each type may be distinguished from the others by appeal to a single criterion of differentiation, that is to say, to traits of precisely the same sort. The indicative traits concern relationship to the redactional purpose of a piece of writing, viewed overall.

(1) Some writings in a given Rabbinic document clearly serve the redactional program of the framers of the document in which those writings occur. These are principal in realizing the documentary design.

(2) Some writings in a given Rabbinic document serve not the

redactional program of the document in which they occur but that of
some other document now in our hands. There is no material difference, as to the taxonomy of the writing of the classics in Judaism,
between the first and second types; it is a problem of transmission of
documents, not their formation.

(3) Some writings in a given Rabbinic document serve not the purposes of the document in which they occur but rather a redactional
program of a document, or of a type of document, that we do not
now have *but can readily envision*. In this category we find the possibility of imagining compilations that we do not have but that could have
existed. Writings that clearly have been redacted in accord with a
program and plan other than those of any document now in our
hands show what I mean. These require no speculation, only a
moment of thought about unrealized redaction. We have ample files
of stories about sages. These were told and recorded, but not com-
piled into complete books, for example, hagiographies about given
authorities. Other religions' canons contain biographies; Rabbinic
Judaism's does not. A second type registers—compilations of exegeses, systematically collected and arranged. Exegetical exercises are
devoted to books of Scripture not subjected to systematic treatment
in any Rabbinic document of late antiquity; we can assemble hypothetical compilations to serve a variety of scriptural books, in the
manner of the medieval *Yalqut* compilers, for example. We can
demonstrate that materials of a given type, capable of sustaining a
large-scale compilation, were available; but no such compilation was
made, so far as extant sources suggest or attest.

(4) Some writings now found in a given Rabbinic document stand
autonomous of any redactional program we have in an existing compilation or of any we can even imagine on the foundations of said
writings.

The distinctions upon which these analytical taxonomies rest are
objective and in no way subjective, since they depend upon the fixed
and factual relationship between a piece of writing and a larger
redactional context.

(1) We know the requirements of redactors of the several documents of the Rabbinic canon because I have already shown what they
are in the case of a large variety of documents. When, therefore, we
judge a piece of writing to serve the program of the document in

which that writing occurs, it is not because of a personal impulse or a private and incommunicable insight but because the traits of that writing self-evidently respond to the documentary program of the book in which the writing is located.

(2) When, further, we conclude that a piece of writing belongs in some other document than the one in which it is found, this too forms a factual judgment.

(3) A piece of writing that serves nowhere we now know may nonetheless conform to the rules of writing that we can readily imagine and describe in theory. For instance, a propositional composition that runs through a wide variety of texts to make a point autonomous of all of the texts that are invoked is clearly intended for a propositional document, one that (like the Mishnah) makes points autonomous of a given prior writing, for example, a biblical book, and that makes points that for one reason or another cohere quite nicely on their own. Authors of propositional compilations self-evidently can imagine this kind of redaction. We have their writings but not the books that they intended to be made up of those writings. Another example is a collection of stories about a given authority or about a given kind of virtue exemplified by a variety of authorities. These and other types of compilations that we can imagine but do not have are dealt with in the present rubric.

(4) And, finally, where we have utterly hermetic writing, sealed off from any broader literary context and able to define its own limits and sustain its point without regard to any canonical document outside itself (other than Scripture, to be sure), we know that here we are in the presence of authorships that had no larger redactional plan in mind. They wrote with no intent to make books out of their little pieces of writing. Here the judgment of what belongs and what does not is not at all subjective.

Do these four types of compilations order themselves in sequence as well? Let me propose, in a tentative way, that they do, then suggest, in a more decisive way, that they do not. We first of all work from end to start in the hypothetical redactional process that culminated in the canon as we know it.

The first of those four kinds of completed units of thought (pericopes), as a matter of hypothesis, fall into the final stage of literary formation. That is to say, at the stage at which an authorship has reached the conclusion that it wishes to compile a document of a given character, the authorship will have made up pieces of writing that serve the purposes of the document it wishes to compile.

The second through fourth kinds of completed units of thought differ from documentary writing. Do they come earlier than this writing during the formation of the classics of Judaism represented by the compilation in which this writing now finds its place?

The second of the four kinds of completed units of thought served a purpose other than that of the authorship of the compilation in which this kind of writing now occurs. Is it therefore, as a matter of hypothesis, to be assigned to a stage in the formation of classics prior to the framing of the document in which the writing now occurs?

The third of the four kinds of completed units of thought clearly presupposes a location in a document of a kind we do not have.

The characteristics of a set of such writings permit us to identify and define the kind of writing that could readily have contained, and been well served by, pericopes of this kind. Compositions of this kind, as a matter of hypothesis, are to be assigned to a stage in the formation of classics prior to the framing of *all* available documents. For, as a matter of fact, all of our now extant writings adhere to a single program of conglomeration and all are served by composites of one sort, rather than some other. Hence we may suppose that, at some point prior to the decision to make writings in the model that we now have but in some other model, people also made up completed units of thought to serve these other kinds of writings. These persist now in documents that they do not serve at all well. And we can fairly easily identify the kinds of documents that they can and should have served quite nicely indeed. Hence this third kind of writing—belonging somewhere but not here in a formal context—signals a stage in the composition of formalized statements prior to the writing for the documents we now have.

Does difference in form signal difference in order? One may argue for and against this proposition, and it seems to me worthwhile to consider both positions. I deem the first the less likely, for reasons that become clear in my exposition of the second.

Difference signals sequence, first unformed, then formed by documentary considerations. It seems to me a plausible view that if people are writing within documentary protocols, they have determined to formalize what earlier was not formalized. Why so? Because the formalization is unusual and the formulation of prose outside a governing pattern is usual. A decision had to have 'been taken to impose a pattern on what was not formerly patterned. In the present context, no decision had to have been taken to remove a pattern from what was formerly patterned. That is why one might propose that unformalized writing is earlier than a writing that has been composed to serve the document in which it now occurs.

Formalization constitutes a literary, not a temporal-ordinal, indicator. But there is a more powerful argument to the contrary. It rests on the established fact that the Mishnah is the first document of Rabbinic Judaism. And that first document of the Rabbinic canon also is the most rigidly formalized. No one can doubt that the Mishnah is unique in the extent and rigidity of its formalization. It furthermore was formalized for mnemonic transmission, in patterns of speech readily memorized. Finally, in its autonomy—unlike any other Judaic document that preceded or any other Rabbinic document that followed—the Mishnah is utterly unique. Since no other document exhibits the mnemonic formalism of the Mishnah, formalization of writing characterizes the Mishnah alone. Other writing went on before, during, and also after the processes that produced the Mishnah. But the other compilations that would emerge did not take shape to facilitate memorization in the way that the Mishnah did. *Sifra* and Tosefta, for example, each in its own way defined by distinctive documentary traits, contrast with the Mishnah in that regard. And the Midrash compilations that succeeded the closure of the Yerushalmi, *Genesis Rabbah* and *Leviticus Rabbah* and their successors, all attest to the process of nondocumentary alongside documentary writing.

The choice between these two conflicting proposals seems to me clear. While formalized writing for documents supersedes freestanding writing not for documents, the high probability is that with the Mishnah the documentary writing came first in sequence and defined a model for the collection and arrangement of non- or other-than-documentary writing. Then both types of writing went forward side by side. No later document would attain the degree and success of formalization achieved in the Mishnah, but no canonical document utterly ignores the task of ordering and regularizing, within a protocol particular to that compilation, the compositions contained therein. Formalized prose for documentary purposes comes at the outset of the canonical process. Writing that was autonomous of documents could have gone on prior to the closure of the Mishnah, though the Mishnah yields only spare evidence of that fact. But what we have are simply two distinct kinds of writing, each responding to its own canonical context.

These, then, are the three stages of literary formation in the making of the classics of Judaism.

What of type four in the list above—writing autonomous of all redactional possibilities, actual, potential, or conceivable? This classification of writing stands beyond the three stages of literary formation because it includes kinds of writings that fall outside any relationship with a redactional program we either have in hand or can even imagine. These freestanding units could have been written at any time—before any sort of documentary redaction (beyond the Mishnah) took place; during such a process but before the selected compilations were designated, so that a variety of others were under construction and materials for them were subject to composition; or after the process had jelled. However we conceive of the process, the redactional tastes of a given set of compilers of documents made no impact upon the writing of such materials. When we find them in existing documents—and they are everywhere—they are parachuted down and bear no clear role in the accomplishment, through the writing, of the redactors' goals for their compilation.

Temporal or Ordinal Position of Writings Autonomous of Any Redactional Program. We can say nothing of the relative temporal or ordinal position of writings that stand autonomous of any redactional program that we have in an existing compilation or of any that we can even imagine on the foundations of such writings. These writings prove episodic; they are commonly singletons in context and can circulate from one document to another without material revision. They serve equally well everywhere because they demand no traits of form and redaction in order to endow them with sense and meaning. Why not? Because they are essentially freestanding and episodic, not referential and not allusive. They are stories that contain their own point and need not invoke, in the making of that point, a given verse of Scripture. They are sayings that are utterly ad hoc. A variety of materials fall into this—from a redactional perspective—unassigned, and unassignable, type of writing.

They not only fall outside the redactional program of any one document; they ignore any such program. They do not belong in documents ("books") at all. An important point follows: *whoever made up these pieces of writing did not imagine that what he was forming required a setting beyond the limits of his own piece of writing.*

For neither the writer of the freestanding composition nor the compiler of the autonomous composite regarded himself as bound by considerations that transcended the actual composition at hand. He wrote without connecting his writing—thought or form—to any other setting or encompassing context. The story is not only complete in itself but could (and did) stand entirely on its own; the saying spoke for itself and required no nurturing matrix; the proposition with its associated proofs in no way was meant to draw nourishment from roots penetrating outside its own literary limits.

Where we have utterly hermetic writing, able to define its own limits and sustain its point without regard to anything outside itself, there we are in the presence of authorships that had no larger redactional plan in mind, no intent to make books out of their little pieces of writing. This proves literary difference. Does it signal ordinal sequence— first unformed, then documentary writing? The formalization of the Mishnah prior to the work of writing compositions for composites that are less formalized than the Mishnah suggests that it does not. Writing simultaneously went on both altogether outside the framework of the editing of documents and within the limits of the formation and framing of documents. Writing of the former kind, then, constituted a kind of literary work on which redactional planning made no impact.

A. *How to Identify Nondocumentary Writing: The Starting Point*

We do not know how the documents of the formative canon took shape. They obliterate formal (rhetorical) idiosyncrasy, excluding the marks of individual contributions, for example, personal style, and imposing a timeless, topical-logical framework upon whatever is said. But two starting points present themselves: (1) the whole document or (2) the smallest irreducible piece of writing.

Consider first starting from the whole and working inward. We may commence our analytical inquiry from a completed document and unpeel its layers, from the ultimate one of closure and redaction, to the penultimate one of joining two or more distinct pieces of writing into a coherent whole, and onward into the innermost formation of the smallest whole units of thought of which a document consists. In so doing, we treat the writing as a document that has come to closure for a purpose at some fixed point and through the intellection of purposeful framers or redactors. We start the analytical process by asking what those framers—that authorship of the whole—wanted their document to accomplish and by pointing to the means by which that authorship achieved its purposes. Issues of prevailing rhetoric and logic of coherent discourse, as well as of the topical program of the whole, guide us in our definition of the document as a whole. The parts, then, come under study under the aspect of the whole. Knowing the intent of the framers, we ask whether and how materials they have used have been shaped in response to the program of the document's authorship. The reading of the parts will be in the light of the program of the whole. We shall define the norm on the baseline of the whole and ask where, how, and why the parts diverge from the norm. This is the mode of comparison and contrast that will generate our hypotheses of literary history and purpose—and also, therefore, our hermeneutics.

The alternative point of entry is to begin with the smallest building block of any and all documents, which is the freestanding sentence or irreducible minimum of completed thought (composition), and to work upward and outward from the innermost layer of the writing. This point of entry ignores the boundaries of discrete documents and, in focusing upon what rarely exhibits documentary markers, asks what we find in common within and among all documents. The norm is defined by the traits of the saying or indivisible composition as it moves from here to there. Within this atomistic theory of the history of the literature, the boundary lines of documents do not demarcate important classifications of data. All data are uniform wherever they occur—or utterly chaotic, it makes no difference. The stress, then, lies not on the differentiating traits of documents but on the points shared in common among them; these points are the same sayings that occur in two or more places. Literary history consists in the inquiry into the fate of sayings, undifferentiated as to origin, as they move from one place to another. The hermeneutics, of course, will focus upon the saying and its history, rather than on the program and plan of documents that encompass also the discrete saying. The advantage of this approach is that it takes account of what is shared among documents, on the one side, and also what exhibits none of the characteristic traits definitive of given documents, on the other.

B. *Nondocumentary Writing: The Case of the Bavli*

To consider blocks of writing that do not show through marks of particularity, documentary origin, we begin with the final canonical document, the Bavli, and ask what the compilers of that document had in hand and how they chose to organize their materials. That is because the Bavli clearly joins together compositions that realize the documentary program and those that ignore that document's, and all documents', program altogether.

The Bavli presents a systematic commentary to the Mishnah-Tosefta-Baraita corpus, on the one hand, and to Scripture, on the other, in both instances imposing its program upon a selection of passages of the received canonical documents. The final organizers of the Bavli had in hand a tripartite corpus of inherited materials awaiting composition into a final, closed document.

The first type of material, in various states and stages of completion, addressed the Mishnah (inclusive of the Tosefta and Baraita corpus) or took up and explored, through diverse cases and legal topics, the principles of laws that the Mishnah had originally brought to articulation. These the framers of the Bavli organized in accord with the order of the Mishnah tractates that they selected for sustained attention.

Second, they had in hand received materials, again in various conditions, pertinent to Scripture, both as Scripture related to the Mishnah and also as Scripture laid forth its own narratives. These they set forth as Scripture commentary. In this way, the penultimate and ultimate redactors of the Bavli laid out a systematic presentation of the two Torahs—the oral, represented by the Mishnah, and the written, represented by Scripture.

And, third, the framers of the Bavli also had in hand materials focused on sages. These, in the received form attested in the Bavli's pages, were framed around twin biographical principles, either as strings of stories about great sages of the past or as collections of sayings and comments drawn together solely because the same name stands behind all the collected sayings. These could easily have been composed into biographies.

Seeing the document whole, how do we describe it? The Bavli as a whole lays itself out as a commentary to the Mishnah. So the framers wished us to think that whatever they wanted to tell us would take the form of Mishnah commentary. But a second glance indicates that the Bavli is made up of enormous composites, themselves closed before inclusion in the Bavli. Some of these composites—around 35 to 40 percent of Bavli's, if my sample is indicative—were selected and arranged along lines dictated by a logic other than that deriving from the requirements of Mishnah (or Tosefta, or legal) commentary.

Joining Mishnah commentary to Scripture commentary represents an innovation and marks the originality and success of the Bavli's framers. The components of the canon of the Judaism of the dual Torah prior to the Bavli had encompassed amplifications of the Mishnah, in the Tosefta and in the Yerushalmi, as well as amplifications for Scripture, in such documents as *Sifra* to Leviticus, *Sifré* to Numbers, *Sifré* to Deuteronomy, *Genesis Rabbah*, *Leviticus Rabbah*, and the like. But there was no entire document, now extant, organized around the life and teachings of a particular sage. Even *The Fathers according to Rabbi Nathan*, which contains a good sample of stories about sages, is not so organized as to yield a life of a sage, or even a systematic biography of any kind. Where events in the lives of sages do occur, they are thematic and not biographical in organization, for example, stories about the origins, as to Torah study, of diverse sages and the death scenes of various sages. The sage as such, whether Aqiba or Yohanan ben Zakkai or Eliezer b. Hyrcanus, never in that document defines the appropriate organizing principle for sequences of stories or sayings. And there is no other in which the sage forms an organizing category for any material purpose.

Accordingly, the decision that the framers of the Bavli reached was to adopt the two redactional principles inherited from the antecedent century or so and to reject the one already rejected by their predecessors, even while honoring it: (1) They organized the Bavli around the Mishnah. (2) They adapted and included vast tracts of antecedent materials organized as scriptural commentary. These they inserted whole and complete, not at all in response to the Mishnah's program.

But, finally, (3) although they made provision for small-scale compositions built upon biographical principles and preserved both strings of sayings from a given master (and often a given tradent of a given master) and tales about authorities of the preceding half millennium, they never created redactional compositions of a sizable order that focused upon given authorities. Still, sufficient materials certainly lay at hand to allow doing so.

In the three decisions, two of what to do and one of what not to do, the final compositors of the Bavli indicated what they proposed to accomplish: to give final form and fixed expression, through their categories of the organization of all knowledge, to the Torah as it had been known, sifted, searched, approved, and handed down, even from the remote past to their own day.

What do we learn about documentary and nondocumentary writing from the Bavli? On the one hand, vast blocks of material realize the program of Mishnah-Tosefta-Halakhah-commentary, in a manner quite distinctive to the Bavli. These blocks we may classify as documentary writing because they adhere to a formal protocol and conventions of logical analysis and argument throughout. On the other hand, vast blocks of material address the systematic exegesis of passages of Scripture. Whether and how these carry out a documentary program devised for the Bavli in particular remains to be investigated. One certainly can make a case that conventions and protocols particular to the Bavli govern here as well; but that case has not yet been made. But there are also blocks of a "biographical" order—compilations of sayings assigned to a single authority; collections of stories about sages, joined by a common theme or even proposition—that hardly exhibit an integral connection to the program of the Bavli's compilers. It is still more difficult to show the documentary intention realized in these blocks of writing.

There is a fourth type of composite in the Bavli, which I call the thematic appendix. These miscellanies are catchalls for diverse materials on a common subject or problem but lack all propositional coherence. In contemporary writing, the counterpart is the appendix of a book, assigned the task of providing data not integrated into the main part of the book but thematically pertinent to it. For the sake of completeness, the author has added the appendix. Why the Bavli's compilers include a fair number of topical miscellanies can generally be determined in context. These invariably are to be classified as non-documentary writing—indeed, composites and aggregates of the same—and any systematic investigation of the nondocumentary writing that went on in the Rabbinic circles will begin with the miscellanies of the Bavli, to which no other document comes close in the proportion of miscellanies.

C. *Freestanding Pericopes Framed without Any Regard to Documentary Requirements*

Let me now generalize about the traits that I see in nondocumentary writing.

The first question is this: does the recognition that some writings responded to documentary conventions and others did not allow us to estimate which kind of writing comes earlier in the formation of the Rabbinic canon? One thing is clear. The nondocumentary kind of writing could have gone on at any time, from the beginning to the end of the process that yielded the entire canon. But are the compositions of this kind, as a matter of hypothesis, to be assigned to a stage in the formation of classics prior to the framing of all available documents? May we suppose that, in some other model at some point prior to the decision to make writings in the model that we now have, people also made up completed units of thought to serve these other kinds of writings? The extant documents contain ample evidences for the existence of compilations in process—with their own distinctive traits of rhetoric, logic of coherent discourse, and especially topic—that did not survive. These evidences persist now in documents that they do not serve at all well. And we can fairly easily identify the kinds of documents that they could and should have served quite nicely indeed. So documentary writing went forward on a broad front, yielding for posterity only part of its heritage of disciplined, completed compilations.

What of parables? We may note that among the "unimaginable" compilations there is not a collection of parables, since in the Rabbinic corpus parables never stand free and never are inserted for their own sake. Whenever in the Rabbinic canon we find a parable, it is meant to serve the purpose of an authorship engaged in making its own point; and the point of a parable is rarely, if ever, left naked and unarticulated. Normally it is put into exhortatory words, but occasionally the point is made simply by redactional setting. It must follow that in this canon the parable cannot have constituted the generative or agglutinative principle of a large-scale compilation. It further follows, so it seems to me, that the parable always takes shape within the framework of a work of composition for the purpose of either a large-scale exposition or, more commonly still, of a compilation of a set of expositions into what we should now call the chapter of a book; that is to say, parables link to purposes that transcend the tale that they tell (or even the point that the tale makes). On this basis, I exclude parables of all kinds; none of them is freestanding; none fails to find a place for itself in accord with the purposes of compilers either of documents we now have in hand or of documents we can readily envisage or imagine.

D. *The Hermeneutics of the Documentary Hypothesis*

Once we recognize that the Rabbinic documents constitute texts, not merely scrapbooks or random compilations of ad hoc and episodic materials, in the documentary framework both the hermeneutics and the (theoretical) history of the texts are recast. For our criteria for interpreting a passage are now defined by the program of the document. Interest in philology (meanings of words scattered over a variety of documents) and ad hoc exegesis (interpretation of phrases and sentences out of narrative or expository context) correspondingly diminishes. The context now predominates; meanings of words and phrases, while interesting, move away from center stage. And the texts now are seen to have histories—the *texts*, that is, the completed documents, and not merely the *materials* that the texts happen, adventitiously, to contain. The hermeneutics for the types of compositions of which Rabbinic compilations are made up rests upon one fundamental premise. It is that Rabbinic documents are texts and not scrapbooks, that we moreover may identify the traits that characterize one compilation and distinguish those traits from the ones that mark another compilation.

Now to spell out a particular realization of the documentary hermeneutics: in my study of *Leviticus Rabbah*, I proposed to demonstrate, in the case of that compilation of exegeses of Scripture, that a Rabbinic document constitutes a text, not merely a scrapbook or a random compilation of episodic materials. A text is a document with a purpose, one that exhibits the integrity of the parts to the whole and the fundamental autonomy of the whole from other texts. I showed that the document at hand therefore falls into the classification of a cogent composition, put together with purpose and intended, as a whole and in the aggregate, to bear a meaning and state a message.

I therefore disproved the claim, for the case at hand, that a Rabbinic document serves merely as an anthology or miscellany or is to be compared only to a scrapbook, made up of this and that. In this exemplary instance, I pointed to the improbability that a document has been brought together merely to join discrete and ready-made bits and pieces of episodic discourse. A canonical document thus does not merely define a context for the aggregation of such already completed and mutually distinct materials. Rather, I proved that a document constitutes a purposive text. So, at issue in my study of *Leviticus Rabbah* is what makes a text a text, that is, the textuality of a document. At stake is how we may know when a document constitutes a text and when it is merely an anthology or a scrapbook.

The importance of this issue for hermeneutics is clear. Let me state the null hypothesis. If we can show that a document is a miscellany, then traits of the document have no bearing on the contents of the document—things that just happen to be preserved there rather than somewhere else. If, by contrast, the text possesses its own integrity, then everything in the text must, first of all, be interpreted in the context of the text, then in the context of the canon of which the text forms a constituent. Hence my hermeneutical program lays heavy stress on the comparison of whole documents, prior to the comparison of the results of exegesis contained within those documents.

Now proponents of the view that redactional, hence documentary, considerations are of negligible importance may claim that powerful evidence contradicts my emphasis on the documentary origin of much writing now located in Rabbinic documents. They point to the fact that stories and exegeses move from document to document, a matter to which we shall return more than once. The travels of a given saying or story or exegesis of Scripture from one document to another validate comparing what travels quite apart from what stays home. And that is precisely what comparing exegeses of the same verse of Scripture occurring in different settings does. Traveling materials enjoy their own integrity, apart from the texts—the documents—

that quite adventitiously give them a temporary home. The problem of integrity therefore is whether a Rabbinic document stands by itself or right at the outset forms a scarcely differentiated segment of a larger and uniform canon, one made up of materials that travel everywhere and take up residence indifferent to the traits of their temporary abode.

The reason one might suppose that, in the case of the formative age of Judaism, a document does not exhibit integrity and is not autonomous is simple. The several writings of the Rabbinic canon do share materials—sayings, tales, protracted discussions. Some of these shared materials derive from explicitly cited documents. For instance, passages of Scripture or of the Mishnah or of the Tosefta, cited verbatim, will find their way into the two Talmuds. But sayings, stories, and sizable compositions not identified with a given earlier text and exhibiting that text's distinctive traits will float from one document to the next.

That fact has so impressed students of the Rabbinic canon as to produce a firm hermeneutical consensus of fifteen hundred years' standing. It is that one cannot legitimately study one document in isolation from others, describing its rhetorical, logical, literary, and conceptual traits and system all by themselves. To the contrary, all documents contribute to a common literature or, more accurately, religion—Judaism. In the investigation of matters of rhetoric, logic, literature, and conception, whether of law or of theology, all writings join equally to given testimony to the whole. For the study of the formative history of Judaism, the issue transcends what appears to be the simple, merely literary question at hand: when is a text a text? In the context of this book, the issue is this: when do the interests of the framers of a text participate in the writing of their text, and when do the framers merely compile from ready-made materials whatever suits their purpose? In the larger context of this question, we shall return in section VII to the issue of "parallels," by which people mean the peripatetic sayings, stories, and exegeses. Then we shall inquire about the testimony that stories occurring in parallel form in diverse documents give to the process of documentary writing and agglutination.

VI. The Question of Literature: B. What Is at Stake in Identifying Other-than-Documentary Writing and Its Traits? The Predocumentary History of Rabbinic Judaism

At stake in differentiating documentary from other-than-documentary writing in the various documents is the recovery of some of the pre-documentary history of Rabbinic Judaism in its normative canon. The question I mean to raise is this: are we able to turn the phenomenology of the components of documents into the makings of a history of the writing down of Rabbinic Judaism? I propose that systematic differentiation between documentary and other-than-documentary components of the several documents affords access to the predocumentary history of the documents of Rabbinic Judaism. A considerable project presents itself. To lay out the main outlines, let me begin from the correct starting point: the facts in hand and differentiating among them.

Start with documentary traits and ask the question: at what point do these register, and when do they govern and take effect—is it at the beginning of the process of documentary formation and agglutination or at the end? By this I mean, do the documentary traits of a given compilation embody a protocol in play at the very outset of writing the completed units of tradition assembled in the document, or do they dictate the formal traits of the writing at the end, in the work of redaction?

To me one answer is self-evidently sound: the documentary traits common to a series of distinct cognitive units are redactional because they are imposed at the point at which someone intended to join together both new writing, serving the documentary program, and also discrete (finished) units on a given theme. Then the document components that do not exhibit the indicative documentary traits— the other-than-documentary writing—represent a stage in the formation of the document that is prior to the stage of redaction.

Let me spell this out. The varieties of traits particular to the discrete units and the diversity of authorities cited therein, including masters considered to have flourished in widely separated times (generations), make it highly improbable that the several units were formulated in a common pattern and then preserved until, later on, still further units, on the same theme and in the same pattern, were worked out and added. That is to say, a sedimentary model does not strike me as a plausible account of the process of formalization of what ends up as the indicative components of a document. In addition, given the fact that nearly all canonical documents exhibit the same high degree of formalization, a sedimentary model requires us to conceive a complex pattern. In accord with that pattern, people writing for document A would have to have had in hand a handbook of formulary rules for whatever they wrote for document A, another for document B under way in the same time frame, a third for document C, and so on. Then we could explain how, within a slow, sedimentary process, the acute formalization of writing could have taken place. But this model seems to me less plausible than one that conceives formalized writing to attest to the conditions of penultimate and ultimate redaction: here are the rules governing the writing of this book at this time, *tout court!*

A further argument against the sedimentary model and in favor of the one I propose—writing for redaction, following rules governing the preparation of the document in hand—derives from another fact characteristic of all the documents: the temporal order of sages does not register. Early and late authorities register opinions side by side, and no one pays attention to the sequence of periods in which they are assumed to have flourished. So the entire indifference to the historical order of authorities and the concentration on the logical unfolding of a given theme or problem without reference to the sequence of authorities make a sedimentary model of accumulation unlikely. It confirms the supposition that, for documentary writing, the work of formulation and that of redaction go forward together.

This interplay of redaction and formulation—writing intended for a document under redaction would conform to the rules in play for that document and no other—yields another observation: what exactly (within the present model) is composed within the redactional process, sentences or paragraphs? That is to say, which defines the redactional phase of the writing: the smallest whole sense units or the composing of sense units into completed propositions in more exact language? The answer yielded by redaction analysis is self-evident: the principal framework of formulation and formalization is the intermediate division, with its repeated patterning of language and corresponding promotion of syllogism, rather than the cognitive unit (freestanding sentence). And what this means for our inquiry is simple: we can tell when it is that the ultimate or penultimate redactors of a document do the writing.

Documentary writing comes later in the formation of materials now preserved in the documentary framework. Non- or extradocumentary writing need not come so late in the process.

Let me articulate my hypothesis and the reasons that generate it, now invoking the typology of writing yielded by documentary criteria that I have already laid out:

(1) The last type of writing in documentary context then in temporal sequence is that carried out in the context of the making of a canonical compilation. This writing responds to the redactional program and plan of the authorship of a document.[1]

(2) The second, penultimate in order, is writing that can appear in a given document but better serves a document other than the one in which it (singularly) occurs. This kind of writing seems to me to fall roughly within the same period of redaction as the first, relative to the time of redaction of the document to whose forms the writing conforms.

(3) The third kind of writing—earliest in the sequence ending with the redaction of the document at hand[2]—is carried on in a manner independent of all redactional considerations such as are known to us. This writing may or may not travel from one document to another;

---

[1] I stress "in documentary context" to make my meaning clear. Looking at all the writing in a given document, I would anticipate that the formalized component of the writing, that which conforms to the documentary protocol, comes last in the process of writing down traditions and that the other-than-documentary writing in that document is prior in closure. But this hypothesis has no bearing on other-than-documentary writing "in general," let alone in other documents. Whether we can differentiate for the entire canon between documentary and other-than-documentary writing is a separate problem. First we have to know what is written for a given document and what is not written for that particular document. Then we have to compare the latter corpus of writing as it derives from more than a single document, for example, nondocumentary writing in the Mishnah and in the Tosefta. What that comparison yields I cannot now guess; I plan to find out in due course. And from that point, the exercise encompasses yet more documents until the entire corpus, Halakhic and Aggadic, has been sorted out. Only then shall we know much about the protocol governing writing for a purpose other than documentary composition (or agglutination).

[2] Once more I stress "sequence ending . . . with the document at hand." After all, the first writing we have in the entire canon is also the most consistently formalized, the Mishnah itself! So these ordinal indications serve only within the limits of a given document, as spelled out just now.

this consideration is not relevant, since it does not exhibit the indicative classificatory traits under study. What matters is not whether it fits one document or another but whether, as the author or authorship has composed a piece of writing, that writing meets the requirements of any document we now have or can even imagine.

How does the present hypothetical discussion lead us into the predocumentary history of ideas now transmitted within canonical documents? The answer comes from a choice. This third kind of writing seems to me to derive from either (1) a period prior to the work of the making of Rabbinic documents, inclusive of the two Talmuds alike, or (2) a labor of composition not subject to the rules and considerations that operated in the work of the making of Rabbinic documents and the two Talmuds.

Because of the considerations already set forth, I tend to prefer the former of the two possibilities. That is, nondocumentary writing is predocumentary writing. A decisive question shows why: *have these writers done their work with documentary considerations in mind?*

I believe I have shown that they have not. Then where did they expect their work to make its way? Anywhere it might because, so they assumed, fitting in nowhere in particular, it found a suitable locus everywhere it turned up. Accordingly, I am inclined to think that the nondocumentary compositions and composites carry us deep into the predocumentary thought of Rabbinic Judaism: writing antecedent to the documentary process.

A simple reason serves: given the documentary propositions and theses that we can locate in all of our canonical compilations, we can only assume that the nondocumentary writings enjoyed, and were assumed to enjoy, ecumenical acceptance. What fits anywhere serves everywhere. So, when we wish to know the consensus of the entire canonical community—I mean simply the sages, anywhere and any time, responsible for everything we now have—we turn not to the distinctive perspective of documents but to the universally acceptable perspective of the extradocumentary compositions. That is the point at which we should look for the propositions everywhere accepted but nowhere advanced in a distinctive way, the "Judaism beyond the texts"—or behind them. So the documentary and the nondocumentary components of the documents are to be distinguished not only in venue but in time, with the latter components assigned a period prior to the former.

We come, then, to writings for a document other than one now in our hands. This kind of writing was first identified by Herbert Basser in 1990, in the following language, which comments on *Leviticus Rabbah* 1:1, the important language being italicized:

> [The passage at hand] is simply a regular Midrashic form explaining a verse in Proverbs. When the Midrash is "transferred" from a Proverb-homily to a Leviticus-homily, we find the Midrash headed by the verse in Leviticus. In other words, what we consider "petihta" is in fact standard exegetical form, nothing else. . . . *There seem to have been collections of Midrash to Proverbs and Psalms that predate these "petihta" Midrashim and were utilized by the preachers. . . . The fact that we have Midrashim defining words in verses in the Writings with no attempt to connect them to Torah suggests that there did exist separate Midrashim on Proverbs and other works.* It is quite likely that these Midrashim were not promulgated in the synagogue but in the academy.[3]

In line with Basser's initial recognition of the implications of the pattern, we may posit the existence of documents we do not have, for which writing went on in the formative age. That too represents documentary writing, not to be ignored. Now let me give a simple, common example of a predocumentary composite in a documentary setting. What is important is for me to spell out the obvious reasons for deeming the composite earlier in formation, not merely different in program, from the documentary setting. I take a random item, a type that occurs in most Midrash compilations, to register the point.

The following passage would serve a systematic exegesis of the book of Psalms. The clauses of Ps. 89:20 are referred to particular Israelite saints: Abraham, then David and Moses. If we set aside the handful of indented compositions—that is, those that gloss or otherwise enrich the exposition—we see a highly systematic exegesis of the cited verse. Viewed in its own terms, the composition does not require us to position it in an exposition of Lev. 1:1—and yet this is precisely what the compilers of *Leviticus Rabbah* have done with the composition/composite. The indented materials are not primary to the composition.

---

[3] Herbert W. Basser, *In the Margins of the Midrash: Sifré Ha'azinu Texts, Commentaries, and Reflections*, South Florida Studies in the History of Judaism 11 (Atlanta: Scholars Press, 1990; reprint, Lanham: University Press of America, 2001), 16–18.

Leviticus Rabbah 1:4

1. A. R. Abin in the name of R. Berekhiah the Elder opened [discourse by citing the following verse]: "'Of old you spoke in a vision to your faithful ones, saying, "I have set the crown upon one who is mighty, I have exalted one chosen from the people"'" [Ps. 89:20].

   B. "[The Psalmist] speaks of Abraham, with whom [God] spoke both in word and in vision.

   C. "That is in line with the following verse of Scripture: 'After these words the word of God came to Abram in a vision, saying . . .' [Gen. 15:1].

   D. "'. . . to your faithful one'—'You will show truth to Jacob, faithfulness to Abraham' [Mic. 7:20].

   E. "'. . . saying, "I have set the crown upon one who is mighty"—for [Abraham] slew four kings in a single night.'

   F. "That is in line with the following verse of Scripture: 'And he divided himself against them by night . . . and smote them'" [Gen. 14:15].

   2. A. Said R. Phineas, "And is there a case of someone who pursues people already slain?

      B. "For it is written, 'He smote them and he [then] pursued them' [Gen. 14:15]!

      C. "But [the usage at hand] teaches that the Holy One, blessed be he, did the pursuing, and Abraham did the slaying."

3. A. [Abin continues,] "'I have exalted one chosen from the people' [Ps. 89:20].

   B. "'It is you, Lord, God, who chose Abram and took him out of Ur in Chaldea'" [Neh. 9:7].

4. A. ["I have exalted one chosen from the people" (Ps. 89:20)] speaks of David, with whom God spoke both in speech and in vision.

   B. That is in line with the following verse of Scripture: "In accord with all these words and in accord with this entire vision, so did Nathan speak to David" [2 Sam. 7:17].

   C. "To your faithful one" [Ps. 89:20] [refers] to David, [in line with the following verse:] "Keep my soul, for I am faithful" [Ps. 86:2].

   D. ". . . saying, 'I have set the crown upon one who is mighty,'" [Ps. 89:20]—

      E. R. Abba bar Kahana and rabbis:

      F. R. Abba bar Kahana said, "David made thirteen wars."

      G. And rabbis say, "Eighteen."

      H. But they do not really differ. The party who said thirteen wars [refers only to those that were fought] in behalf of the need of Israel [overall], while the one who held that [he fought] eighteen includes five [more, that David fought] for

>   his own need, along with the thirteen [that he fought] for the
>   need of Israel [at large].
> I.   "I have exalted one chosen from the people" [Ps. 89:20]—"And
>   he chose David, his servant, and he took him . . ." [Ps. 78:70].
> 5. A. ["Of old you spoke in a vision to your faithful one . . ."] speaks
>   of Moses, with whom [God] spoke in both speech and vision, in
>   line with the following verse of Scripture: "With him do I speak
>   mouth to mouth [in a vision and not in dark speeches]" [Num.
>   12:8].
> B.   "To your faithful one"—for [Moses] came from the tribe of
>   Levi, the one concerning which it is written, "Let your
>   Thummim and Urim be with your faithful one" [Deut. 33:8].
> C.   ". . . saying, 'I have set the crown upon one who is mighty'"—
> D.   The cited passage is to be read in accord with that which R.
>   Tanhum b. Hanilai said, "Under ordinary circumstances a
>   burden which is too heavy for one person is light for two, or
>   too heavy for two is light for four. But is it possible to sup-
>   pose that a burden that is too weighty for six hundred thou-
>   sand can be light for a single individual? Now the entire
>   people of Israel were standing before Mount Sinai and say-
>   ing, 'If we hear the voice of the Lord our God any more,
>   then we shall die' [Deut. 5:22]. But, for his part, Moses heard
>   the voice of God himself and lived" [= I:I.6.B–D].
> E.   You may know that that is indeed the case, for among them
>   all, the word [of the Lord] called only to Moses, in line with
>   that verse which states, "And [God] called to Moses" [Lev.
>   1:1].
> F.   "I have exalted one chosen from the people" [Ps. 89:20]—"Had
>   not Moses, whom he chose, stood in the breach before him to
>   turn his wrath from destroying them" [he would have destroyed
>   Israel] [Ps. 106:23].

The composition, with or without the secondary materials that are
inserted, means to expound the cited verse of Psalms, linking the passage to the figures of Abraham, David, and Moses. It can best serve
as a component of a Midrash compilation for Psalms, which we do
not have for late antiquity. It also could serve for an exposition of the
figure of Abraham or of David or of Moses, but we have no such
compilations devoted to named saints of Scripture. In one or the
other of these hypothetical documentary venues, the passage would
be classified as a documentary writing. The one destination that the
writers could not have contemplated is *Leviticus Rabbah*, an exposition
of passages of the book of Leviticus, or even a construction in *Leviticus
Rabbah* devoted to the figure of Moses as a prophet. The passage

intersects with the theme of its location, and that is all. The composition (with or without its intruded materials) existed prior to its inclusion in *Leviticus Rabbah* and I would claim—in something very like its present articulation—*also prior* to the writing of the compositions and composites of *Leviticus Rabbah* that serve the program of the compilers of *Leviticus Rabbah*.

Let me state the matter in more theoretical terms. When people went about the work of making documents, they did something fresh with something inherited. They made cogent compositions, documents, texts enjoying integrity and autonomy. But they did so in such a way as to form of their distinct documents a coherent body of writing—of books, a canon; of documents, a system. And this they did in such a way as to say, in distinctive and specific ways, things that, in former times, people had expressed in general and broadly applicable ways. Nondocumentary writing that is now located in a documentary setting, then, seems to me to originate in a period prior to the documentary writing. It ignores documentary issues altogether. Thus it should derive from a time when redactional considerations played no paramount role in the making of compositions and composites. A brief essay, rather than a sustained composition, was then the dominant mode of writing.

Writing such as the passage before us, which does not presuppose a secondary labor of redaction, for example, in a composite, probably originated when authors or authorships did not anticipate any fate for their writing beyond their particular labor of composition itself. What this means is that the author (or authorship) does not imagine a future for his (or their) writing. What fits anywhere is composed to go nowhere in particular. In the nondocumentary writing, then, we deal with a literary period in which the main kind of writing was ad hoc and episodic, not sustained and documentary. To state matters plainly: writing that can fit anywhere or nowhere is prior to writing that can fit somewhere but does not fit anywhere now accessible to us, and both kinds of writing are prior to the kind that fits only in the document in which it is now located.

Future inquiry will have to refine that hypothesis and show in detail how it accounts for the history—literary and intellectual—of Rabbinic Judaism in its predocumentary statement. Specifically, the predocumentary component of a specific document—the compositions and even composites that do not conform to the documentary protocol—requires specification, its principal ideas or propositions articulated. A labor of comparison of the propositions conveyed by the documentary components of the compilation with those of the nondocumentary components of the same compilation must follow, yielding the comparison and contrast of the two orders of writing: what ideas are particular to the document, what ideas are commonplaces, representative of other-than-documentary opinion as well. Then one must ask how, if at all, the (allegedly) later ideas, representing the opinion of the framers of the document, engage with, relate to, the (supposedly) earlier layer of ideas, representing the generality of Rabbinic opinion (the counterpart to anonymous, therefore normative, Halakhic rulings). I cannot now predict the outcome, but I do believe that such an analytical process will yield interesting results.

To close with the obvious, the labor of comparing and contrasting the ideas and propositions of the two types of writing in a given document will have to be carried out for all canonical documents, inclusive of the two Talmuds. Then, and only then, the results over time will yield the promise of a well-grounded history of the unfolding of Rabbinic doctrine by objective, replicable methods of ordinal differentiation, perhaps even in temporal sequence. A massive labor of detailed inquiry, document by document, awaits.

VII. The Question of Literature: C. Other-than-Documentary Writing: The Matter of Proportion and Purpose

The question remains: what proportion of the Rabbinic document is made up of non- and extradocumentary writing? A sample of the other-than-documentary components of the Bavli, Mishnah, Tosefta, *Sifra*, and *Genesis Rabbah*[4] shows that, for the analyzed samples of Bavli, Mishnah, Tosefta, and *Sifra*, the extra- and nondocumentary writing forms a paltry proportion of the whole. Freestanding compositions, furthermore, undertake no critical documentary task within the document(s) in which they occur. They take a subordinated role,

---

[4] For *Genesis Rabbah* the proportion of freestanding compositions is not paltry. But the autonomous writing in it is of a single classification and yields a workable hypothesis on one type of non- and predocumentary writing.

illustrating or filling out a proposition, not inaugurating one. So the canonical documents overall come out of a process of documentary formation that has imparted shape and structure to the larger proportion, by far, of what is in the documents. And that process has admitted nondocumentary writing only occasionally and episodically. So the nondocumentary testimonies are not only sparse but also unfocused—random evidence, the best kind for assessing the state of Rabbinic opinion beyond (and before!) the documentary process (or the several documentary processes, respectively!). That in all five compilations, Bavli, Mishnah, Tosefta, *Sifra*, and *Genesis Rabbah*, the role of freestanding compositions proves entirely peripheral is not a subjective opinion. It is a fact that is founded on the basis of objective criteria of analysis. The results of the sample can be replicated by others interested in the problem. Further work on the other canonical documents is called for. But I anticipate comparable outcomes.

Let me spell out the urgency of the matter of proportion and purpose. Why do the facts produced by the sample on which I report make a difference, and to whom? The answer lies in an ongoing debate about the fundamental characterization of the canonical documents of Rabbinic Judaism in its formative age. Let me review the matter, already adumbrated earlier. Two theories of the formation of the Rabbinic canon presently contend. One, broadly held, regards documentary bounds as null. The other deems them consequential and determinate. At stake is the possibility of characterizing Rabbinic Judaism as a cogent structure and system, a contextual description based on coherent canonical documents. These are matters that require considerable amplification.

The former theory sees the Rabbinic tradition as a vast corpus of disorganized bits and pieces— a mass of contradictory opinions about we know not what, yielding no category formations, let alone temporal aggregates of focused opinion. The compilations of Rabbinic writing begin with the smallest whole units of discourse, and these are random and unformed. These freestanding stories and other composites, now collected in a random manner in the compilations of the Rabbinic canon, form a body of evidence that points to an extradocumentary origin of the compositions and composites of the Rabbinic compilations of late antiquity. First came the bits and pieces, and only later on the agglutination of these bits and pieces into the compilations we now have. Everything floated free in its day. Then, for reasons we know not, in some arbitrary manner, people collected and arranged this ready-made writing in the posterior collections now in our hands. On this theory of agglutination, we cannot hope to discern cogent category formations of coherent opinion, building blocks of a religious structure, components of a religious system: Judaism. By definition, the formal building blocks and components are null, mere accidents and random composites, not purposive statements of a propositional character.

The contrary theory—already set forth here—maintains the opposite, beginning at the end of the process, not at the start. It differentiates by redactional traits exhibited by some compositions and composites but not others. As I argued at some length, those that exhibit redactional traits come later in the process; those that do not, earlier. So at stake is the differentiation, by temporal categories, between documentary and nondocumentary writing, and I hold that such differentiation is called for, with promising results for the history of the formation of Rabbinic Judaism in its canonical phase.

I believe my analyses of all the canonical documents have yielded these results. The canonical compilations are purposive. Rabbinic writing begins in the whole units formed by documents with their definition of distinctive rhetoric, topic, and logic of coherent discourse. The consequent documents register convictions, prove propositions, and speak to a particular time and place and in behalf of a determinate corporate body. This characterization of the canonical writings adopts for itself a historical-temporal model of a determinate character. First came the program of forming a document with determinate qualities of rhetoric (form), topic (proposition), and logic of coherent discourse (how matters form coherent statements). Then came the preparation of compositions and composites exhibiting the determinate traits of the document.

This contrary theory therefore contains an important qualification. It also recognizes that variable proportions of the Rabbinic documents are made up of non- and extradocumentary writing. By no means do all of the units of coherent thought and expression ("paragraphs") in the several canonical writings adhere to the indicative traits of the documents in which they appear. The documentary reading of the canonical compilations accommodates this fact without difficulty. According to this theory of the formation of the Rabbinic tradition, along the way—perhaps before writing *for* documents, *within the rules of* particular documents, began—writings of a non- and extradocumentary character were undertaken. Then these too found their way into the nascent documents. The non- and extradocumentary compositions generally supplement the expositions to which they are tacked. They do not take a primary part in the documentary exposition of propositions.

One way or another, the parties to the debate take up the same data. But they evaluate it differently. Specifically, advocates of the documentary reading of the canonical writings must address the free-standing components of the documents—the other-than-documentary writings, whether external to all documents or to a particular compilation. The advocates of an atomistic reading of the same compilations must deal with the distinctive traits of rhetoric and topic and logic of coherent discourse that, all together, define a given document and no other. Since they build upon the freestanding compositions, they have to account for the disciplined, rhetorically formal, and propositionally purposive compositions and composites. The outcome is simply stated:

(1) The proportion of extra- or nondocumentary writing in the canonical compilations in most of the sampled documents is negligible.

(2) The role of this writing in all of them is peripheral. So, while the documentary hypothesis of the Rabbinic canon makes provision for other-than-documentary writing, it assigns to this classification of compositions and composites a subordinate role in the process of documentary formation.

The model that I invoke is simple. Whatever the state of Rabbinic writing of compositions and composites, the canonical documents, for their part, begin whole. They commence in a definitive plan and program that form analysis discerns. The several documents originate in that initial decision (1) to write a document ("book") on a given topic, (2) to impose upon the writing particular traits of formalization, and (3) to join the bits and pieces of composed writing into composites by appeal to one theory of logical coherence rather than some other.

The greater part by far of each of the several documents is made up of precisely this sort of documentary writing. But circulating probably before, but certainly at the time of, the compilation of the canonical documents was a body of non- and extradocumentary writing. Materials of that corpus were chosen for, or found their way into, the canonical documents—I repeat, *ordinarily in modest proportion, always in a peripheral role.*

A. *Documentary, Nondocumentary, and Extradocumentary Writing: The Case of* Genesis Rabbah

Let me take a single document and review what I have found out about the types of writing that make up the document and how they relate to one another. I have chosen *Genesis Rabbah,* a complex and diverse compilation.

1. *Documentary Writing in* Genesis Rabbah

Documentary writing in *Genesis Rabbah* accomplishes the goals of the compilers of that document, conforms to the pattern that predominates throughout, and delivers the messages, makes the statements, that the compilers have created the document to set forth. In *Genesis Rabbah* documentary writing takes the basic forms of the intersecting-verse/base-verse construction and the exegetical composition. More to the point, the passages that register the main propositions of the document viewed whole, propositions that will be specified shortly, fall into the category of documentary writing.

2. *Nondocumentary Writing in* Genesis Rabbah

Freestanding compositions and composites ignore the definitive traits of rhetoric and topic (and even logic of coherent discourse) that characterize a particular document, whether *Genesis Rabbah* or any other. They fall into two principal classifications, narratives and exegetical sets (a verse of Scripture and some words of amplification or generalization of the proposition yielded by that verse). The document further yields compositions that do not conform to the formal or topical program governing the whole. In theory these compositions could have found a position elsewhere than in *Genesis Rabbah,* and it could have been for a purpose other than that which defines the composition and compilation of *Genesis Rabbah.* But these find no parallels in other documents and hence require classification as nondocumentary, even though they are unique to this compilation.

3. *Extradocumentary Writing in* Genesis Rabbah

Some compositions occur in other documents in addition to *Genesis Rabbah*. They are, by definition, extradocumentary ("parallels"). They violate all documentary lines and definitions. They represent a kind of writing not generated by the program of making a coherent statement through cogent propositions set forth in a fixed repertoire of forms. These have been amply instantiated. They are of two sorts: comments on verses, and stories. The former are ordinarily brief and stereotypical. The latter are striking for their fixed wording.

4. *The Documentary Complex*

Genesis Rabbah is a composite document. It is made up of writing undertaken in accord with the distinctive conventions of the document itself. But it contains, in addition, compositions that could have served, and did serve, in other compilations as well. As with the Talmud that it accompanies, the Yerushalmi, so in *Genesis Rabbah*, some of the material in the compilation can be shown to have been composed before that material was used for the purposes of the compilers of this particular document. Many times a comment entirely apposite to a verse of Genesis has been joined to a set of comments in no way pertinent to the verse at hand. Proof for a given syllogism, furthermore, will derive from a verse of Genesis as well as from numerous verses of other books of the Bible. Such a syllogistic argument therefore has not been written for exegetical purposes particular to the verse at hand. On the contrary, the particular verse subject to attention serves that other, propositional plan; it is not the focus of discourse; it has not generated the comment but merely provided a proof for a syllogism. This is what it means to say that a proposition yields an exegesis.

B. *Do Nondocumentary Compositions Matter? 1. The Negligible Proportion of Freestanding Stories in Rabbinic Documents*

First, the peripatetic sayings and freestanding stories form a negligible proportion of the crafted and purposive documents where they do occur. Documents defined by characteristic traits of rhetoric, topic, and logic of coherent discourse do not depend, except for a tiny fraction of their compositions and composites, upon writing shared with other compilations. When we ask just how significant a proportion of a document is made up of stories autonomous of a particular document and common to two or more, the answer is, a minor proportion.

C. Do Nondocumentary Compositions Matter? 2. The Tangential Position, in Documentary Context, That Is Assigned to the Freestanding Composition

Second, when we ask about the importance of freestanding stories in the canonical documents, we find that they play a tangential role. They provide useful information, they illustrate, they amplify, they constitute a topical appendix or a footnote. But they do not bear the principal burden. They do not carry the documentary message where they do occur. How do we know this fact? It is by identifying the main lines of exposition and argument of a given composite. If we outline a composite, we see that the freestanding story always takes a subordinate position and never defines a principal part in the composite in which it figures. This I have done for *Genesis Rabbah*, which illustrates the rule for the other comparable compilations. Let me spell out my main result with appropriate emphasis.

Genesis Rabbah is a composite document. It is made up of writing undertaken in accord with the distinctive conventions of the document itself. But it contains, in addition, compositions that could have served, and did serve, in other compilations as well. As with the Talmud that it accompanies, the Yerushalmi, so in *Genesis Rabbah*, some of the material in the compilation can be shown to have been composed before that material was used for the purposes of the compilers of this particular document. Many times a comment entirely apposite to a verse of Genesis has been joined to a set of comments in no way pertinent to the verse at hand. Proof for a given syllogism, furthermore, will derive from a verse of Genesis as well as from numerous verses of other books of the Bible. Such a syllogistic argument therefore has not been written for exegetical purposes particular to the verse at hand. On the contrary, the particular verse subject to attention serves that other, propositional plan; it is not the focus of discourse; it has not generated the comment but merely provided a proof for a syllogism. That is what it means to say that a proposition yields an exegesis.

Why all this? What relationship do I discern between the forms of a document and its program? The answer for *Genesis Rabbah* is clear. The document's framers have chosen a particular, appropriate book of Scripture to make their statement, and they could have accomplished their goals only in the setting of that book and no other. So the topical program, the exegesis of the book of Genesis, is critical to the documentary definition. Then it is time, at the end, to ask what specifically is the fundamental proposition, displayed throughout *Genesis Rabbah*, that yields the specific exegeses of many of the verses of the book of Genesis and even whole stories. It is that the beginnings point toward the endings, and the meaning of Israel's past points toward the message that lies in Israel's future. The things that happened to the fathers and mothers of the family Israel provide a sign for the things that will happen to the children later on. To this program, documentary writing is essential, but other-than-documentary writing is tangential, an add-on—paltry in proportion, subordinate in function.

VIII. The Question of Literature: What Is Now at Stake?

What literary questions await investigation, and how should I define future inquiries? I see three distinct tasks, each of them able to absorb an entire generation of work. First comes a fresh, form-analytical exegesis of the canonical documents, from the Mishnah through the Bavli. Second, we require historical research into the predocumentary writing that is preserved in the documentary corpus. Third, we shall have to establish the premise that we can speak of documents at all. That is through a systematic presentation, with full reason and justification, of what scholarship conceives to constitute the definitive version of each document: critical editions, constituting more than compilations of variant readings. Let me explain what I see as the three principal parts of the literary question that awaits.

A. *A Fresh, Form-Analytical Exegesis of the Canonical Documents*

First, renewing the exegetical task requires a clearer picture of the formation of the documents than is presently in hand. In Chapter One, I introduced the notion of a fresh exegesis of the Bavli. In the present context, I offer a more general prescription of what is to be done to render the documents accessible to the intellectual enterprise of contemporary learning.

This is required because until now we have been reading these documents within rules of interpretation that do not pertain to the reading of the generality of documents out of ancient times and ancient Judaism. The premises that govern, govern only here. At present the exegesis of the Rabbinic canon carries forward the premises and presuppositions of the received tradition. It means that words and phrases require explanation, but context and construction, the logic of coherent discourse and the sheer sense of sentences in their larger setting, do not. This characterization captures the state of extant exegesis. What is the alternative that I propose? It is time to ask the texts to dictate the kind of exegesis—commentary, explanation, and therefore also translation—that they favor. This exegesis, in accord with interior rules of intelligibility and logic, is defined by the documents themselves—when we understand how they work, in what ways they convey their deepest messages. The established exegesis represented by atomistic readings of words and phrases does not even attempt to read the texts as coherent statements. Whether in the original Hebrew or Aramaic or in German, Hebrew, English (British or American), or Spanish, the translations of the twentieth century are themselves systematic exegetical exercises and, by definition, do not begin to tell us what these documents mean, read as coherent statements. All they do is render words and phrases, allowing the context, without mediation, in all its muteness to speak for itself.

This answer will surprise. People assume, after all, that the established exegetical tradition suffices. They take for granted that we now know pretty much what we need to know about what the texts are saying, because the centuries of exegetical work behind the contemporary consensus have established the final meanings. What remains are improvements and corrections of details, clarifications of readings, definitions of words and phrases. Apart from one or two canonical compilations—the Tosefta, for instance—no fundamentally contemporary reading of the canonical writings, based on contemporary theories of the character of these writings, their contents and continuity, has taken place. The commentaries in the modern critical editions, for example, of *Genesis Rabbah* or *Leviticus Rabbah* or *Pesiqta deRab Kahana*, are episodic and unsystematic. The best exegetical work of modern times on any Rabbinic text, that pertaining to the Tosefta, still is prolix, unfocused, and unsystematic, and it goes without saying—rubbish heap of unsifted possibilities and untested bright ideas though it is—still it is even incomplete! It is a model of erudition and paraphrase, where the whole adds up to a bit less than the sum of the parts. And nothing else competes with it.

The conception that a document contains a key for its own decipherment, inviting as it is, has been realized only partially for the Mishnah and, in substantially diminished measure, for the other Rabbinic canonical writings; but this work is primitive relative to what is required. The progression from the traits of a document to the rules of compilation, to the laws of composition, to the details of cogency and coherence—starting at the outset and proceeding to the end—none has really taken this road to the end for even one document, including the Mishnah. But if the basic hypothesis—hermeneutics yields exegetics—is familiar in the literary study of religion, a fresh exegesis of the entire canon, to compete with the incessant paraphrastic enterprise that passes for scholarship in Rabbinics, has yet to establish itself as a principal task of learning. When everyone concurs that we know what we need to know, a field of learning has paralyzed itself through self-indulgence and self-praise. So the first question of literature in the study of Rabbinic Judaism is this: do we really know, on the basis of internal evidence, what these texts mean?

B. *The Predocumentary History of the Ideas Set Forth in the Canonical Documents*

Second, any kind of historical research that seeks predocumentary patterns and stages and trends—that is, that plans to provide any sort of narrative at all—is going to require the results. But precisely what results do I have in mind? I have already set forth, in laying out the question of history, one approach to the history of ideas, viewing ideas as components of entire systems of thought, for example, constituents of established category formations (a matter we shall revisit presently). Here I deal with something entirely distinct from ideas constructed in systems: random, notional evidence. Let me explain.

In Chapter Two, I discussed the predocumentary history of systems of ideas. In the present context, I point to a particular method for identifying the predocumentary corpus of ideas (inclusive of narratives, laws, exhortations, and exegeses). These two matters do not go over the same ground, but their results do converge. The predocumentary history of systems of ideas concerns the logical steps by which a given conclusion emerged at the end of a sequence of logical steps of analysis and reasoning. Here we take up a formal problem: what evidence does a document yield concerning its utilization of compositions not originally composed by the document's own compilers? The predocumentary history of systems of ideas deals in abstracts of coherent constructions. The predocumentary history of ideas addresses random data, not constructed into compositions and composites at all. The former is hypothetical but supplies its own context of coherence. The latter is based on tangible evidence but then requires us to impose patterns of order and meaning (if any) upon the consequent random data that emerge. The latter, a question of literature and its forms and conventions, bears its own promise and rests on its own foundations. I believe the value, for the study of how documents cohere and accomplish their goals and for the larger formative history of Rabbinic Judaism, is self-evident.

C. *Validating the Documentary Reading of the Canon against the Nihilistic Denial That We Possess More than Compilations of Diverse Readings of This and That*

Third, the very claim of Rabbinic Judaism to derive from a historical venue rests on establishing the specific occasions to which the documents attest, both in the aggregate and in detail. Some scholars are so impressed by the diversity of the manuscript evidence for some of the Rabbinic documents that they have concluded that, for antiquity, there is nothing we may call "Judaism," a religious system realized in its canonical writings. That is because there are no timely documents, only diverse manuscripts of indeterminate location in time and space. We cannot speak of *Genesis Rabbah*, for example, but only of a variety of manuscripts that, one by one, present themselves as *Genesis Rabbah*, and so throughout. The condition of the manuscript evidence for a given compilation (such as I have called here "document") is so parlous, so uncertain, that we cannot position a piece of writing of a determinate character in time or circumstance. All we have are much later representations of a corpus so inchoate as to lack all determinate definition. If we were to judge from the publications of that school of thought, indeed, when it comes to Rabbinic Judaism, there is neither a structure of ideas nor a system for generating and solving fresh problems. There is only a vast corpus of variant readings, which add up to nothing in particular, a hodgepodge and a mess of gibberish.

At stake in the debate is the possibility of defining Rabbinic Judaism as a coherent religious structure and system. With determinate documents, each with its proposition and program, we may discern a structure that is embodied in cogent statements, a system that addresses determinate questions and solves them. To summarize: those who deny the documentary character of the canonical writings also neglect the study of Rabbinic Judaism, and those who claim to discern in the writings a structure and a system also undertake the description, analysis, and interpretation in context of that Judaism.

The documentary hypothesis requires the reading of the writings start to finish and the systematic categorization, by reference to rhetoric, topic, and logic of coherent discourse, of each of the components of each of the writings. This work has been done and has produced sustained results. The rejectionists call attention to the indeterminacy of the manuscript evidence, rich as it is in variant readings, as an argument that the entire documentary enterprise is hopeless to begin with: there are no documents susceptible of characterization, only diverse manuscript testimonies to we know not what. They further point to compositions and composites, as well as singleton sayings, that are shared among two or more documents. These by definition testify against the documentary hypothesis of the Rabbinic canon.

D. *Where to Begin?*

If, in an appropriate circumstance, a beginning scholar, doctorate in hand, dissertation in print, were to interview me, then, about work I think worth doing, what should I suggest for a starting point?

The three components of the literary question of Rabbinic Judaism equally promise important results. But the place to start answering the literary question should be signaled by a single consideration: where are there models, and where is there none? To a young scholar I would advise that you strike out on your own, now that your dissertation is in print and you have learned what the passing generation has to teach you. That means, use what you have learned, for essentially your own program.

It also means, do not recapitulate what others have done, and still more so, do not go over problems you have already solved. The worst thing you can do is more of the same. In the present context of study of the Rabbinic canon as a corpus of literature, what I recommend within the program I have outlined is that you go where there are no models, either in person or in the library. What are the consequences for the tasks outlined here?

1. *Defining Documents out of Diverse Manuscript Testimonies*
The definition of documents by reference to the manuscript evidence requires reasoned critical texts—not merely the compilation of variant readings but evaluation of them. We already have models of how this work should—and should not—be carried on. I would regard these models as definitive. Do not ask machines to solve problems requiring taste, judgment, and intelligence and erudition. And do turn to existing editions—reasoned catalogues in the French sense—for how to define a document of Rabbinic Judaism out of its manuscript testimonies (and the interior logic they embody).

2. *Contemporary Commentaries on Classic Documents*
Access to the meanings of the texts can be improved but is well developed. No generation is orphaned in the study of Rabbinic writings of antiquity. The various received and contemporary commentaries offer more than a preliminary reading of most, though not all, documents. Here people can build upon what is in hand. Even though I cannot point to an acutely contemporary, systematic, and orderly exegesis of a single Rabbinic document, I can identify important examples, even though of a notional or episodic character, of what is to be done. If I had to lay down a general warning, it would be in this simple language: there are two mistakes—assuming we know less than we know and assuming we understand more than we really do. Of the two, the more pernicious is to impute to a text clarity and accessibility beyond the capacities of what is before us: to assume we can make sense of what is gibberish.

3. *The Predocumentary History of Ideas*
Third comes the question that to date lacks all models; neither how the question is to be answered nor what we can hope to find out has as yet been realized, even in a partial or primitive manner. For the predocumentary history of ideas now conveyed in documentary set-

ting stands at its most elementary stages. I cannot point to a single systematic exercise in identifying ideas within a given document that, by the document's own evidence, antecede the formation and redaction of the document. That is where, all other factors being equal, I should advise people to commence: what is truly fresh and lacking in precedent.

4. *Where There Are No Models, Go, Define a Model—but Then Do the Work!*
My message, if I were asked the long, long questions of youth such as I asked Goodenough and Wolfson, would be this: where there are no models, go, devise your own model—and then do the work completely and thoroughly. The worst you can do is pass on your opinion and supply suggestive examples of what you would do if you had the time, the energy, and the ambition. That is to say, the worst you can do is what most people do who do anything at all.

But if I were asked what I personally intend to take up when I have completed my account of the three questions of formative Judaism, the answer would be that it is none of the above. The most basic task I now intuit is *systematically and thoroughly to discover the protocols of non-documentary writing, document by document.* And that is the work that I shall do. For the one thing I have learned in almost fifty years is that the canonical documents are best approached line by line, in detail. The regularities yielded by detailed classification await discovery— and all else starts there. From the literature of formative Judaism we learn the history and the religion. I cannot repeat too often that the character of the evidence predetermines the nature of the inquiry, dictating the starting point.

CHAPTER FOUR

THE QUESTION OF RELIGION

I. Defining the Question of Religion for Rabbinic Judaism

The character of the evidence predetermines the nature of an inquiry. So far as we may phrase a question of religion that is appropriate to the canon of formative Judaism, it concerns ideas viewed in their interior framework. In more general language: by the religious study of a religion, I mean the analysis of the logic and the categorical structure of a religious system of the social order, in particular as that system is portrayed by a canon of documents. In composing a definition, aware of the obvious limitations and unsolved problems, I work from specifics to generalizations. So when I say that the character of the evidence predetermines the nature of an inquiry, I generalize by reference to the character of the evidence in hand, recognizing that evidence of other kinds will then yield their own generalizations.

What exactly, in the context of studying the Rabbinic canon, do I mean by studying religion—*religion*, and not history or literature? By "religion," I mean to describe, analyze, and interpret a very specific phenomenon: ideas, accorded supernatural origin or status, that define the system and structure of the social order set forth as God's will for humanity in community. In the present context, "religion" refers to the corpus of ideas and practices that define that social entity under divine sponsorship and dominion. When, faced with a multiplicity of Judaisms, I speak of "Judaism," I refer to the intellectual system and structure for holy Israel's social order that animate the canonical documents of formative Rabbinic Judaism. "System" and "structure" pertain to how bodies of religious facts, for example, things God said and did and demands and plans, hold together (structure) and generate principles of broad public pertinence (system). At stake is how facts sustain syllogisms and how these form out of facts a coherent statement of religious truth. The question of religion more broadly stated, then, concerns how ideas pertaining to God's imperatives make a large and cogent statement—a matter of intellectual interest, subject to public analysis and debate. The religion program, accordingly, differs from the historical one in its inner-facing perspective. It differs from the literary one in its effort to cross documentary boundaries and find out what the documents, all together, set forth as a coherent statement.

So, to recapitulate, the nature of the evidence—documents accorded authoritative status in a canon—therefore imposes severe limits on the question of religion, restricting us to the examination of religious ideas, not religion in the actualities of the social order and politics of its day. But the restrictions are still narrower, for we take up not ideas in general but a particular statement of them, one made within clear limitations. For, in the canon of formative Judaism, we deal with a public statement of a textual community, set forth in terms of ideas given tangible form in narrative, law, exhortation, and exegesis. That corporate statement conveys *what* the faithful are supposed to have thought and *how* they are represented as having thought: norms of attitude and conviction, norms of action and conduct of intellect. That is what we know about Rabbinic Judaism in its formative age, and it is all we know.

We do not know much about how the imperatives of the religious system Rabbinic Judaism were realized in society and politics. Accordingly, as I shall explain, we may ask about (1) the organizing principles of thought, the governing category formations (below, in this section), and (2) the rules that governed the articulation of thought, the generative logic everywhere active in the documents (sections II and III).

We further may compare the religious system set forth by Rabbinic Judaism with the systems set forth by other Judaisms of the same venue (section IV). These in general represent the principal questions of religion that the formative canon of Rabbinic Judaism, when viewed on its own and when brought into juxtaposition with other canonical formations of religious affines, sustains.

In these remarks I have given a minimalist estimate of what the religious study of the religion before us permits us to ask. But does the Rabbinic canon, which alone attests to that Judaism, truly limit itself to public, corporate, and purely intellectual matters to the exclusion of what is private, personal, and emotional or experiential? Indeed it does—by definition. The documents derive from, and are preserved by, textual communities for whom they speak, so they are public, not personal. If they encompass opinion assigned to named individuals, this ordinarily, though not always, is meant to signify a schismatic view. They concern public duties and corporate attitudes, not private emotions or idiosyncratic experiences. Stories are exemplary, rarely particular, when they concern persons and events. That is why, although the range of issues important in the study of religion is broader than what is public, corporate, and intellectual, the character of the evidence imposes limitations on the questions we may appropriately present.

Yet the question presses: is there really no testimony to what is outside the documentary corpus and what is before it, to the world beyond and the world within? In the present evidence, I find none. That is, little leads us to the actualities of the world of Rabbinic Judaism beyond the texts thereof. As to the world beyond that of Rabbinic Judaism represented by the same canonical writings, the documents say much about the realm beyond their rule, but all is shaped within the logic of the system. In the documents' account of how things outside the circle of the faithful are supposed to have been, there is no pretense at portraying the random happenings of an ordinary, unimagined world. All is selected, and a fair measure fabricated. In the canon, therefore, I do not know how to gain access to a social culture autonomous of the texts but to which the texts attest. So, as to what lies within and before the canonical portrait, the documentary formulation of Rabbinic Judaism does not tell us about interior feelings, attitudes, or motivations, for everything is formulated for public presentation.

The canon, then, sets forth only how the systemic logic of rigorous thinkers leads them to portray the world: facts of religious experience rendered by philosophy into broad syllogisms, the consequential truths of religious conviction. The canonical evidence conveys the intangible realities of the religion only so far as these take intellectual form. Emotions and inner experiences, intuitions and insights, when portrayed by the canon, form elements of the social culture of a public system. All experiences, emotions, attitudes, memories, and hopes are recapitulated and reconstructed in the intellectual construction of a system of ideas: laws and lore and exegesis and exhortation that hold together (so I maintain) in a cogent construction. What the question of religion addresses is therefore readily answered: the intellectual presentation of the religion's principles—in the case of Rabbinic

Judaism, a formulation of the society and culture in which God takes up an abode, with its generative logic as set forth by God in the Torah and with a complete account of how it is articulated in law and theology.

As I said, the evidence dictates the definition of an inquiry. In the aspect of religion, then, I see two fundamental questions. In the model of interior, then exterior, perspectives as set forth in Chapter Two, the first question leads us into the interior of the structure and system, and the second leads us outward toward its exterior relationships and context in comparison with other kindred systems.

(1) CATEGORY FORMATIONS: Can we speak of a cogent corpus of religious belief and practice out of the inchoate data supplied by the canonical documents? Out of the mass of details, how are we able to discern the operative category formations, and can we see how the several category formations come together to function as a working system: the design of holy Israel's social order, God's Kingdom in this-worldly terms?

(2) STUDY OF RELIGION, COMPARISON OF RELIGIONS: With such a system in view, within the established discipline of the academic study of religion, which insists on comparison and contrast, can we situate the Judaic construction in the context of comparison and contrast, both with other Judaisms and with other religions of the same time and place?

(3) STUDY OF RELIGION, STUDY OF HISTORY: Finally, how, in the case of formative Judaism, does the study of religion part company from the study of history? What questions engage the one, and what questions the other?

To these specific questions, brief answers suffice. Let me now spell out the tasks undertaken in sections II and III of this chapter, the description of the religion Rabbinic Judaism as represented by its canonical documents. In the same context, I distinguish the issues of religion from those of history, the ones of Chapter Four from those of Chapter Two.

A. *The Religious Study of Religion in the Case of Rabbinic Judaism*

The religious study of religion represented by a canon of books, and that alone, seeks to describe systems mainly by working back from their end products, the writings. Such a study promises an account of the ideas that animate these writings and an explanation of how these ideas cohere. That is, the religious study of religion embodied only in a complex of writings concerns itself with the category formations of a system—how they cohere and how a systemic logic defines them. The category formations, which join fact to fact to form a syllogism and which turn facts into truth, form the building blocks of the system, its definitive structures.

The task therefore is to work one's way back from the canon to the system embodied in those category formations, not to imagine either that the canon is the system or that the canon creates the system. Contrast, in this context, the historical with the religious study of religion. To the historical study of religion, the canon is the given, the phenomenon to be accounted for in the world beyond the canon. To the religious study of religion, the canon is the problem to be solved in its interior architectonics: how does the whole hold together, how do the parts function to create order and meaning? This shades over into a problem of logic: what are the rules of making connections (between and among data) and drawing conclusions (out of the agglutination of data into patterns).

Still, the religious study of a religion will want to ask for whom the canonical writings speak. But the answer is only marginally illuminating, for we cannot get beyond their limits. They speak, in particular, for those to whom that logic of connection and conclusion is self-evident. On account of perspicacity, this corporate intellect defines the social entity, the systemic community. The community ("Israel"), then, comprises the group whose social system ("way of life") is recapitulated by the selected canon ("worldview"). The group's exegesis of the canon in terms of the everyday imparts to the system the power to sustain the community in a reciprocal and self-nourishing process of detail. The community, through its exegesis, imposes continuity and unity on whatever is in its canon. The writings, then, yield a different kind of information from data that conventional historians require. Most of the questions of origin and development that historians claim to solve cannot find answers in the evidence canonical writings provide. But the canonical evidence answers other and, in the view of many, more urgent and formidable questions of religious persistence: why this, not that?

This brings us to what is at stake in the religious study of religion. While we cannot account for the origin of a religious-social system now conveyed in its canon, we can explain the workings of the logic that provides its power to persist. It is a symbolic transaction in which social change comes to expression in symbol change. That symbolic transaction takes place in its exegesis of the systemic canon, which, in literary terms, constitutes the social entity's statement of itself. That is how the texts recapitulate the system, although the system does not recapitulate the texts. That is because the system comes before the texts and is expressed by them and so implicitly defines the canon. The exegesis of the canon, then, forms the ongoing social action that sustains the whole. I repeat: the system does not recapitulate its texts; it permeates, generates, selects, and orders them. A religious system imputes to the texts as a whole the cogency that the documents' original authorships may not have expressed in and through the parts; and through the documents a religious system expresses its deepest logic *and joins religious system to practical circumstance.* The whole works its way out through exegesis, and the history of any religious system—that is to say, the history of that religion writ small—is the exegesis of its exegesis.

What exactly do I mean when I stress that *the system does not recapitulate the canon, the canon recapitulates the system?* It is that the system forms a statement of a social entity, specifying its worldview and way of life in such a way that, to the participants in the system, the whole makes sound sense, beyond argument. So in the beginning are not words of inner and intrinsic affinity but (as Philo would want us to say) "the Word": the transitive logic, the system, all together, all at once, complete, whole, finished—the word awaiting only that labor of exposition and articulation that the faithful, for centuries to come, will lavish at the altar of the faith. A religious system therefore presents a fact not of history but of the immediacy of the social present.

So the historical questions of origin and survival, which we took up in Chapter Two and meet again in part B of this section, take a subordinate position in the religious study of a religion. To the religious study of a religion the issue of why a system originates and survives or fails proves impertinent, by itself, to the analysis of a system—but still is necessary to our interpretation of it. A system on its own is like a language. A language forms an example of language if it produces communication through rules of syntax and verbal arrangement. That paradigm serves full well however many people speak the language or however long the language serves. Two people who understand each other form a language community, even, or especially, if no one beyond them understands them. So too, by definition, religions address the living, constitute societies, and frame and compose cultures.

For however long and at whatever moment in historical time it may be, a religious system, viewed on its own terms, always grows up in the perpetual present, an artifact of its day, whether today or of a long-ago time. The only appropriate tense for a religious system is the present. A religious system always *is*, whatever it was, whatever it will be. Why so? Because its traits address a condition of humanity in society, a circumstance of an hour—however brief or protracted the hour and the circumstance. To the historians working on the writings of Rabbinic Judaism in its formative age, these considerations prove baffling; to scholars of religion, they recapitulate the banalities and truisms of an active scholarly inquiry. Then what about a system is to be studied? It is the active category formations, which take inert facts and transform them into coherent compositions of truth. These are matters to which we return in section V.

B. *The Religious Study of Religion: The Analytical Program*

So much for the religious description of religions through their category formations. What of the work of analysis, the religious analysis of religions in context? The answer is self-evident to everyone who studies religion through the study of exemplary religions: to study religion is to compare religions. In the comparison of religions, aiming at insight into all of them equally, the study of a religion gains depth and perspective as we ask, "Why this, not that? If we know this, what else do we learn?" These are the givens of the comparative study of religions, the analytical phase of the religious study of religion. The study of religion, accordingly, pursues a distinct program all its own. The perspectives of interiority and exteriority, so useful in situating our inquiry in history, serve once more, but in different ways.

What I contribute to the analytical program of the comparison of religions in the present instance is simple: just as one religion sustains comparison with another, so (1) the constituent components of one and the same religion are to be compared with one another (here: Halakhah and Aggadah), and, furthermore, so (2) the competing systems of one and the same religion—the several Judaisms, in simple language—are to be subjected to comparison and contrast. To spell this out: (1) Rabbinic Judaism is made up of two massive native categories, as I shall explain at some length—Halakhah, law; and Aggadah, lore. These work together to make the complete systemic statement. How are they to be described if not through comparison and contrast? This would represent a process of comparing interior components of one and the same system. (2) Moreover, in late antiquity, a number of Judaic systems took shape in response to the same heritage of Scripture and tradition. These Judaisms demand comparison and contrast. This would represent the process of exterior comparison within the systemic framework of Judaism. Both of these exercises, of analysis through comparison and contrast, represent promising directions for learning.

Take the interior framing of the matter. The question of religion concerns, first of all, the interior architectonics, by which I mean the category formations that impose order on the canonical data and that turn facts into truth. What are the category formations that animate the canon and sustain it through all its components? How does one principal part compare with, relate to, another? An inquiry into the religious structure and system of Rabbinic Judaism, then, will identify the governing category formations that structure the documentary evidence: the lines of order and proportion and balance that make of the whole more than the sum of the parts—that is, impart significance to raw facts.

Seen from the documentary perspective, the category formations can be shown to remain constant in structure but evolve in program as one document takes up one set, and another document a partially revised set, of category formations. Thus the comparison and contrast of the documentary phases of stable category formations demand attention. Sections II and III of this chapter will discuss how the shifts, from one set of documents to another, in the definition of category formations and their contents are to be coordinated and shown to reveal an encompassing pattern. The comparison of the systemic components of Rabbinic Judaism begins with the identification of the category formations and the comparison of those of the Halakhah with their Aggadic counterparts (sections II and III, respectively).

The exterior framing—the comparison and contrast of Judaisms—presents no surprises (section IV). Once we acknowledge that other collections of documents embody other Judaic systems for the social order, we naturally want to relate these to the one in hand.

Comparison and contrast commence when we have identified a category formation common to two or more Judaic systems—indeed, ideally, to all of them. For three systems besides the Rabbinic—the one set forth by the apostle Paul, the one portrayed in the library found at Qumran, and the one adumbrated in the writings of Philo—we ask about the definition and function of "Israel." In this context I propose general laws that emerge from the comparison and may serve for the analysis of other religions besides Judaism and for the comparison and contrast of the constituent systems of those religions. This is accomplished in section IV.

C. *The Historical Study of Religion and the Religious Study of Religion:*
The Differences

To readers of these pages, the present formulation of matters, with its stress on comparison and contrast of religions, will sound familiar. Since in Chapter Two I asked how Rabbinic Judaism situates itself in relationship to paganism and Christianity, it would appear that I repeat for the question of religion my framing of the question of history: a labor of comparison and contrast, the one focusing on synchronic comparison, the other—the interior comparison of Judaic systems or components of a Judaic system—on diachronic or synchronic, as the case requires. So the question presses: how does the historical study of formative Judaism differ from the religious study of that same Judaism if issues of context, comparison, and contrast of religious systems of the social order once more dictate the agenda?

A simple answer presents itself. The question of history, as shaped in Chapter Two, concerns matters of origins and development. Historical questions trace sequences of patterns: scriptural roots, the history of ideas, and their predocumentary history. The study of the history of Rabbinic Judaism addresses exterior matters of religion and society, on the one side, and the extradocumentary contexts of ideas, on the other. What of comparison of religions? That external perspective requires us to compare Rabbinic with Christian teachings about the social order—a model for other such exterior comparisons that await. The question of religion, by contrast, does not ask about time and change and negotiation with the world beyond. Rather, it asks about system and structure, the interior logic and its power of self-evidence. The question of religion asks about the coherence, proportion, balance, interior structure, and order of the construction of the social order that history traces in its temporal accidents, the external relationships and patterns.

Exterior perspectives on religions define a familiar program, supplied as they are by the comparative study of religions. Everyone concurs that, without comparing one religion to another, we understand little about any one religion. But precisely what do we contemplate comparing? And how in this context does the religious comparison of religions differ from the historical comparison of religions?

Starting from the second question, here too we find ourselves obligated to distinguish the religious from the historical comparison of religions. The latter, in the models laid out in Chapter Two, entailed presenting in sections VI and VII, pagan and Christian cultural and social policy compared with the Rabbinic. The historical comparisons concerned doctrines of the organization of religion, on the one side, and the relationship of religion to the social order, on the other. The study of religion aims at the comparison of substantive doctrines, large-scale constructs, of different religions, not just the formal effects of those doctrines. What that means in concrete terms is simple. It would concern how Christianity and Zoroastrianism take up the same questions that Rabbinic Judaism addresses. What comparisons and contrasts emerge when we ask entire, roughly synchronic religious systems to speak to a common agenda? These are questions that arise from the religious study of religion, as distinct from the historical study of religion in the context of culture and society.

II. An Interior Perspective: 1. The Category Formations of the System Viewed Whole—the Halakhah

The canon of Rabbinic Judaism sets forth its data within two massive native categories, norms of behavior (Halakhah, law) and norms of belief (Aggadah, lore), encompassing in the latter case narratives, exhortations, and exegeses of Scripture. The Halakhah, set forth in continuous documents, the Mishnah-Tosefta-Yerushalmi and the Mishnah-Tosefta-Bavli, defines its own native categories. When we understand how these take shape, we can follow the logic of the religious system portrayed by the canon, its modes of thought conveyed through making connections and drawing conclusions. And this intellectual dynamic infuses the religious experience organized and given meaning through the Halakhah. That is because through the Halakhah a corporate, social system of culture is conveyed in rules governing everyday conduct. By reason of their rational organization in the native categories of the Halakhah, these rules are not random and episodic but coherent and systematic. In imposing requirements of omission and commission, they all together form a massive, cogent pattern. The study of the category formations of Rabbinic Judaism commences with those of the Halakhah. With these in hand, we grasp the context in which the Aggadic counterpart is to be portrayed. What is at stake is an account of the categorical construction of the Rabbinic system.

When we grasp the organizing categories native to Rabbinic Judaism in its Halakhic canon, we confront the Rabbinic system, whole and complete, *as it is realized in normative conduct or action.* As just now indicated, these are definitively set forth for us by the first document of Rabbinic Judaism, the Mishnah. Only the concluding canonical composite, the Bavli or Talmud of Babylonia, which is the most important document of the formative canon, encompasses both Halakhic and Aggadic category formations. It is so organized as to spell out the Halakhah in its larger Aggadic setting.

So the interior perspective that the system affords of itself, for itself, begins in the Halakhah, and to understand Rabbinic Judaism requires a clear grasp of the Halakhic system, specifically its organizing category formations and the logic that animates them. How does it do the work? It is through topics subjected to a distinctive program of questions—not merely topical expositions about this and that but analytical expositions of topics, aimed at answering penetrating questions concerning these topics. The native category formations of the Halakhah organize data around topics, with a topic so defined as to highlight a particular aspect, to answer a distinct question about the topic. I cannot overstress the pointed character of the organizing program, which identifies, in connection with a topic, a particular problematic: what the Halakhah concerning that topic wishes to explain or explore. So in the shaping of the Halakhic category formations, we see the collaborative working of the twin principles of cogency: (1) the analysis of (2) a particular topic.

A. *Unrealized Theories of the Halakhic Category Formation*

In accord with the fully realized theory of category formation of Rabbinic Judaism, the Halakhah is defined by analytical-topical category formations. Information on a given subject is shaped into the answer to one or more propositional or analytical questions of broad interest, generally transcending the subject matter altogether. We should be able to account, within this theory, not only for the category formations that govern but also for the omission of those that could have served but do not play a role in Halakhic exposition of corporate Israel's culture and social order. What are these unrealized theories of Halakhic category formation? Besides the Mishnah's normative theory of topical-analytical category formation, I identify in the canonical compilations of the Halakhah these other theories, which account for anomalous composites and turn out to form variations on the initial theory—and not very influential ones at that.

1. *The Mishnah's Anomalous Tractates*

Besides the tractates, that is, the category formations, that are organized topically-analytically, I find in the Mishnah anomalous tractates, or sizable components of tractates, that serve, as the normative ones do, to select and arrange data in coherent constructions. These are the principles and the pertinent tractates (or sizable components of tractates):

> ORGANIZE HALAKHIC MATERIALS BY THE NAMES OF CITED AUTHORITIES: *Eduyyot*
>
> ORGANIZE HALAKHIC MATERIALS TOPICALLY, NOT ANALYTICALLY, SO THAT THEY COHERE IN A NARRATIVE OF HOW THINGS ARE DONE: *Tamid, Middot*
>
> ORGANIZE HALAKHIC MATERIALS CIRCUMSTANTIALLY, FOR EXAMPLE, BY THE OCCASION ON WHICH RULINGS WERE ADOPTED: *M. Yadayim* 4:1–4

The topical-not-analytical tractates tell the story of the divine service of the Temple and the building itself. What we learn in *Eduyyot* is how the preferred approach to category formation would *not* be carried out. But the Talmuds, particularly the Bavli, would find useful the agglutinative principle of the collection of composites around attributive formulas, whether or not limited to a particular Halakhic topic or problem. The collection of Halakhic compositions into composites identified by a common circumstance—attributive authority, topic,

passage of Scripture—defined matters only episodically. Laws were
not linked to events because the entire institutional foundation of the
legal system—as it is portrayed by the documents themselves—did
not frame the presentation of the law. Where a law was set forth mattered little; which authority sponsored it, still less. What made a law
normative was the power of logic, not the legislative body behind it
or the sponsorship of a prominent legal authority. Indeed, a law cited
in the name of a particular authority is more often than not deemed
schismatic.

2. The Mishnah's Anomalous Composites

In addition to substantial components of tractates, I find sets of anomalous composites of data, and these also indicate the operation of
principles of category formation other than the normative one.

> TOPICAL-NOT-ANALYTICAL: NARRATIVE OF HOW THINGS ARE DONE: *M.
> Sheqalim* 3:1–4; *M. Yoma* 1:1–7:5; *M. Suk.* 5:1–7; *M. Rosh Hashanah* 2:3–7;
> *M. Taanit* 2:1–4; *M. Nazir* 6:7–9; *M. Sot.* 1:4–2:5; *M. Neg.* 14:1–10; *M.
> Par.* 3:1–10
>
> ANALYTICAL-NOT-TOPICAL: ORGANIZE HALAKHIC MATERIALS AROUND AN
> ANALYTICAL PROBLEM, WITHOUT A UNIFORM TOPICAL CORE: *M. Pes.* 4:4;
> *M. Meg.* 1:4–11; *M. Git.* 4:1–5:9; *M. Men.* 10:3; *M. Hul.* 1:5–7; *M. Ar.*
> 2:1–3:5; *M. Par.* 8:2–7

The topical-not-analytical approach to category formation in the
Mishnah limited its interest to matters concerning the cult; the use of
narrative to convey the Halakhah through a description of how things
are done served for a particular subject. But no other rhetorical convention took over in presenting any other particular subject.

3. The Tosefta's Anomalous Composites

We proceed to the Mishnah's first commentary, the Tosefta, and ask
how it forms category formations other than through the topical-
analytical method of the Mishnah:

> TOPICAL-NOT-ANALYTICAL: *T. Ber.* 4:8–11; 5:6; *T. Shab.* 6:1–7:18; *T. San.*
> 2:2–13
>
> ANALYTICAL-NOT-TOPICAL: *T. Sheb.* 7:2–8; *T. B.Q.* 6:29–31; *T. Shebu.*
> 4:1–5; *T. Shehitat Hullin* 1:12–25; *T. Men.* 1:2–4; *T. Tem.* 1:18–22; *T.
> Zab.* 3:1–5:1; *T. Tebul Yom* 1:4–7

The division of the topical-analytical method of category formation into
its components characterizes the Tosefta's anomalous composites.

4. The Yerushalmi's Anomalous Composites

The Yerushalmi, drawing upon the Tosefta and the Mishnah to make its systematic presentation of its chosen category formations, relies on the Mishnah's method of category formation in all but a few instances.

> TOPICAL-NOT-ANALYTICAL: *y. Ber.* 2:2–3 II:2–3; *y. Naz.* 9:2 I.3–7
> ANALYTICAL-NOT-TOPICAL: *y. Sheb.* 3:1 I–IV

The Yerushalmi's contribution proves negligible.

5. The Bavli's Anomalous Composites

The Bavli, at the end, employs the topical-not-analytical mode of category formation in some volume.

> TOPICAL-NOT-ANALYTICAL: *b. Ber.* 2:1–2 I:2–11; [*b. Ber.* 3:4 II:2–13;] *b. Ber.* 7:1–2 I:16–24; *b. Ber.* 7:1–2 XII:8–24; *b. Shab.* 2:1 IX:6–36; *b. Shab.* 2:1 X:3–6; *b. Pes.* 3:7–8 I:3–17; *b. Yoma* 1:1 IV:3–7; *b. Rosh Hashanah* 1:1 II:2–9; *b. Meg.* 3:1–2 I:13–44; II:7–19, 20–49; *b. Ket.* 6:5 I:2–17; *b. Git.* 4:4A–D I:8–24; *b. B.Q.* 7:7 I:12–55; *b. B. B.* 1:5 IV:4–48; *b. San.* 7:5 I:2–22; *b. Zeb.* 2:1A–C VI:3–13; *b. Men.* 3:7 II:5–52; *b. Men.* 3:7 I:2–11; *b. Men.* 3:7 III:2–39; *b. Men.* 4:1 I:10–69
>
> (PROPOSITIONAL OR) ANALYTICAL-NOT-TOPICAL: *b. Zeb.* 5:1 IV:2–14; *b. Men.* 1:1 I:5–13

The Bavli proves remarkably fecund in the presentation of topical-not-analytical composites, an observation that takes on meaning when we examine the topical program that the Bavli realizes.

B. The Four Plausible Theories of Category Formation and the One That Was Chosen

The Halakhic category formation through purposeful analysis of a topic produced fifty-nine topical-analytical category formations as set forth by the Mishnah and adopted by the Tosefta. Four other theories episodically surfaced in the Mishnah and the Tosefta, if not in entire tractates, then in large composites:

(1) select and organize data topically, without imposing a purposeful set of questions upon the presentation of those data;

(2) select and organize data to investigate an abstract theory or proposition of Halakhah, without restriction as to the topics that instantiate that theory or proposition;

(3) collect laws that cohere by reason of the authority behind them
   or the event that precipitated their promulgation (a given occasion or session, comparable to a given document [!]);
(4) select laws of a common subject, and order them in a narrative,
   with a beginning, middle, and end—a variation of the first option.

The first, second, and fourth alternatives simply represent variations
on the established theory of category formation, the topical-analytical
one. The third produced negligible results. The first with its variations
accounts for the category formations of an other-than-topical-analytical character. It follows that the normative theory of category formation is to choose data deemed to constitute a single subject, where
possible forming the data into answers to theoretical questions or
where necessary simply gathering data deemed to cohere as a topic.

1. *Other Judaic Modes of Category Formation besides the Rabbinic Halakhic*
Even at this point, comparison with other Judaic systems comes into
play. It is an interior and diachronic comparison, beginning with
Scripture, and it alerts us to what is novel in familiar principles of
category formation, those we encounter in ordinary thought in Western philosophical contexts. Indeed, the present mode of thought is
so familiar as to obscure its rejection of a perfectly plausible past
mode of doing the same. Scripture, in the Pentateuchal law, set forth
alternative approaches to the selection and interpretation of established rules and the construction of those rules into compositions
deemed to cohere. Other collections and arrangements of laws into
large conglomerates were produced by other Israelite heirs of
Scripture, exemplified by the law codes of the Dead Sea Scrolls, the
Elephantine papyri, and the like. But in fact nothing comparable to
the Mishnah-Tosefta-Yerushalmi/Mishnah-Tosefta-Bavli—either in
analytical character or (all the more so) in sheer scope, volume, and
coverage—emerges out of any other Judaic system and its writings.
We look in vain to Scripture, to the Dead Sea library, to the writings
of Philo, for compositions of equivalent comprehensiveness. Let me
state with appropriate emphasis: *in the Judaic corpus of antiquity, from
Moses to Muhammad, the Mishnah-Tosefta-Yerushalmi-Bavli are unparalleled,
both severally and jointly.*

The Halakhah, the continuous statement of law formed by the
foundational documents of Judaism all together, is unique; to its

grandeur no other legal system among ancient Judaic writings aspires, to its comprehensive reformation of Israelite society none presents a counterpart, not the laws of the Dead Sea library read as a coherent composite, nor the adumbration of the laws set forth by Philo, nor, self-evidently, the lesser compilations. The upshot is simply put. The Halakhah in its category formations represents a labor not only of recapitulation and reformation of Scripture's law but also of reconstruction, systematization, and renewal. The purpose of the Rabbinic sages, as revealed through the shape and structure of their work in the Halakhah of the Mishnah-Tosefta-Yerushalmi, and the Bavli, is to translate the narratives, case law, stories, sayings, and rules of Scripture into a coherent, cogent statement: a system meant to realize God's grand design for Israel's social order.

Diachronic comparison then raises this question: why innovate by means of the topical-analytical theory of category formation? We cannot appeal to an available model to account for it. If the intent of the Halakhah, from the Mishnah forward, is to systematize and concretize the received laws of Scripture and to transform them into a coherent design of the Israelite social order (whether in theory, whether in actuality), how otherwise were the sages to turn laws into jurisprudence and cases into rules—and effectively to present the results as a paradigm? Scripture offered no model, with its tight adherence to the mythic mode of presenting law: all coherent by reason of God's instruction to Moses, never re-formed, recast into the regulations of the holy society that this instruction intended.

Let me present a concrete problem. How, for example, someone could have turned the laws of Deuteronomy 12–26 into a design for the social architecture of Israel I cannot say. Scripture's heaviest emphasis lies in the origin of the laws with God, not in demonstrating the proportion, balance, coherence, and rationality of the laws. Moses left that task for his successors in the oral Torah. His sole principal "category formation," the one thing that holds together many things and imparts coherence to the whole, lies in his language, "The Lord spoke to Moses saying, 'speak to the children of Israel and say to them,'" and in the counterpart allegations, both formulaic and narrative, that all together characterize the law of the written Torah and endow it with cogency.

Moses left open that task for the sages who framed the Halakhah by the theory of analogical-contrastive analysis yielding topical-analytical category formations. Once, beyond the closure of Scripture, people determined to carry forward the Halakhic enterprise, to provide Israel with God's plan for the social order of a kingdom of priests and a holy people, the design of God's dominion, what were they to do? At issue now was not the origin and authority of the law; those questions were settled by the Pentateuchal portrait. The question now was this: *how do the rules derive from cases, the laws join together into jurisprudence; and whence the logic and the order of the system seen whole?*

It was for the solution of precisely this problem, the sifting of discrete facts in quest of their proper position and proportion in the order of things, that natural history undertook its work of classification through comparison and contrast, through the identification of a genus and the species thereof.

From the very fundamental trait of the Halakhah, its organization into its six divisions and fifty-nine topical-analytical subdivisions, we see how the sages solved the problem of rendering Scripture (and such oral tradition as they possessed therewith) into a systematic statement. Were we to ask the framers of such law "codes" as Exodus 20–23, Leviticus 1–15, or Deuteronomy 12–26, for a "table of contents" to their codes, the list of topics would show, for Exodus 20–23 and Deuteronomy 12–26, no accessible logic to account for the choice and sequence of subjects, just this and that in no apparent order of self-evidence. Considerations of narrative may play a role, but no logic intrinsic to the laws and attentive to their details enters in. The snippets of laws in the former, the wildly diverse program of the latter—these exercise no power of organization and effect no coherence among their data at all. And even Leviticus 1–15, which does produce a logical sequence of well-executed category formations, proves truncated and insufficient to the task of yielding generalizations for the Israelite social order in all its dimensions. The Pentateuch provides the data for the social task undertaken by the sages, but no model to guide them in their work. And from this perspective, we are able to answer the question of why this, not that: why the topical-analytical approach to Halakhic category formation?

2. *The Generative Logic of the Halakhic Mode of Category Formation*
The answer to this question of systemic rationality (why this, not that?) comes in response to this question: how, then, faced with the choices the Rabbinic sages contemplated for themselves, were they to

proceed? Once we recognize their purpose—and the Halakhah, seen whole, embodies the realization of that purpose, which, consequently, we may define with some certainty—the question answers itself. If we wish to know the law that a case exemplifies, the rule that governs diverse cases, we have no choice but to ask the analytical questions of taxonomic logic: what species encompass the exempla, the cases; and what genus, the species? Natural history defined the sole solution to the sages' assignment: a logical, not a mythic, re-presentation of the Halakhah.

This meant extending the revealed law according to its own principles of logic and laws of articulation. The species embody the law for like things; the genus sets down the rule to hold together, to control, the variables between and among the species thereof. Then the taxic indicators, the variables that we require, present themselves as signals of an inner order, a logic realized in the traits of things and their taxic power. For this labor of turning Scripture's commandments, in their narrative setting, into a design for Israel's social order, such as the sages accomplished in the Halakhah as we know it, only one theory of category formation could have served.

This was the analogical-contrastive analysis that yielded the hermeneutics of selection and interpretation of data and thus produced the indicated category formations. The Mishnah recast the givens of Scripture into its category formations, working from the whole to the parts, because the framers of the category formations that are realized in the Mishnah found, in the logic of natural history, the medium for accomplishing God's purpose in setting forth the Pentateuchal laws.

That logic—identify the data that constitute a topic; form of the data a species like but unlike another (hypothetical) species so as to form a common genus, sustaining a process of analogy and contrast to set forth an analytical program of problems and their solution—produced what God's purpose required. This is the self-evident order, the rationality, that turned the bits and pieces, the discrete parts, into a transcendent whole.

3. *The Self-Evidence of Analytical-Topical Category Formations Yielded by Hierarchical Classification: A Null Hypothesis*
When (in secular language) from two received bits of information the sages could generate a fresh point, when two cases produced a rule

encompassing many more cases, in that syllogistic exercise the Rabbinic sages accomplished their purpose.

And the only way to accomplish that wonder of intellect lay along the topical-analytical path through the lush fields of Pentateuchal cases, laws, and commandments.

What follows?

Once we know why this, we realize there is no *that.*

If this theory of the purpose and context of category formation in the Halakhah serves, then what should we anticipate in the successor documents, the Mishnah having accomplished its goals from the outside to the inside, the whole to the parts? Here I offer my null hypothesis: from what we should (and do) find, we extrapolate what we should not (and do not) encounter as well. My hypothetical reconstruction of the modes of thought is therefore to be tested against the actualities of canonical-systemic Halakhic data. What should we not find is category formations other than those defined by the Mishnah or, more to the point, category formations that do not take shape around the constituent principles—cogent topics subjected to analysis of a determinate problematics. Two hypotheses require testing.

1. First, we should expect that a theory of category formation so powerfully responsive to the tasks and purposes of the sages would govern the formation of new categories. For at issue is not a problem of detail, one merely of organizing facts into convenient rubrics, but a task critical to the very construction of the system. We should not find any other theory of category formation that solves the problem facing sages, only variations on the one that they have chosen. For, once the governing logic takes over, it should force from view all alternatives: anything else is illogical.

2. Second, we should anticipate a very limited expansion of the range of category formations, and for the same reason. The category formations that impose structure and order on the Halakhah—approximately threescore in all—and that are before us represent not random but highly predetermined selections. Why predetermined? I state with heavy emphasis the hypothesis and the null hypothesis: *a category formation could take shape only for data susceptible to analogical-contrastive analysis, for formation into a species with a hypothetical counterpart within a common genus.*

How shall we know whether this theory of matters works?

(1) We should find no material expansion of the Halakhic category formations of the topical-analytical sort.

(2) We should accommodate the new topical category formations within the existing structure.

(3) Where we do find a topical-analytical category formation beyond the initial system's account of matters, we should find it possible to explain it—why this, not that?

It further follows that a singleton species, lacking a counterpart to make possible a process of Halakhic comparison and contrast, according to this theory should prove rare and essentially exceptional. To put it differently, the Halakhah can accommodate an unlimited number of new topics as circumstances require and can create required laws or recast existing laws to form coherent statements; but such new topics would represent ad hoc add-ons, not systematic category formations comparable to those in hand.

If the category formations that we do have actually took shape within the present hypothesis, then the work on the parts should flow from the framing of the whole, and there should be no reason within the Halakhah for a large number of further category formations deriving from analogical-contrastive analysis of the givens of Scripture and tradition. What sets the outer limits on the expansion of the Halakhah's repertoire of category formations is Scripture (with tradition) itself.

To state my thesis simply: the work, once commenced along the lines proposed here, also came to fruition and closure at the very outset. The category formations commence as a whole and themselves speciate, first by (in literary terms) divisions, then by tractates. In light of the task undertaken by the sages and the logic selected by them to accomplish this task, one could set aside received category formations, as the Tosefta, Yerushalmi, and Bavli did. But with the data of Scripture (and tradition), one would not find possible the definition of new topical-analytical category formations. The generative logic ought to prevent it.

The first of the two expectations (we should expect that a theory of category formation so powerfully responsive to the tasks and purposes of the sages would govern the formation of new categories) is confirmed in the summary that follows in section C, below. That is, the method of category formation embodied in the Mishnah's repertoire of category formations necessary and sufficient to the task that the sages carried out would dominate thereafter. Its domination is signaled in two ways.

First, it could exclude all category formations shaped by other than the topical-analytical method.

Second, it could itself osmose—break apart into its two components, topical and analytical.

Within the large structures defined by the topical-analytical method of category formation, the Halakhah could and did accommodate topical-not-analytical composites. That is because these, after all, hardly violated the generative logic but only refined it.

But no fundamentally *new* approach to category formation could have found its way into the Halakhic system, so far as the Mishnah-Tosefta-Yerushalmi-Bavli portrayed this system, because, to accomplish its goals, the system could approach data in only one way. And that was to recapitulate, whether reading Scripture or tradition or contemporary custom, to collect data in accord with its topical classification and order those data in a manner that would yield general rules from cases, and laws of broad application from problems. To explain the syllogistic process that is hypothetically reconstructed here: Scripture gave the sages the information that two apples and two apples equal four apples. The sages conceived that two and two equal four. A theoretically unlimited corpus of cases produced the simple rule, which theoretically could be extended to an unlimited corpus of unimagined cases.

That is why, the work having come to closure when the system made its initial and authoritative statement through the Mishnah, the governing logic could mutate and osmose within its narrow, initial limits. In this context, speaking of plausible theories of category formation, we may say, in answer to the question of why this and not that, the reason for the "this" is that *there is no "that."*

The second expectation is that we should anticipate a very limited expansion of the range of category formations, and for the same reason. What about the *topical* expansion of the Halakhah? Within the theory just now set forth, we should find severe limitations on the topical repertoire of the Halakhah, not an infinity of possibilities, such as logic, unlimited by the topical program of Scripture and tradition, might have suggested. If the task of the Halakhah is what I claim it to have been—to transform the narratives, cases, and exhortations of Scripture into a systematic statement of Israel's social order—then the possibilities of topical category formations find their definition solely in the initial provision of Scripture and tradition. We should find among new topics mainly category formations adumbrated by Scripture (or tradition) itself, and in an ideal world, we also should find a very limited number of these.

We shall now find that these anticipated results match the reality of Mishnah-Tosefta-Yerushalmi-Bavli. The number of new topical-not-analytical category formations is, in proportion to the whole, negligible; all of them fit within the existing program of category formations. And only a single topical-analytical category formation will present itself: an authentic candidate for inclusion within the structure of the Halakhah on equal terms with the initial repertoire of such formations, based on the interplay of topicality and analytical potentiality. And within the theory set forth in these pages, this single candidate proves critical to this structure, finding a place at its very heart and center.

C. Testing the Null Hypothesis: The Expansion of the Halakhah—the Identification of New Topical or Analytical Category Formations

As explained, we have now to take up the topical expansion of the Halakhah in the Mishnah-Tosefta-Yerushalmi and Mishnah-Tosefta-Bavli, viewed whole.

1. The Mishnah's Anomalous Tractates

In the case of the Mishnah, excluding tractate *Abot*, we have four anomalous tractates, not formed around the hermeneutics of analysis (comparison and contrast) of determinate topics: *Eduyyot*, *Tamid*, *Middot*, and *Qinnim*. In them I find no expansion of the topical program of the Halakhah. *Tamid* and *Middot* remain well within the topical program of the conventional category formations; and in the main, *Eduyyot* goes over compositions that occur in the topical-analytical tractates. Nor do abstract analytical propositions figure. *Qinnim* is a handbook of special problems of Halakhic analysis, utterly without parallel in the Mishnah. It is best compared to an exercise: given these premises, how do we analyze and solve the following cases/problems? Euclid would have found himself intellectually at home among the Temple priests, for whose education such a wonderful workbook was fabricated.

2. *The Mishnah's Anomalous Composites*

I. New Topics
In addition, we find in the Mishnah sizable composites that are of materials of an other-than-topical-analytical character. Though not entire tractates, they should register. Here I do not list composites that contribute to an established category formation, for example, to *Yoma, Sukkah,* and the like. These do not represent the expansion of the topical program of the Halakhah. I list only a topical narrative lacking all analytical program:

> √ the narrative on collecting the shekel offering

But this is familiar from the counterparts in *Yoma, Sukkah,* and the like. The established pattern—use of narrative for Temple topics—governs. The narrative on collecting the shekel offering does not embody a new category formation but shows a different way of setting forth an existing one.

II. New Propositions or Analytical Principles
What about propositions that are not encompassed in the topical-analytical framework, for example, propositions set forth not topically but embodied and instantiated in a variety of unrelated topics? Here analysis sustains itself outside the framework of a particular topic and its exposition—not common in the Mishnah but also not unknown:

> √ Established custom prevails
> √ A fixed difference forms the variable between the species of a common genus
> √ Where considerations of the common good, for example, the good order of the world, intervene, the law is guided by those considerations
> √ No classification yields one-sided results, but circumstances or contexts govern consequences
> √ The paradox: $B/A \neq C/B$, but $C/B = B/A$

The new analytical principles encompass both legal truisms—established custom prevails, and the common good prevails, other things being equal—and important principles of natural history and its logic. The latter could have formed chapters in a handbook on constructing category formations. But they did not attract imitation beyond the Tosefta's continuation of the Mishnah's initiatives, as we shall now see. The logical anomaly of the final entry has already been noted.

3. The Tosefta's Anomalous Composites

We proceed to the Tosefta's composites—the Tosefta covers most, though not all, of the Mishnah's tractates but has none of its own—and ask about new topics or propositions yielded by the companion continuation document, the Mishnah's first "talmud."

I. New Topics

Does the Tosefta expound topics not represented by the Mishnah's topical-analytical program? These are new topics:

√ order of the meal, washing hands
√ reciting a blessing when performing a commandment
√ twenty-four priestly gifts belonging to Aaron and to his descendants according to a general statement (Num. 18:8) and a specific enumeration (Num. 18:9–18) and the covenant of salt (Num. 18:19)
√ what matters constitute "the ways of the Amorites"
√ intercalating the year
√ the commandments of the children of Noah

All the new topics but two fit into the received program of the Mishnah: Temple topics stand without an analytical dynamics. The two fundamentally new category formations, fully articulated and impressive in sheer volume, are the companions—the children of Noah and "the ways of the Amorites." These open a new path, one that the Mishnah's category formations hardly contemplated, concerning the gentiles. But of the two, the remarkable composite "the ways of the Amorites" produced no secondary expansion, no indication of recognition, in the Talmuds, of a major construction. So it did not function as a Mishnah-Tosefta tractate for the Yerushalmi or Bavli. The other category formation, the children of Noah, embodied in the Halakhah of the commandments of the children of Noah, will come to the fore presently and prove to lead us right to the core of the topical question. We will return to the children of Noah when we reach the Bavli.

II. New Propositions or Analytical Principles

Does the Tosefta set forth propositions or analytical principles outside the framework of topical-analytical category formations? These qualify:

√ There is a stringency that applies to . . . that does not apply to . . .
√ That which is valid in wringing the neck is invalid in slaughtering. That which is valid in slaughtering is invalid in wringing the neck—a fixed variable differentiates the two species of a common genus and suffices for that purpose

The Tosefta does signal an interest in carrying forward the exposition of analytical category formations, contributing its own candidates for the handbook that, on the strength of the Mishnah's evidence, could have taken shape. As noted earlier, what we have here is a reworking of the received category formations into larger composites still, a task that a commentary such as the Tosefta would find natural to its assignment.

4. *The Yerushalmi's Anomalous Composites*

Do we find anomalous composites in the Yerushalmi? I find a negligible representation. But that should not obscure a clear documentary decision: the Yerushalmi systematically comments on only thirty-nine of the Mishnah's sixty-three tractates. This represents a systemic decision of considerable daring.

I. New Topics

New topics are these:

√ tefillin
√ the grave in the nethermost depths

The Yerushalmi's framers, in their recapitulation of the Halakhah, dropped *many* more category formations than they added. But given the continuous character of the Halakhic presentation—Mishnah-Tosefta-Yerushalmi—we cannot interpret that decision as a judgment on the system, only a decision on the task to be undertaken by a particular set of continuators of the system.

II. New Propositions or Analytical Principles

I find only one new analytical principle:

√ the contrived distinction in the Halakhah

It is difficult to see how a rule of law can serve as an analytical category formation; all we have here are cases that illustrate the same principle. The Yerushalmi once more emerges as essentially a commentary to selected tractates of the Mishnah and selected passages of the Tosefta; when it comes to the problem of category formation, its framers appear not to have engaged.

5. *The Bavli's Anomalous Composites*

Now we come to a sizable corpus of new topics, articulated in a manner different from the Mishnah's austere, disciplined presentation. These should be set into the perspective of the Bavli's selection, for systematic exegetical work, of only thirty-seven of the Mishnah's sixty-three topical-analytical composites.

I. New Topics

I find in the Bavli a considerable corpus of well-articulated topical expositions, and they are hardly random or episodic:

√ rules on the recitation of the Shema'
√ the rules and regulations of a meal
√ further rules on saying grace
√ the Hanukkah lamp; the festival of Hanukkah
√ Hanukkah in the liturgy
√ the unlettered person and the disciple of the sage
√ the mezuzah
√ improperly postponing the fulfillment of vows beyond the passage of the year in which they are taken
√ the laws that govern the mourner
√ marrying off orphans, support of the poor
√ freeing slaves
√ rules on correct management of the land of Israel
√ the rules of philanthropy: Who contributes? Who receives?
√ the religious obligations of the children of Noah: idolaters and slaves
√ the religious duty of sanctifying hands and feet by washing
√ the Halakhah of writing the Torah scroll
√ on the lamp-stand and candlestick
√ tefillin: rules and regulations in general
√ sisith (show-fringes)

The Mishnah's Halakhic category formations—its six principal divisions—accommodate all of the individual category formations I can identify in the Bavli. I see no break-out toward a primary Halakhic division beyond the established ones.

II. New Propositions or Analytical Principles
I find only two candidates:

√ When do cases form a series?
√ A wrongful intention that is not obviously wrong is treated by the All-Merciful as an intention that can invalidate an offering, but one that is obviously wrong is treated by the All-Merciful as incapable of invalidating the offering

The former of the two analytical exercises focuses on a particular topic, and it generates no new or secondary problems for solution. The latter is theoretical in form but particular in application, pertaining, as it does, to the Temple offerings.

D. *The Rules of Choosing Topics*

These results produce a striking perspective on the stability of the Rabbinic system of category formations and of the principles that define this system. To explain: a culture in theory may identify an unlimited range of category formations, but in practice it chooses to build with a finite number of building blocks. That is, a system organizes data in some few ways, within a determinate body of category formations. But these then are refined in a vast range of variations. This fact may be expressed in terms of food. A given culture selects from a long menu of possible sources of nourishment the few items it wishes to utilize, but then prepares those items in a singularly broad selection or set of pots and pans. A few types of grain are deemed legitimate to yield bread, but bread from the selected types of grain comes in many variations. And this carries us back to our null hypothesis: we should not find a vast expansion of new topics, and those we do find should conform to the principles of formation of comparison and contrast that are in play throughout.

Once we realize that the entire corpus of new topics fits into the large divisions of the received ones, we recognize the primary position of the Mishnah's formulation of the Halakhic category formations. Its method governs. What we see is that an item treated casually in the Mishnah may attract attention later on; rules for a familiar topic take shape and come together. But I cannot point to a single case of a new topic that falls entirely outside the topical repertoire of the Mishnah.

In addition—the null hypothesis now collapses—as to the identification of a category formation that selects data and interprets them in the way in which the Mishnah's category formations do, the topics added beyond the Mishnah's program present exactly one instance.

The Mishnah defined all *the topical-analytical category formations conventionally spun out from the whole to the parts.*

The one important corpus of anomalous data—new topical/not-analytical category formations—that requires attention comes to us in the Bavli. Let us take up that, in context, formidable catalogue and ask this: where do we move beyond the limits of the Mishnah's topical program? (In my catalogue I specify in parentheses the tractate that encompasses the topic.) We eliminate forthwith the following items, which simply develop topics treated in the Mishnah's category formations in the context defined thereby. These all are matters to which the Mishnah makes casual reference but to which the continuator documents, particularly the Bavli, supply a sizable body of laws:

> rules on the recitation of the Shema' (*Berakhot*)
> rules and regulations of a meal (*Berakhot*)
> rules on saying grace (*Berakhot*)
> improperly postponing the fulfillment of vows beyond the passage of the year in which they are taken (*Nedarim/Rosh Hashanah*)
> the laws that govern the mourner (*Moed Qatan*)
> marrying off orphans (*Ketubot*)
> support of the poor (*Peah*)
> freeing slaves (*Gittin*)
> rules on correct management of the Land of Israel (*Baba Qamma*)
> the rules of philanthropy: Who contributes? Who receives (*Peah*)
> the religious duty of sanctifying hands and feet by washing (*Yadayim*)
> the unlettered person and the disciple of the sage (*Horayot*)

What the Bavli adds is commonly a topical appendix, spelling out a variety of rules on existing topics. Rarely do these expositions respond to a generative problematic. Most of the new topics then find a place within an established category formation, and what the continuator documents, particularly the Bavli, do is enrich the corpus of data, not recast its main lines of structure and order. The hermeneutics of comparison and contrast does not subject these items to analogical-contrastive analysis.

This reduces the list of genuinely new items to a handful. In all, I find these freestanding and essentially inert topics, each of them autonomous and lacking counterparts:

> the Torah scroll
> the lamp-stand and candlestick
> tefillin; sisith; mezuzah
> Hanukkah

The first three are holy objects, each accorded a full Halakhic account. Hanukkah is the one holy day that the Mishnah's program of category formations omits but that requires attention in its own terms. That is because it is unlike the pilgrim festivals, the days of awe, the Sabbath, and so on; like Purim, it produces (or is comparable to) no occasion for Temple offerings, but on other bases it is readily differentiated from Purim. So it is sui generis. And this provides a key to the other new topics of the Bavli.

Anyone can concur that the holy objects (and the specified holiday) demand legal definition and regularization. But a second glance tells us that they all are sui generis, not species of a common genus. Each is unique in categorical context. Let me spell this out. What other species forms a common genus with the Torah scroll or tefillin or sisith or the mezuzah? None of the specified items affords the opportunity hypothetically to designate a counterpart species for the formation of a common genus and a process of analogical-contrastive analysis. The Torah scroll stands for them all, and having said that, I need say nothing more. The Torah scroll is unique; the rules for writing and protecting it have no analogue. And the same observation covers the rest. Tefillin, sisith, and the mezuzah bear no counterparts that sages would acknowledge, for example, among the "ways of the Amorites"!

The rules of choosing topics therefore are two: the new topic will be an established fact in Israel's holy life (1) that is not accommodated by the Mishnah's category formations and (2) that is sui generis and not accessible to analogical-contrastive analysis.

So we can answer the two critical questions that together frame the rule for selecting new topics. That is, we explain both the "why not that," meaning the omission of these items from the Mishnah's categorical foci, and the "why this," meaning their identification and inclusion later on:

(1) None of them could have generated a category formation by the criteria that govern in the Mishnah: a topic bearing a counterpart species of a common genus, therefore, susceptible of hermeneutical development through analogical-contrastive analysis. And none of them, as a matter of fact, does sustain analogical-contrastive analysis; each is unique in categorical context.

But (2) all of them form components of the system, indeed of the holy objects of the system, data that are treated tangentially by the Mishnah's category formations (for the reasons just now spelled out). But they are then endowed with a rich factual amplification by the continuator document, the Bavli. That explains why each of the topical composites is made up of inert information, presented in random order. No topical composite is focused on the solution of a theoretical problem. None is animated by an issue that transcends the facts and imparts consequence to them. The very character of the Bavli's representation of the new topics conforms to the rule: not coherent and logically well-ordered but merely miscellaneous laws, stories, precedents, exegeses about a required topic. Now to the one exception to these rules: the children of Noah.

1. *The Children of Noah: Explaining the Categorical Anomaly*
And this rule to account for new topics brings us back to the Bavli's critical exception, noted but ignored until now. It is the single item among the new topics that violates the rule of choosing new topics just now set forth. The anomaly, "the children of Noah," lays out, in particular, the religious obligations of the children of Noah, idolaters, and slaves, a category formation fully articulated in the Bavli but, neglected in the Mishnah, initially presented in the Tosefta's presentation of *Abodah Zarah* as well.

This category formation does invite sustained analogical-contrastive analysis. For what species of a genus more tightly fits the hermeneutics of the Halakhah, is better served thereby, than humanity, divided into Israel and the gentiles (therefore the children of Noah as against the children of Israel)? To be sure, the category formation/tractate *Abodah Zarah* deals with gentiles, who are defined, as a matter of fact, simply as idolaters pure and simple. But the generative problematic

of that tractate concerns the relationship between Israelites and gentiles on gentiles' occasions of active idolatry. The Halakhah uses the
occasion of idolatry to contemplate a condition entirely beyond the
imagination of Scripture: the hegemony of idolatrous nations and
the subjugation of holy Israel. The Halakhah of *Abodah Zarah*, fully
considered, makes of the discussion of idolatry the occasion for the
discussion of Israel's place among the nations of the world and of
Israel's relationships with gentiles.

The Mishnah's framing of the category formation of idolatry and
the gentiles has not a word to say about the gentiles' relationship with
God. But this forms the center of the discussion of the obligations of
the children of Noah in the Tosefta and Bavli. That category forma-
tion/tractate does not take up the problematics of the genus, human-
kind, divided into the species, Israel and the children of Noah (there
are no other gentiles any more besides Noah's children), nor does any
other. So we must ask why.

That brings us back to the hypothesis and the null hypothesis. Our
rule is that the new, post-Mishnaic, category formations will be principally topical. The Mishnah will have defined all of the conventional,
topical-analytical category formations. The rule confronts its exception: why not that? Specifically, why does the Mishnah devote no
work to the comparison and contrast of Israel and the nations in relationship to God, not only in relationship to one another?

As soon as we ask the question, the answer presents itself. The
Mishnah—and the Halakhah generated by the Mishnah—takes as its
task the concretization, the contextualization, of the Pentateuch's
design of God's Kingdom to be realized by Israel. It therefore concerns itself with Israel's inner life, and its category formations are
dictated, in the end, by the tasks of rendering a systematic and comprehensive account as the design of the social order of the Pentateuch's cases, discrete laws, narratives, and exhortations. But what
place, then, for gentiles' relationship with God anyhow? They have
none; they rejected the Torah and do not recognize God's sovereignty. That is what marks them as gentiles. For, so far as the
Pentateuch is concerned, gentiles play no part, have no place, in
Israel's social order.

In addition, the Halakhic category formations beginning with the
Mishnah rarely attend to gentiles in other contexts; Israel is conceived
as a people dwelling wholly alone. The Mishnah does not contem-

plate Israelites outside the Land realizing the kingdom of priests and the holy people such as the Pentateuch contemplates. That, by definition, will take place only in the Land. So, within that same view, Israel will not dwell among the nations but only in the Land of Israel, the Land uniquely Israel's. Hence the Pentateuch's account, recapitulated in the systematic way in which the Mishnah's category formation recasts matters, will not require a category formation of gentiles but only a category formation to deal with Israel and the nations on special occasions—gentile celebrations, to be exact. How to explain the appearance of something whose absence we can account for: if why *not* that, then *why* that?

As soon as the Mishnah's Halakhic system extended its reach to the Israel in Babylonia—and therefore anywhere beyond the limits of the Land, including also Syria, that interstitial territory—Israel's circumstance exposed the need to frame a category formation of the Mishnah's type, a topic shaped by a powerful problematic deriving from an analogical-contrastive reading of the species of a common genus. And this is the category formation that, quite appropriately, the Bavli fully articulated but that the Tosefta—serving *Abodah Zarah*, quite appropriately—adumbrated.

Here—to make matters explicit—is our answer to the question of why this and not that, both in particular and in general:

(1) Why this? In general, the topics of Scripture that invite speciation and analogical-contrastive analysis will yield category formations through the hermeneutics now fully exposed. And the topics of the Pentateuch that do not will find their place, within the Halakhah, within the framework of those that do generate category formations.

(2) Why not that? To take the case at hand, why *Abodah Zarah* but not a category formation on the children of Noah? Why "Israel and the gentiles—idolaters" but not "Israel and the children of Noah"? Because category formations take shape through a process of comparison and contrast, which *Abodah Zarah* sustains; "the children of Noah," however, viewed as comparable to Israel, does not sustain the analytical process. This massive omission, best understood by reference to the task of Pentateuchal systematization that the Halakhic system took for itself to begin with, would be addressed by the continuator documents—the Tosefta in brief, the Bavli at length.

Scripture takes for granted that Israel will live all by itself in the Land of Israel, and its final solution to the gentile problem is to eliminate the idolaters from the Land of Israel. The Mishnah's category formation recapitulates that datum in *Abodah Zarah*, which recognizes the presence of gentiles in the Land but does not legitimate it. Only in the post-Mishnaic (or extra-Mishnaic, it hardly matters) articulation of the category formation children of Noah does the Halakhah accord recognition to the presence, within the framework of its systemic building blocks, of gentiles. And then the contents of the Halakhic topic are predetermined. In play is the criterion that the same Halakhah that governs Israel defines the variables: Israel is subject to many hundreds of commandments, the gentiles to seven. The Aggadic counterpart to the Halakhah would then supplant the Pentateuchal-Mishnaic solution: at the end of days the gentiles (all idolaters) will revert to death, but Israel (those who live in God's Kingdom and accept his rule) will ascend to eternal life. But for that time, the Halakhah in its category formations does not legislate, as the Rabbinic canon repeatedly underscores.

E. *Why This, Not That? The Premises and Goals of the Halakhah in Its Category Formations*

The outcome of this protracted analysis may be succinctly stated. The question of why this and not that encompasses both the method of category formation and the message conveyed therein through the repertoire of topics. At issue are ways of category formation not taken and Halakhic categorical possibilities not realized in the normative statement of the Halakhah: the Mishnah's fifty-nine topical-analytical category formations as mediated by the Tosefta, Yerushalmi, and Bavli. The regularities characteristic of the data of anomalous method and of new topical composites explain why this and not that—specifically, why this method of Halakhic category formation and not other methods that could have been chosen, why these particular category formations and no others in the Mishnah-Tosefta-Yerushalmi-Bavli.

From scattered evidence of alternative methods of category formation, I extrapolate the rejected alternatives: theories of category formation that could have served but were not utilized in the Halakhic construction that defines the norm. When it comes to the new topical or analytical or topical-analytical category formations, we are able to account for two facts.

First, all but one of the new category formations are either topical or analytical but not both; then the question of why this and not that, concerning topics, centers on why only a single topical-analytical category formation beyond the initial repertoire.

Second, I can account for all of the new topical category formations by a familiar labor of classification: comparison and contrast to the established category formations of the initial structure.

From the expansion of the program of the category formations beyond the Mishnah's particulars, therefore, I set forth the rules of choosing topics. From a theoretically unlimited number, the Halakhah that is set forth in the Mishnah chose threescore, and the successor documents added remarkably few to this number. To state matters simply: of topics available for a religious theory of the social order to address, there is in theory no necessary limit. But the Halakhic category formations actually number, at the end, not a great many more than at the outset.

Why this, not that? Because Scripture and tradition and the logical requirements for the articulation of the cases of Scripture and tradition as laws—the logic of comparison and contrast for the purpose of hierarchical classification—dictated the category formations that would take shape. They eliminated those that would not. Given what the sages set out to accomplish, an assignment that, by its composite character, the Pentateuch inevitably would impose upon its heirs, the sages accomplished precisely what the logic and consequent hermeneutics of category formation of the Halakhah required.

Then—the question cannot be avoided—what about the Mishnah category formations that do not begin in Scripture? They are *berakhot*, *taanit*, *demai*, *tohorot*, *uqsin*, *ketubot*, and *qiddushin*. No passage of the Pentateuch enters into the formation of the Halakhah of those tractates, whether in principle or in detail. Still, all but two of them fit well into the mode of thought that the Halakhah entailed. These are to be classified as follows:

CATEGORY FORMATIONS THAT CONCERN SUPEREROGATORY ACTS OF PIETY OUTSIDE THE CULT: *berakhot, taanit*

CATEGORY FORMATIONS THAT DEAL WITH INTERSTITIAL PROBLEMS, FOR EXAMPLE, MIXTURES, DOUBTS: *demai, tohorot, uqsin*

CATEGORY FORMATIONS THAT, ALONG THOSE SAME LINES, DEAL WITH THE SPECIAL PROBLEM OF THE WOMAN VIEWED AS AN INTERSTITIAL DATUM: the transfer of a woman from one established status to another: *ketubot, qiddushin,* to which we could well add *gittin,* that is, the woman in the interstitial circumstance, neither in the father's nor in the husband's house

We have already dealt with *Tamid* in context. So apart from *Berakhot* and *Taanit,* which build on the givens of the Shema', the Prayer, the Grace after Meals, and other rites performed in the village and the home in divine service in correspondence with that of the Temple, the other-than-scriptural category formations all deal with problems of interstitiality, which attract the attention of the framers of the Mishnah in their paramount enterprise of hierarchical classification. All other category formations begin in Scripture, some simply recapitulating, others vastly reworking, Scripture's own data.

To conclude: I promised at the outset to account for the character of the Halakhah's category formations and its generative hermeneutics for the selection and interpretation of data in the received structure of category formations. By appeal to the fundamental task undertaken by the sages of the Halakhah, I have done so. I planned also to explain the advent of new topics for systematization in category formations. By invoking the established category formations of the initial statement, I have done so. If the Pentateuch, encompassing the oral traditions identified with Sinai by the sages, contains topics that remain outside the structure and the system of the Halakhah, I cannot say what they might be, and many centuries of highly perspicacious exegesis of the Pentateuch support the judgment that there is none. Once the sages undertook, in line with Scripture's plain message, to explore the requirements of the restoration of Adam and Eve to Eden within the social formation of Israel in the Land of Israel, the method and the media were predetermined. The Halakhah, through its category formations, systematically transformed particular topics into occasions for reflection upon principles. That is to say, the Halakhah brings about transformation of the here, the now, and the occasion (place and time and event, mostly in nature) into the embodiment, the exemplification, of the abstract ground of being that is captured in the regularities of nature and Israel's social order.

Here we see how the category formations, properly understood, yield a statement of religion: a theory of the social order resting on the divine imperative. Through the provision of norms of conduct and conviction such as Scripture itself sets forth or logically invites, the Halakhah lays out an account of how the entire social order may be constructed to realize Eden once more, this time under God's rule. This restoration comes about not in the end of days, when the Messiah comes, but in the here and now of the workaday world. It is there that the Israelite, formed by the discipline of the Torah, learns both to atone for and to overcome his natural propensity willfully to rebel against God. Within the social order of an enlandised Israel, moral man constructs a godly society. This reading of the written Torah and translation of its law into the canons of ordinary life speaks in category formations of the Halakhah, as initially realized by the Mishnah-Tosefta-Yerushalmi-Bavli, that is, by the Mishnah. It is the Judaism that this set of category formations would construct and sustain. So much for the interior perspective afforded by a comprehensive theory of the Halakhic category formations, building blocks of the religious system of the social order we call Rabbinic Judaism. But what of the other native category essential to that same Judaism, the Aggadic corpus? To this we now turn.

III. An Interior Perspective: 2. The Halakhic and Aggadic Category Formations in Comparison and Contrast

The other native category of the canon of formative Judaism, Aggadah—narrative, exhortation, exegesis of Scripture to yield moral rules—finds its place in compilations of scriptural exegesis, Midrashim, and also in fully realized compositions and composites located in the two Talmuds. As indicated, Aggadah takes up a subject matter different from that of the Halakhah. It concerns itself with norms of belief and attitude, in contrast to the Halakhah's norms of behavior and action. Aggadic discourse commonly comments on a received text, tells a story, or advocates a proposition of normative conviction and conscience, whereas Halakhic discourse expounds and analyzes a topic of normative conduct.

No more fundamental question concerning formative Rabbinic Judaism awaits answers than this one: How do the two kinds of discourse hold together in a single cogent system? Where, systemically viewed, are the points of complementarity and correspondence? Critical to the religious study of Rabbinic Judaism is the issue of how norms of action realize norms of attitude or, in literary terms, how the Halakhic and the Aggadic compositions, composites, and category formations constitute a coherent construction. The question of religion demands that we explain how, at the interior points of meeting, the principal native categories of the religion before us cohere.

That question cannot be answered with any systematic demonstration at the present time. How the Halakhic category formations cohere with the Aggadic ones is difficult to discern because the Halakhic category formations are articulately defined by the Halakhic documents, Mishnah-Tosefta-Yerushalmi and Mishnah-Tosefta-Bavli, whereas corresponding constructions of Aggadic data—large-scale expositions of topics in response to a distinctive analytical program—do not present themselves at all. The Aggadic constructions are topical, expounding a proposition about a given subject. Or they demonstrate a proposition through exegesis of Scripture. But the Aggadic topical and propositional expositions do not follow documentary lines, as the Halakhic ones do. They are generally ad hoc and not comparable to the sustained, systematic topical expositions, start to finish, such as the Halakhic category formations supply.

Above all, if we seek to build on the basis of the category formations of the Aggadah laid out in documentary units in the manner of the topical-analytical Halakhic documents with their topical-analytical program, we cannot succeed. The Aggadic documents and non-documentary compositions and composites rarely tell us what it is about a topic that they wish to explore. At most, they are propositional, but they are seldom analytical in the manner of the Halakhic presentations. I cannot say what I think the problematics of a topical proposition and exposition might be.

A single example suffices. What it is about "Israel" that an Aggadic composition or composite wishes to explore, its analytical program, rarely comes to the surface. By contrast, what the Halakhic authorities wish to know about, for example, *sanhedrin-makkot* or *ohalot* or *shebiit* is always readily to be discerned. The proposed problematics is easily tested and shown to inhere and energize the exposition. All efforts at expounding the problematics of Aggadic presentations of topics are stymied by the failure of the documents to devote their major expository exercises to coherent topics, let alone propositions concerning them. All expositions of topics within a hypothetical problematic in the manner of the Halakhic category formations prove post facto and deductive, including my *Theology of the Oral Torah: Revealing the Justice of God*, which is a demonstration of a proposition concerning the logical coherence of the Aggadic compositions within a single large and generative problem—how God's justice is to be revealed through the Torah—that is formed otherwise than through a systematic sifting of small bits of evidence in quest of patterns. So, while each organizes its presentation in large building blocks, the Halakhic ones do not match the Aggadic ones in morphology or structure, nor do the Aggadic composites invoke Halakhic composites, let alone category formations, within their own.

That is why I identify the issue of how the Halakhah and the Aggadah compare and correspond as one of the great unsolved problems of systemic analysis of Rabbinic Judaism. How they work together is difficult to document in formal terms. I know of no way to do the work properly—how systematically and comprehensively and inductively to describe in proper detail that collaborative venture. What I find troubling is a simple fact. Occasionally the Halakhic presentation will invoke Aggadic facts, less commonly vice versa. But the respective types of systemic building blocks, the composites of Aggadic topical expositions and the Halakhic topical-analytical category formations, do not commonly intersect. The topics of the latter scarcely correspond with those of the former. Since, however, within the Halakhic structure of category formations Aggadic compositions and composites occasionally figure, we may ask about the cogency of the Halakhah and the Aggadah at the points at which, by their own testimony, they intersect. For the intersection indicates markers of inner unity between the Halakhah and the Aggadah. It signals the point at which Rabbinic Judaism, as a unitary construct, emerges out of its diverse, distinctive sectors and their building blocks. That is our starting point.

At issue is not the very occasional reference to a Halakhic fact in an Aggadic exposition, or the somewhat more commonplace resort to an Aggadic datum in a Halakhic one, for example, for purposes of illustration or exhortation to keep the law. What is at stake is the context of thought and expression established by systematic constructions of topical or even propositional composites, compilations of many discrete facts in the service of a coherent argument. The Aggadic documents rarely introduce Halakhic materials in their exposition of Aggadic propositions. And the contrary is also the case. The exposition of the Halakhic components of the Halakhic documents—nearly the entirety of the Mishnah, most of the Tosefta, much of the

Yerushalmi, and the greater part (I estimate 60 percent) of the
Bavli—only rarely requires Aggadic complements or supplements.
Yet whereas the Aggadic documents rarely resort to Halakhic materials to make the case they wish to set forth, in some of the Rabbinic
documents of the formative age the presentation of the Halakhah is
accompanied by a massive Aggadic component. We occasionally find
the intersection of large aggregates of well-composed Aggadic data in
a Halakhic composite or of Halakhic ones in an Aggadic setting—not
discrete texts but articulated contexts of thought. Where and why do
these intersect when they do?

A. *The Uses of the Aggadah by the Halakhah*

In Rabbinic literature, rarely indeed does a fully articulated Halakhic
category formation encompass and utilize, to make its point, a fully
articulated Aggadic composite. Granted, an Aggadic composition
may find a place in proximity to a Halakhic exposition. But the
Halakhah, within its own categorical bounds, will not then exploit the
Aggadic discourse for its purpose—for example, allude to the Aggadic
fact to make the Halakhic point. That is so, even though the rare
exceptions to this rule show that the Halakhic discourse could have
done so. Conversely, when the Aggadic category formation defines
the primary discourse, for example, in a Midrash compilation, the
Halakhah, in its cogent category formations, still less commonly
occurs in Aggadic composites. That is the case, moreover, even
though, when it does, the Halakhic composition serves to render the
Aggadic exhortation more compelling and concrete. But the actual
occasions prove remarkably few in number and negligible in proportion. Aggadic discourse rarely asks the Halakhah to contribute norms
of practical conduct to its expositions of its propositions of an other-
than-concrete character, for example, the moral rules and their consequences. So, how do the two media of Rabbinic discourse, Halakhic
and Aggadic, with their two distinct bodies of data, form a complete
and cogent whole: the statement of Rabbinic Judaism as a coherent
structure and system?

A simple fact makes possible the beginnings of an answer to the
question of the unity of the Aggadah and the Halakhah. In some of
the Halakhic documents of Rabbinic literature, Aggadic compositions
and composites take a position side by side with Halakhic ones. And

when a Halakhic exposition within the Halakhic category formation is juxtaposed to Aggadic compositions that articulate the categorical constructions of the Aggadah viewed whole, we sometimes see a remarkable fact. It is that the Aggadah makes the Halakhic discourse more profound and encompassing. Then who has seen the implicit correspondence of the Halakhic and the Aggadic category formations and so effected the juxtaposition, if not the union, of the two? Clearly, the framer of the document, not the author of the composition or composite, whether Halakhic or Aggadic, conceived that the Aggadah intersects with and vastly enriches the Halakhic discourse.

These established facts carry us to the problem at hand. Since in the Halakhic documents—Mishnah, Tosefta, Yerushalmi, Bavli—we find Aggadic compositions and composites, we want to know how the Aggadic contribution affects the Halakhic discourse: what holds them together? These Aggadic components of Halakhic documents stand on their own. But since, at some points, though the Aggadic discourses are freestanding, they contribute to the Halakhic exposition within the category formations defined by the Halakhah, an interesting question arises. It is one that is systematic and not merely episodic in character: *in Halakhic discourse viewed in its entirety, what does the Aggadah provide that the Halakhah cannot say in its own terms but that nevertheless the compositor of the document deemed essential to the presentation of the Halakhic statement?*

The answer to this question carries us deep into the profound unities of Halakhic and Aggadic discourse, which define Rabbinic Judaism at its core. Finding the answer requires exploring the generative conception behind the juxtapositions, reconstructing its principles by working back from the data to the premises and presuppositions. The question of religion is this: case by case, what connections did the compiler of the Halakhic documents perceive between the Halakhic and the Aggadic category formations that he has juxtaposed, often with great effect?

For the Halakhah is normative in deed, definitive in practice. The Aggadah, people generally maintain, allows for greater latitude in conviction than the Halakhah does in conduct. So, when we find that a compositor has encompassed in his Halakhic repertoire an Aggadic corpus, we identify elements of the Aggadah that participate in the normative statement of the Halakhah. Accordingly, given the issue at hand, when we assess the role of the Aggadah in the Halakhah, it is the Halakhah that defines the basis for coherent discourse, the

governing category formation. Therein Aggadic compositions occasionally find a place. So it is for the Halakhah to explain why the
selected Aggadic composite belongs. But then, with that explanation,
the Halakhah also encompasses the Aggadic selection within its
penumbra of what is authoritative and obligatory—thus, once more,
the religion Rabbinic Judaism.

B. *An Illustrative Case: Aggadah in the Halakhah of* Taanit,
*the Law of Fasting in Times of Crisis and of the Village Cohort
That Participates in the Temple Cult*

Let me illustrate the potential for asking the question of religion in
the present manner. I present a single model of inquiry, the case of
Mishnah-Tosefta-Yerushalmi-Bavli tractate *Taanit*, taking up the four
documents one by one in succession and systematically answering the
same questions out of the resources of each.

1. *Aggadic Compositions in Mishnah-Tosefta* Taanit
Here are the Aggadic compositions that are utilized by the compositors
of the Mishnah and the Tosefta in the presentation of the Halakhic
rule. Indentations signal the intrusion of material not primary to the
documentary program—in this case, the Halakhic exposition. Further
indentation indicates a gloss of a gloss, and so on throughout.

Mishnah *Taanit* 3:8

A. On account of every sort of public trouble (may it not happen) do
they sound the shofar,
B. except for an excess of rain.
C. M'SH S: They said to Honi, the circle drawer, "Pray for rain."
D. He said to them, "Go and take in the clay ovens used for
Passover, so that they not soften [in the rain which is coming]."
E. He prayed, but it did not rain.
F. What did he do?
G. He drew a circle and stood in the middle of it and said before
Him, "Lord of the world! Your children have turned to me, for
before you I am like a member of the family. I swear by your
great name—I'm simply not moving from here until you take
pity on your children!"
H. It began to rain drop by drop.
I. He said, "This is not what I wanted, but rain for filling up cis-
terns, pits, and caverns."
J. It began to rain violently.

K. He said, "This is not what I wanted, but rain of good will, bless-ing, and graciousness."

L. Now it rained the right way, until Israelites had to flee from Jerusalem up to the Temple Mount because of the rain.

M. Now they came and said to him, "Just as you prayed for it to rain, now pray for it to go away."

N. He said to them, "Go, see whether the stone of the strayers is disappeared."

O. Simeon b. Shatah said to him, "If you were not Honi, I should decree a ban of excommunication against you. But what am I going to do to you? For you importune before the Omnipresent, so he does what you want; like a son who importunes his father, so he does what he wants.

R. "Concerning you Scripture says, 'Let your father and your mother be glad, and let her that bore you rejoice' [Prov. 23:25]."

I now proceed to ask a systematic set of questions, which are repeated in subsequent analyses as well.

(1) What is the context, in Halakhic discourse, of the Aggadic com-position or composite?

The Aggadic narrative illustrates the rule, A–B, that the alarm is sounded for every crisis except an excess of rain. But the narrative does not qualify as a legal precedent; the incident is treated as excep-tional in every way. On the basis of the Aggadic narrative, we could not have reconstructed the Halakhic ruling. But with this ruling in hand, we are informed by the Aggadah how exceptional a case would have to be to trigger the exception to the rule just now given.

(2) What links do we discern between the Aggadic composition and the Halakhic composite in which it has been situated?

The link between the Aggadic composition and the Halakhic com-posite is intimate. The Aggadah, as noted, contradicts the rule, giv-ing a case in which the alarm is sounded for an excess of rain.

(3) Does the Aggadah play a role in the documentary presentation of the Halakhah, and if so, what task does it perform?

So far as the Halakhah requires an expression of the remission of the law, the Aggadah provides that expression. On the basis of this instance, we may say, the Halakhah states the rule; the Aggadah, the exception.

(4) Can we explain why the compositor of the Halakhic document (or its main components) found it necessary to shift from Halakhic to Aggadic discourse to accomplish his purposes?

The function of the Aggadah is to illustrate, in extreme terms, the working of the Halakhah: where the Halakhah is remitted. It is not possible to frame a case for the union of the Halakhah and the Aggadah more fitting than this one.

Now to Tosefta. Italics here signify a citation of the Mishnah, which is indicated.

T. Taaniyyot 2:12–13

2:12   A.   A <i>town which gentiles besieged, or a river</i> [M. <i>Ta.</i> 3:7B]—

       B.   and so too, a ship foundering at sea,

       C.   and so too, an individual pursued by gentiles or by thugs or by an evil spirit—

       D.   they are not permitted to afflict themselves in a fast, so as not to break their strength [but only to sound the shofar].

       E.   And so did R. Yosé say, "An individual is not permitted to afflict himself in a fast,

       F.   "lest he fall onto the public charity, and [the community] have to support him."

2:13   A.   M'SH B: To a certain pious man did they say, "Pray, so it will rain."

       B.   He prayed and it rained.

       C.   They said to him, "Just as you have prayed so it would rain, now pray so the rain will go away."

       D.   He said to them, "Go and see if a man is standing on Keren Ofel [a high rock] and splashing his foot in the Qidron Brook. [Then] we shall pray that the rain will stop [cf. <i>M. Ta.</i> 3:8].

       E.   "Truly it is certain that the Omnipresent will never again bring a flood to the world,

       F.   "for it is said, 'There will never again be a flood' [Gen. 9:11].

       G.   "And it says, 'For this is like the days of Noah to me: as I swore that the waters of Noah should no more go over the earth, so I have sworn that I will not be angry with you and will not rebuke you' [Is. 54:9]."

       H.   R. Meir says, "A flood of water will never be, but a flood of fire and brimstone there will be, just as he brought upon the Sodomites.

       I.   "For it is said, 'Then the Lord rained on Sodom and Gomorrah brimstone and fire from the Lord out of heaven' [Gen. 19:24]."

       J.   R. Judah says, "A flood affecting all flesh there will never be, but a flood affecting individuals there will yet be.

       K.   "How so?

       L.   "[If] one falls into the sea, and he drowns, or if one's ship sinks at sea, and he drowns, lo, this is his [particular] flood."

M. R. Yosé says, "A flood affecting everything there will not be, but a flood of pestilence there will be for the nations of the world in the days of the Messiah,

N. "as it is said, 'And I took my staff, and I broke it, annulling the covenant which I had made with all the peoples' [Zech. 11:11].

O. "What does it say? 'So it was annulled on that day' [Zech. 11:12]."

(1) What is the context, in Halakhic discourse, of the Aggadic composition or composite?

Here is a case in which the Tosefta has its version of the Mishnah's story, but the Halakhic setting is lost. We may, then, say that the Tosefta's formulation of the tale is prior to the Mishnah's version and the Mishnah's version improves by supplying details, or that the Mishnah's version has been removed from the Halakhic setting that affords context and meaning and has been treated in a generalized way by its heirs in the Tosefta, or that we have two independent formulations of the same theme. But we need not waste time on petty historical questions that in the end cannot be definitively settled.

(2) What links do we discern between the Aggadic composition and the Halakhic composite in which it has been situated?

In Tosefta's version, there is no connection between the Halakhic statement at T. 2:12 and the Aggadah of T. 2:13; that is explicit.

(3) Does the Aggadah play a role in the documentary presentation of the Halakhah, and if so, what task does it perform?

No.

(4) Can we explain why the compositor of the Halakhic document (or its main components) found it necessary to shift from Halakhic to Aggadic discourse to accomplish his purposes?

The documentary program of the Tosefta is different from that of the Mishnah. The Halakhic focus of the Mishnah has secured a Halakhic reference point for the story as set forth by the Mishnah. The Tosefta's compositor had no such interest—at least not at this point.

Mishnah *Taanit* 4:5

[A] The time of the wood offering of priests and people [comes on] nine [occasions in the year]:

[B] on the first of Nisan [is the offering of] the family of Arah b. Judah [Ezra 2:5, Neh. 2:10];

[C] on the twentieth of Tammuz [is the offering of] the family of David b. Judah;

[D] on the fifth of Ab [is the offering of] the family of Parosh b. Judah [Ezra 2:3, Neh. 2:8];

[E] on the seventh of that month [is the offering of] the family of Yonadab b. Rekhab [Jer. 35:1ff.];

[F] on the tenth of that month [is the offering of] the family of Senaah b. Benjamin [Ezra 2:35, Neh. 7:38];

[G] on the fifteenth of that month [is the offering of] the family of Zattu b. Judah [Ezra 2:8, Neh. 7:13];

[H] and with them [comes the offering of] priests, Levites, and whoever is uncertain as to his tribe, and the families of the pestle smugglers and fig pressers.

[I] On the twentieth of that same month [is the offering of] the family of Pahat Moab b. Judah [Ezra 2:6, Neh. 7:11].

[J] On the twentieth of Elul [is the offering of] the family of Adin b. Judah [Ezra 2:15, Neh. 7:20].

[K] On the first of Tebet the family of Parosh returned a second time [with another wood offering].

[L] On the first of Tebet [Hanukkah] there was no delegation,

[M] for there was Hallel on that day, as well as an additional offering and a wood offering.

T. Taaniyyot 3:5–9

3:5 A. Why did they set aside [special times for] the wood-offering of priests and people [*M. Ta.* 4:5A]?

B. For when the exiles came up, they found no wood in the wood-chamber.

C. These in particular went and contributed wood of their own, handing it over to the community.

D. On that account prophets stipulated with them that even if the wood-chamber should be loaded with wood, even with wood belonging to the community, these should have the privilege of contributing wood at this time, and at any occasion on which they wanted,

E. as it is said, "We have likewise cast lots, the priests, the Levites, and the people, for the wood-offering, to bring it into the house of our God, according to our fathers' houses, at times appointed, year by year, to burn upon the altar of the Lord our God, as it is written in the law" [Neh. 10:34].

F. And it says, "For Ezra had set his heart to study the law of the Lord and to do it, and to teach his statutes and ordinances in Israel" [Ezra 7:10].

3:6 A. Those days [of the wood-offering, *M. Ta.* 4:5] it is prohibited to conduct the rite of mourning or to have a fast,

B. whether this is after the destruction of the Temple or before the destruction of the Temple.

C. R. Yosé says, "After the destruction of the Temple it is permitted [to lament or to fast], because it is an expression of mourning for them."

D. Said R. Eleazar b. R. Sadoq, "I was among the descendants of Sana'ah [*M. Ta.* 4:5F, Ezra 2:35] of the tribe of Benjamin. One time the ninth of Ab coincided with the day after the Sabbath, and we observed the fast but did not complete it."

3:7 A. What was the matter having to do with the families of the pestle smugglers and the fig pressers [*M. Ta.* 4:5H]?

B. Now when the Greek kings set up border-guards on the roads, so that people should not go up to Jerusalem, just as Jeroboam the son of Nebat did, then, whoever was a suitable person and sin-fearing of that generation—what did he do?

C. He would take up his first-fruits and make a kind of basket and cover them with dried figs,

D. and take the basket with the first-fruits and cover them with a kind of dried figs,

E. and he would put them in a basket and take the basket and a pestle on his shoulder and go up.

F. Now when he would come to that guard, [the guard] would say to him, "Where are you going?"

G. He said to him, "To make these two rings of dried figs into cakes of pressed figs in that press over there, with this pestle which is on my shoulder."

H. Once he got by that guard, he would prepare a wreath for them and bring them up to Jerusalem.

3:8 A. What is the matter having to do with the family of Salmai the Netophathites (cf. I Chr. 2:54: "The sons of Salma: Bethlehem, the Netophathites")?

B. Now when the Greek kings set up guards on the roads so that the people should not go up to Jerusalem, just as Jeroboam the son of Nebat did,

C. then whoever was a suitable and sin-fearing person of that generation would take two pieces of wood and make them into a kind of ladder and put it on his shoulder and go up.

D. When he came to that guard, [the guard] said to him, "Where are you going?"

E. "To fetch two pigeons from that dovecote over there, with this ladder on my shoulder."

F. Once he got by that guard, he would dismantle [the pieces of wood of the ladder] and bring them up to Jerusalem.

G. Now because they were prepared to give up their lives for the Torah and for the commandments, therefore they found for themselves a good name and a good memorial forever.

H. And concerning them Scripture says, "The memory of a righteous person is for a blessing" [Prov. 10:17].

I. But concerning Jeroboam son of Nebat and his allies, Scripture says, "But the name of the wicked will rot" [Prov. 10:17].

3:9 A. R. Yosé says, "They assign a meritorious matter to a day that merits it, and a disadvantageous matter to a day of disadvantage."

B. When the Temple was destroyed the first time, it was the day after the Sabbath and the year after the Sabbatical year.

C. And it was the watch of Jehoiarib, and it was the ninth of Ab.

D. And so in the case of the destruction of the Second Temple.

E. And the Levites were standing on their platform and singing, "And he has brought upon them their own iniquity, and he will cut them off in their own evil" [Ps. 94:23].

F. Now tomorrow, when the Temple-house will be rebuilt, what will they sing?

G. "Blessed be the Lord, the God of Israel, from everlasting to everlasting" [I Chr. 16:36].

H. "[Blessed be the Lord, the God of Israel] who alone does wondrous things. Blessed be his glorious name [forever; may his glory fill the whole earth! Amen and Amen]" [Ps. 72:18–19].

(1) What is the context, in Halakhic discourse, of the Aggadic composition or composite?

The Halakhah, *M. Ta.* 4:5A, refers to particular times for wood offerings presented to the Temple by priests and people, as catalogued. The Tosefta's Aggadic amplification then provides a narrative account of the origin of those details of the cult. We have found counterpart instances in which Aggadic tales explain the origins of cultic regulations, broadly construed. To this point, we have not found, in Aggadic compositions, etiologies, in the form of narrative, of the origin of other than Temple rites and procedures. The explanation is not only generic but particular and detailed, as T. 3:7–8 show. T. 3:9 is tacked on.

(2) What links do we discern between the Aggadic composition and the Halakhic composite in which it has been situated?

The link concerns not the detail of the Halakhah to be explained but the occasion for the making of the Halakhah in general terms. The bias of the Aggadah favors a narrative explanation for cultic rites, as noted.

(3) Does the Aggadah play a role in the documentary presentation of the Halakhah, and if so, what task does it perform?

The Mishnah's presentation of the Halakhah does not require the Aggadic picture of historical, one-time origins but derives support from it.

(4) Can we explain why the compositor of the Halakhic document (or its main components) found it necessary to shift from Halakhic to Aggadic discourse to accomplish his purposes?

The framer of the Tosefta fills out the picture given by the Mishnah in the manner set forth above.

2. *Aggadic Compositions in Yerushalmi* Taanit

What about the Yerushalmi's use of Aggadic compositions within its Halakhic composites? Italics here signify the use of Aramaic, rather than Mishnaic Hebrew.

Yerushalmi *Taanit* 3:9 III.1–2

[III:1 A] And he prayed, but it did not rain [M. 3:9E]:

[B] [Why did the rain not come properly?] Said R. Yosé b. R. Bun, "Because he did not come before God with humility."

[III:2 A] Said R. Yudan Giria, "This is Honi the circle drawer [of M. 3:9], the grandson of Honi the circle drawer. *Near the time of the destruction of the Temple, he went out to a mountain to his workers. Before he got there, it rained. He went into a cave. Once he sat down there, he became tired and fell asleep.*

[B] "*He remained sound asleep for seventy years, until the Temple was destroyed and it was rebuilt a second time.*

[C] "*At the end of the seventy years he awoke from his sleep. He went out of the cave, and he saw a world completely changed. An area that had been planted with vineyards now produced olives, and an area planted in olives now produced grain.*

[D] "*He asked the people of the district, 'What do you hear in the world?'*

[E] "*They said to him, 'And don't you know what the news is?'*

[F] "*He said to them, 'No.'*

[G] "*They said to him, 'Who are you?'*

[H] *"He said to them, 'Honi, the circle drawer.'*

[I] *"They said to him, 'We heard that when he would go into the Temple courtyard, it would be illuminated.'*

[J] *"He went in and illuminated the place and recited concerning himself the following verse of Scripture: 'When the Lord restored the fortune of Zion, we were like those who dream'"* [Ps. 126:1].

(1) What is the context, in Halakhic discourse, of the Aggadic composition or composite?

The point of Halakhic intersection is attenuated; it is at III:1, which is then expanded at III:2.

(2) What links do we discern between the Aggadic composition and the Halakhic composite in which it has been situated?

None.

(3) Does the Aggadah play a role in the documentary presentation of the Halakhah, and if so, what task does it perform?

No.

(4) Can we explain why the compositor of the Halakhic document (or its main components) found it necessary to shift from Halakhic to Aggadic discourse to accomplish his purposes?

The Yerushalmi's final compositor has provided a topical appendix on the figure of Honi. The story does not bear on the Halakhah in any direct way. I have omitted from the repertoire a large mass of Honi stories and counterparts set forth by the Bavli; these connect to the Halakhah only via the name of Honi (!).

3. *Aggadic Compositions in Bavli* Taanit

B. to *M. Taanit* 2:12 XII.1, 3 17b–18a

[XII.1] [A] As to any [day concerning which] in the Fasting Scroll [*Megillat Taanit*] it is written [in Aramaic:] "not to mourn"—on the day before, it is prohibited to mourn. On the day after, it is permitted to mourn:

[XII.3] [A] The master has said: *From the eighth of Nisan until the close of the Festival of Passover, during which time the date for the Festival of Pentecost was reestablished, fasting is forbidden:*

[B] *Why say, "until the close of the Festival of Passover"? Why not say simply, "until the Festival," and since the Festival itself is a festival period, mourning is forbidden at that time anyhow?*

[C] Said R. Pappa, "It is in line with what Rab said, [18a] 'That formulation was required only to extend the prohibition to the preceding day.'" Here too that formulation was required only to extend the prohibition to the preceding day.

[D] *In accord with the view of what authority does that position conform?*

[E] *It conforms to the position of R. Yosé, who has said,* "It is forbidden to mourn both on the day prior and on the day following the specified occasions."

   [F] *If that is the rule, it should be forbidden to mourn also on the twenty-ninth day of Adar also—why do you determine to focus on the consideration that it is the day before the Daily Offering was established, when you can derive the rule governing that day from the fact that it is the day after the twenty-eighth of Adar?*

   [G] *For it has been taught on Tannaite authority:*

   [H] *On the twenty-eighth of that [month, that is, Adar], good news came to the Jews, that they need not separate themselves from [practice of] the law.* "For the government had decreed that they may not involve themselves with [study and practice of] Torah, that they may not circumcise their sons, and that they must profane the Sabbath." What did Judah b. Shammua and his associates do? They went and took council with a certain matron with whom all of the notables of Rome were familiar. She said to them, "Tonight, come and cry [to the Roman government] for help!" That night, they came and cried out: "In the eyes of [God in] heaven, are we not your brothers? And are we not all the children of a single father? And are we not all the children of a single mother? How are we different from every other people and language that you enact harsh decrees upon us?" Now, as a result [the government] annulled those [decrees], and [as for] that same day—they designated it a feast.

[I] Said Abbayye, "That formulation was required only to deal with the case of a month that is full [that has thirty days, not twenty-nine]. [In that case the thirtieth of Adar would be the last day of the month and could only be included in the restriction on the ground that it precedes the first of Nisan and not that it follows the twenty-ninth of Adar, since a day, the twenty-eighth, intervenes]."

[J] R. Ashi said, "You may even maintain that it pertains to a month that is lacking [and is only twenty-nine days]. On a day following a festival day, fasting alone is forbidden, but mourning is permitted, but as for the twenty-ninth of Adar, situated between two festival days, it is treated as though it were a festival day itself, with mourning forbidden on that day too."

(1) What is the context, in Halakhic discourse, of the Aggadic composition or composite?

The Aggadah H is essential to the argument of F, which makes reference to the clause of the mourning scroll that pertains. Then the Aggadic narrative explains the background of the celebratory occasion. We note the very favorable representation of Roman government—accessible, as it is alleged to have been, to rational argument on humanitarian grounds!

(2) What links do we discern between the Aggadic composition and the Halakhic composite in which it has been situated?

The Aggadic narrative forms evidence in the Halakhic argument and makes a contribution to the corpus of facts on which the argument is built.

(3) Does the Aggadah play a role in the documentary presentation of the Halakhah, and if so, what task does it perform?

The Aggadah is integral to the Halakhic presentation.

(4) Can we explain why the compositor of the Halakhic document (or its main components) found it necessary to shift from Halakhic to Aggadic discourse to accomplish his purposes?

Only by appeal to the Aggadah at hand (or a comparable story) could the case have been made for the position that is maintained by a party to the discussion.

M. Taanit 3:1–2

3:1

[A] The conduct of these fast days which have been described applies in the case of the first rainfall.

[B] But in the case of crops that exhibit a change [from their normal character]

[C] they sound the shofar on their account forthwith.

[D] And so [if] the rain ceased between one rainstorm and the next for a period of forty days,

[E] they sound the shofar on that account forthwith,

[F] for it represents the blow of famine.

3:2

[A] If the rain fell sufficient for crops but not for trees,
[B] for trees but not for crops,
[C] for this and that, but not for [filling up] cisterns, pits, or caverns,
[D] they sound the shofar on their account forthwith.

B. to *M. Taanit* 3:1–2 III.1–6 19b–20a

[III.1] [A] If the rain fell sufficient for crops but not for trees, for trees but not for crops, for this and that, but not for [filling up] cisterns, pits, or caverns, they sound the shofar on their account forthwith:

[B] *Now it is so that rain sufficient for crops but not for trees does happen, when it rains gently and not heavily; so too, rain that is good for trees but not for crops happens, when it rains heavily and not gently; and there can be rain that is good for both crops and trees but not fill up cisterns, ditches, and caves, if it falls heavily and gently but not yet sufficiently. But how is it possible for sufficient rain to fall to fill cisterns, ditches, and caves, yet not to be good for crops and trees, in accord with the Tannaite formulation?*

[C] *It would be a case of torrential rain.*

[III.2] [A] *Our rabbis have taught on Tannaite authority:*

[B] They sound an alarm for rain for trees if it has not rained by half a month prior to Passover [that is, the new moon of Nisan], and for cisterns, ditches, and caves even half a month prior to Tabernacles; and whenever there is not sufficient water for drinking, it is done at once.

[C] What is the definition of "at once"?

[D] On the following Monday, Thursday, and Monday.

[E] They sound the alarm only in their own province [*T. Ta.* 2:8C–F].

[F] In the case of croup, they sound the alarm only if deaths result. If no deaths result, they do not sound the alarm.

[G] They sound the alarm in case of locusts, however small the sample.

[H] R. Simeon b. Eleazar says, "Even on account of grasshoppers [do they sound the alarm]" [*T. Ta.* 2:9D–E, 2:10A–B].

[III.3] [A] *Our rabbis have taught on Tannaite authority:*

[B] They sound the alarm on account of the condition of the trees [needing rain] through the other years of the Sabbatical cycle [but not in the Seventh Year], and for cisterns, ditches, and caves, even in the Sabbatical Year.

[C] Rabban Simeon b. Gamaliel says, "Also on account of trees in the Sabbatical Year [do they sound the alarm], because they provide support for the poor [who then are permitted freely to take the fruit]."

[D] *It has further been taught on Tannaite authority:*

[E] They sound the alarm on account of the condition of the trees [needing rain] through the other years of the Sabbatical cycle [but not in the Seventh Year], and for cisterns, ditches, and caves, even in the Sabbatical Year.

[F] Rabban Simeon b. Gamaliel says, "Also on account of trees in the Sabbatical Year [do they sound the alarm]."

[G] For the scrub in the field they sound the alarm even in the Seventh Year because it provides support for the poor."

[III.4] [A] *It has been taught on Tannaite authority:*

[B] From the day on which the house of the sanctuary was destroyed, rains have turned irregular for the world: there is a year in which the rain is abundant, and there is a year in which the rain is scanty; there is a year in which the rain falls at the anticipated time, and there is a year in which the rain does not fall at the anticipated time.

[C] To what is a year in which the rain falls at the anticipated time to be compared? To the case of a worker who is given his week's food in advance on Sundays: the dough is well baked and edible.

[D] To what is a year in which the rain does not fall at the anticipated time to be compared? To the case of a worker who is given his week's food at the end of the week on Fridays: the dough is not well baked and is inedible.

[E] To what is a year in which the rain is abundant to be compared? To the case of a worker who is given his week's food all at once. The waste in grinding a qab [thirty seahs] is no more than the water in grinding a qab [a sixth of a seah], and the waste in kneading a kor is no more than the waste in kneading a qab.

[F] To what is a year in which the rain is scanty to be compared? To the case of a worker who is given his food bit by bit. The waste in grinding a qab is no less than the waste in grinding a kor; so too with kneading a qab, it is no less than kneading a kor.

[G] Another matter: to what is a year in which the rain is abundant to be compared?

[H] To the case of a man kneading clay. If he has plenty of water, then the clay is well kneaded, but not all of the water is used up; if he has only a little water, then the water will be used up, but the clay still won't be well kneaded.

[III.5] [A] *Our rabbis have taught on Tannaite authority:*

[B] One time all Israel ascended to Jerusalem for the festival, and they didn't have enough water to drink. Naqedimon b. Gurion went to a certain lord. He said to him, "Lend me twelve wells of water for the pilgrims, and I shall pay you back with twelve wells of water, and if I don't do it, then

I'll give you instead twelve talents of silver," with a fixed time for repayment.

[C] When the time came for repayment and it did not rain, in the morning he sent him a message, "Send me the water or the money that you owe me."

[D] He sent word, "I still have time, for the rest of the entire day belongs to me."

[E] At noon he sent him word, "Send me the water or the money that you owe me."

[F] He sent word, "I still have time, for the rest of the entire day belongs to me."

[G] At dusk he sent him word, "Send me the water or the money that you owe me."

[H] He sent word, "I still have time today."

[I] That lord ridiculed him. He said to him, "The whole year it hasn't rained, [20a] and now is it going to rain?"

[J] He cheerfully went off to the bath house.

[K] While the lord was cheerfully going to the bath house, Naqedimon sadly went to the house of the sanctuary. He wrapped himself in his cloak and stood up in prayer, saying before him, "Lord of the world, it is obvious to you that it was not for my own honor that I acted, not for the honor of my father's house did I act, but I acted for your honor, to provide ample water for the pilgrims."

[L] At that moment the skies darkened with clouds and it rained until water filled twelve wells and more.

[M] As the lord was going out of the bath house, Naqedimon b. Gurion was leaving the house of the sanctuary. When the two met, he said to him, "Pay me the cost of the extra water that you owe me."

[N] He said to him, "I know full well that the Holy One, blessed be he, has disrupted his world only on your account. But I still have a legitimate gripe against you to collect the money that is owing to me! The sun has already set, so the rain has fallen in the time that belongs to me [after the end of the specified time limit]."

[O] He once more went into the house of the sanctuary, wrapped himself in his cloak, and stood up in prayer, saying before him, "Lord of the world, let people know that you have loved ones in your world."

[P] At that instant the clouds scattered and the sun shone at that moment.

[Q] The lord said to him, "Had the sun not broken through, I still would have had a legitimate gripe against you to collect the money that is owing to me."

[R] A Tannaite statement:

[S] His name wasn't Naqedimon, it really was Boni, and why was he called Naqedimon? For the sun broke through [*niqedera*] on his account.

[III.6] [A] *Our rabbis have taught on Tannaite authority:*

[B] In behalf of three persons the sun broke through: Moses, Joshua, and Naqedimon b. Gurion.

[C] *As to Naqedimon b. Gurion, we have a tradition.*

[D] *As to Joshua, there is a verse of Scripture:* "And the sun stood still and the moon stayed" [Josh. 10:13].

[E] But how do we know that that is so of Moses?

[F] Said R. Eleazar, "*It derives from the use of the words,* "I will begin," *in the two instances. Here we find,* 'I will begin to put the dread of you' [Deut. 2:25], and in connection with Joshua, 'I will begin to magnify you' [Josh. 3:7]."

[G] R. Samuel bar Nahmani said, "*It derives from the use of the word 'put' in both cases. Here we find,* 'I will begin to put the dread of you' [Deut. 2:25], and in connection with Joshua, 'In the day when the Lord put the Amorites' [Josh. 10:12]."

[H] Said R. Yohanan, "*From the verse itself the lesson is to be derived:* 'The peoples that are under the whole heaven who shall hear the report of you and shall tremble and be in anguish because of you' [Deut. 2:25]: And when did they tremble and feel anguish on account of Moses? This is when the sun stood still for him."

(1) What is the context, in Halakhic discourse, of the Aggadic composition or composite?

The theme of the Mishnah rule, M. 3:2, and the Bavli's compositions in amplification of that rule, III.1–2, is sounding the alarm for a dearth of rain, which accounts for the formation of the composite, III.1–5. In this composite, what is the role of the Aggadah? The story translates the general allusions to a situation of drought into a particular case and how Israelite ingenuity, resting on divine grace, solved the problem. The miracles compound as the story unfolds. Then, III.6 adds, the exceptional situation is comparable to occasions involving Moses and Joshua. The whole, III.5–6, is formed around Naqedimon's name and inserted because of the general thematic interest in drought. But while the Halakhah deals with routine response to the crisis, the Aggadah explicitly deals with the one-time and extraordinary.

(2) What links do we discern between the Aggadic composition and the Halakhic composite in which it has been situated?

The links are attenuated and merely thematic, but placing the Aggadic narrative into this context bears a theological implication of considerable weight.

(3) Does the Aggadah play a role in the documentary presentation of the Halakhah, and if so, what task does it perform?

The Aggadah articulates what is implicit in the Halakhah, which is, in the end, that Israel has to make itself worthy of Heaven's provision of miracles.

(4) Can we explain why the compositor of the Halakhic document (or its main components) found it necessary to shift from Halakhic to Aggadic discourse to accomplish his purposes?

The Halakhah prescribes certain activities to that end, but the decision remains in the hands of God and is not to be coerced. That is the message involving both Naqedimon and Honi. Joining the Aggadic stories to the Halakhic rules allows the compositor to make a statement that the Halakhah, on its own, cannot make; and to correct an impression that the Halakhah willy-nilly might leave.

B. to *M. Taanit* 3:11 XVI.1–4 25b–26a

[XVI.1] [A] If they were fasting and it rained for them before sunrise, they should not complete the fast. [If it rained] after sunrise, they should complete the day in fasting:

[B] *Our rabbis have taught on Tannaite authority:*

[C] "If they were fasting and it rained for them before sunrise, they should not complete the fast. [If it rained] after sunrise, they should complete the day in fasting," the words of R. Meir.

[D] R. Judah says, "It if rained before noontime, they need not complete the fast. If it rained after noontime, they should complete the day in fasting."

[E] R. Yosé says, "If it rained before the ninth hour, they need not complete the fast, if after the ninth hour, they must complete it. For lo, we find in the case of Ahab, king of Israel, that he did fast from the ninth hour onwards:

'See you how Ahab humbles himself before me' (1 Kgs. 21:29)."

[XVI.2] [A] R. Judah the Patriarch decreed a fast and it rained after dawn. He considered that people should complete the fast. Said to him R. Ammi, "We have learned: 'before noontime . . . after noontime.'"

[XVI.3] [A] Samuel the Younger decreed a fast and it rained before dawn. The people thought that it was a gesture of praise for the community. He said to them, "I shall tell you a parable: To what is the matter to be compared? To a slave who asked his master for a favor, and the master said to them, 'Give it to him, so I don't have to hear his voice.'"

[XVI.4] [A] Again Samuel the Younger decreed a fast, and it rained after sunset. The people thought that it was a gesture of praise for the community. He said to them, "This is not a gesture of praise to the community. But I shall tell you a parable: To what is the matter to be compared? To a slave who asked his master for a favor, and the master said, 'Let him wait until he is submissive and upset and then give him his favor.'"

[B] And then, from the viewpoint of Samuel the Younger, *what would represent a case that* involved a gesture of praise to the community at all?

[C] He said, "A case in which they recited the prayer, 'he causes the wind to blow,' and the wind blew; 'he causes rain to fall,' and rain fell."

(1) What is the context, in Halakhic discourse, of the Aggadic composition or composite?

The Halakhah, XVI.1, provides for the occasion of Heaven's immediate response to prayers for rain: do the people have to complete the fast day that has early on accomplished its purpose? I should distinguish between the precedent, XVI.2, and the Aggadic narratives, XVI.3–4. The former involves the law as articulated; the latter move beyond the Halakhah and raise exactly the point paramount elsewhere in the Halakhic exposition: does Israel coerce Heaven by these rites? The answer is this: not only does Israel not have the power to coerce Heaven, but even though Israel's prayers for rain are answered, this is not a mark that Israel enjoys special favor in Heaven. So here, as is often the case, the Aggadah moves beyond the this-worldly limits of the Halakhah.

(2) What links do we discern between the Aggadic composition and the Halakhic composite in which it has been situated?

The Aggadah directly addresses the facts of the Halakhah but changes the focus of analysis.

(3) Does the Aggadah play a role in the documentary presentation of the Halakhah, and if so, what task does it perform?

The power of the Aggadah to disclose a deeper layer of theological thinking provoked by the Halakhah could not be more dramatically articulated.

(4) Can we explain why the compositor of the Halakhic document (or its main components) found it necessary to shift from Halakhic to Aggadic discourse to accomplish his purposes?

The Halakhah permitted him to raise the deeper question that, in his view, the Aggadah resolves. Only together, in their counterpoint relationship, do the Aggadah and the Halakhah make the entire statement that the compositor had in mind for the topic at hand.

4. *The Aggadic Role in the Halakhic Discourse of* Taanit

At each point in the unfolding of Mishnah-Tosefta-Yerushalmi-Bavli *Taanit*, the Aggadah and the Halakhah work together, each carrying out its particular task, to present a cogent and proportionate picture for the topic before us. The topic, fasting in times of crisis in order to win Heaven's favor, bears within itself the obvious dilemma: does God respond automatically when Israel fasts, or does God exercise mercy as an act of grace, in which case, why fast? The Halakhah, then, sets the stage, defines the activity, and so raises the question, and the Aggadah responds time and again to that deeper question implicit in the very provisions of the Halakhah for human activity in response to evidences of divine displeasure. In this context, the Mishnah's story about Honi underscores the uncertainty of importuning Heaven. That is something Honi could accomplish, but not many others. The secondary expansion of the Honi materials in the Tosefta and Yerushalmi need not detain us. A still more explicit statement emerges in the compositors' union of *M. Ta.* 3:1–2, with their secondary exposition at B. to *M. Ta.* 3:1–2 III.2–4, at III.5–6: such events of divine intervention are exceedingly rare. And then, at the end, comes the explicit response to the challenge of the Halakhah in the Aggadic narratives of B. to *M. Ta.* 3:11 XVI.1–4.

A more familiar role of the Aggadah is to account for the origin of Halakhic rules for the Temple cult and its extensions in the village and household; so B. to *M. Ta.* 2:12 XII.1, 3. How do the Halakhah and the Aggadah relate in shared discourse? The four documents— through the Aggadah that intersects with the Halakhah in the native category formation *taanit*—do make a single, coherent statement, one in which the Halakhah sets the norm and the Aggadah the exception. Here the Halakhah deals with the ordinary, the Aggadah with the extraordinary. A single religious system of the world order comes to expression, for the particular Halakhic system at hand, only when the Aggadah and the Halakhah are each permitted to make their distinctive contribution. Separately they produce cacophony, together coherence and cogency—Judaism, whole and complete.

This example limits the inquiry to points at which the Halakhah requires Aggadic compositions to register its message. The Halakhah then controls the discourse; the Aggadah is carefully chosen for the Halakhic purpose. Why not conduct the exercise in a less restrictive manner? Because the generative, fundamental category formations of the Halakhah and those of the Aggadah are incompatible, as I shall now show, and this creates the unsolved problem I set forth as a question of religion in the study of formative Judaism and its canon.

C. *Aggadic and Halakhic Incompatibility in Category Formations*

Mere proximity of an Aggadic to a Halakhic composition, by itself, does not settle the matter. The occurrence of a freestanding sentence here or there hardly suggests that to the Aggadah in that context is assigned a vital role in the Halakhic discourse. Only when we can establish a large-scale intrusion of the one into the other does the question before us arise. That is to say, we have to establish that an Aggadic construction, itself fully cogent, has entered into the Halakhic context. But that is not always self-evident.

Why the uncertainty about whether the presence of an Aggadic composite in a Halakhic context makes a difference? It is because the category formations of the Aggadah and those of the Halakhah are incompatible. Viewed from afar, both the Halakhah and the Aggadah select data and construct of them coherent statements within category formations that impart cogency and context for the discrete pieces of information. But that is from a distance. From close up, the very model of category formations of the one bears little in common with those of the other. The Halakhic topics and the Aggadic ones do not intersect or even correspond in formal expression, let alone in principles of coherence. The fundamental theory of category formation governing for Halakhic data does not explain the construction of the category formations that serve for the Aggadic data, and the opposite is also the case. If the Halakhic category formations define the model of discourse that imparts sense and coherence to data, then the Aggadah yields no larger constructions that qualify as category formations at all—and vice versa. It is therefore noteworthy when, as we just saw, the category formation of the one accommodates the presence of a cogent composition of the other.

As we have now seen in detail, the Halakhic documents define the Halakhic category formations, topical, analytical, and cogent. The category formations match literary divisions, tractates, with the classification of data by topic and problematic. Not so the Aggadah. The documents of the Aggadah are not topically organized, and the compositions and composites of the Aggadah set forth in the Talmuds rarely attain the dimensions of a Halakhic tractate, for example, in the Mishnah. The upshot is simple. While the Halakhah announces its category formations for us, the Aggadah requires us to define them on our own, as best we can. But they do not emerge out of the Aggadic documents, and so far they are topical, the topics derive from an a priori expectation of how Aggadic discourse should take shape. That is to say, given the character of Aggadic discourse in the Midrash compilations, we have no problem in proposing obvious

Aggadic topical category formations—God, Torah, Israel, idolatry, sin, atonement, the gentiles, and so on. But while propositional, these are rarely analytical and argumentative; they prove propositions, they do not explore them. And, a concomitant fact, the lines of definition of the Aggadic category formations do not coincide with the documentary boundaries of the Aggadah, let alone the topical composites preserved by the Talmuds. The matter is neatly illustrated by the Aggadic units of the Halakhic expositions of *Taanit* just now surveyed. Like those in hand, so in general, none of the topical composites we find in the Aggadic compilations or in the Aggadic composites of the Talmuds actually constitutes a category formation or is topically divided into category formations that correspond in function to those of the Halakhah.

But, for the sake of argument, let us list the topics that we deem native categories of the Aggadah: God, Torah, Israel, idolatry, sin, atonement, and the rest. Then turn to the Halakhic category formations *sanhedrin, shebiit, and kelim*, for example. We immediately realize that the topical program of the Halakhah and that of the Aggadah scarcely correspond. Law does not translate itself into lore, norms of conduct into norms of conviction. That is obvious. What Halakhic category formation corresponds to, or deals with the issues inherent in, the topic Torah, or Israel, or God, to name principals? And what Aggadic composition or composite takes shape around the topic *sanhedrin*, or the laws of the Seventh Year (*shebiit*), or the laws of the susceptibility to uncleanness of various utensils (*kelim*)? The incompatibility is fundamental; the native categories of the one are unable to correspond to, or even connect with, those of the other.

So the foundations of systemic cogency of the native categories of Rabbinic Judaism, the Halakhic and the Aggadic, remain to be explored. And that requires not merely the kind of comparison of the narratives yielded by the category formations of the Halakhah and of the Aggadah read as a continuum, such as just now set forth. It demands a detailed analysis of where the two bodies of writing do not intersect at all, an explanation of why to one is assigned a particular part of the systemic statement viewed whole that the other is not asked to convey at all, in any terms. One example suffices: the Halakhah bears nearly the entire burden of the statement on cleanness and uncleanness; the Aggadah, practically none. Why this, not that? I do not know.

IV. An Exterior Perspective: The Comparative Study
of Judaisms—the Category Formations of the Rabbinic
System in Comparison and Contrast to Those of
Other Judaic Systems

The upshot is clear: the question of religion addressed to Rabbinic
Judaism, with its comparisons and contrasts of Halakhah and Aggadah, gains depth when we extend to its domain the exercise of comparative study. But this tells us we cannot leave the matter when we
have taken up only the comparison of the principal parts, the native
categories, of the Rabbinic system and structure, the Halakhah contrasted with the Aggadah. Exterior to Rabbinic Judaism are corresponding Judaic systems awaiting attention in this same context. For,
as I pointed out in section I of Chapter One, people commonly recognize that diverse bodies of data attest to different Judaic systems of
the social order, diverse Judaisms. If the religious study of religion
requires the comparison of religions, then the religious study of
Judaism(s) demands the comparison of one Judaic religious system of
the social order with others.

What justifies the comparison to yield the possibility of contextual
contrast? All Judaisms are formed into a common genus by a
definitive trait, which characterizes all of the religious systems bearing the same indicative category and excludes all that do not. That
is the common indicator: Scripture received as the exhaustive and
complete account of God's self-manifestation. This indicator characterizes all Judaic religious systems of antiquity but no other-than-
Judaic religious system in that or any other age. Thus excluded are
all pagan cults, which do not acknowledge this Scripture's authority,
as well as the Christianities that possess another Testament besides
what they called the Old, and all the more so the ones of Gnostic
character that reject Scripture altogether.

What is at stake? In comparing Judaic systems, we gain perspective
on the system at hand, identifying the choices it has made, discerning
its distinctive points of emphasis. Specifically, when we have identified
what they have in common, we are ready to contrast what is thereby
available for comparison. To show how the comparison of religions
takes place within the framework of Judaisms, I take up how various
well-documented systems of antiquity define one Aggadic topic that
is common to them all and that, further, is required for any Judaism.

It is the native category Israel, which every Judaic system invokes. In investigating the theories of Israel presented by the documentary evidence of that Judaism, I have a very particular question in mind.

What, specifically, do I wish to learn? It is how, with reference to the common category Israel, the several systems position themselves. What are the choices that they make in defining and utilizing this category, and what do we learn about the whole system from this indicative detail? So through the common topic Israel, defined in all cases by a common Scripture, we compare Judaic systems with one another, affording perspective on all of them. What we see is how a given component of a system serves as a systemic indicator, a detail bearing the statement of the whole.

That labor of comparison and contrast, then, shows the way in which I propose to enter into processes of thought concerning the social consciousness of a given group as important statements of that consciousness come before us. When they speak of "Israel," to what sort of social group do they refer, and how do they think about that group? Ultimately at stake in the answers is insight into the solution of a much larger problem, the way in which religious systems take shape, the relationship, in the formation of religious systems, between circumstance and context, contents and convictions. That is what is at stake in the comparative study of Judaisms in the context of religion study.

A. *Defining "Israel" in Systemic Context*

What I shall now show is a proposition bearing interesting implications for the study of religion. An "Israel" will find its definition entirely within the Judaic system that it serves. The category will prove wholly congruent to the shape and structure of that system and will be formed of materials selected by the systemic authorship out of Scripture's data and a miscellaneous repertoire of possibilities. The opposite proposition is that the social entity, Israel, will appeal to facts dictated by the social world "out there," so that the system will struggle to absorb and assimilate the givens of a politics and imagination dictated by social realities and not formed by the system itself. That opposite but quite plausible proposition is false for the data we examine. An "Israel" within a given system is the invention of the system builders, with those traits found relevant to the larger system—

without appeal to facts or realities beyond the range of systemic control.

The outcome is obvious. Any notion that the character of "Israel" will find definition in a received corpus of facts not subject to the system's own processes of selection is false. Any conception that the system builders—the Rabbinic sages, in the present instance, over a period of centuries—composed their "Israel" through the collection of information and the generalization of what they found is improbable. The system responds to its inner logic and makes things up from there. That is why neither the social data nor the repertoire of available "Israels" make a contribution on their own initiatives. The simple fact is that religious ideas—systems—constitute what in sociology are called independent variables. Ideas matter and make the world.

B. *Israel in Rabbinic Judaism: The Two Stages in the Formation of the Judaism of the Dual Torah*

The canonical writings of formative Judaism fall into two groups, each with its own plan and program, the first produced in the second and third centuries, before Constantine, the second in the fourth and fifth, after him. The first of these groups of writings begins with the Mishnah and encompasses *Abot*, the Tosefta, and the Tannaite Midrash compilations. The second set of the same writings begins with the Yerushalmi and reaches the Rabbah-Midrash compilations and their companions, and the Bavli. Each division of the canon sets forth its own conception of Israel. The Rabbinic sages did not merely describe a group; they portrayed it as they wished to. They did not assemble facts and define the social entity, the social group, as a matter of mere description of the given. They imputed to the social group Jews the standing of the systemic entity Israel. They furthermore assigned to this entity indicative and definitive traits that, to begin with, take form in the distant reaches of the mind, for example, belief in the resurrection of the dead as a scriptural doctrine (*M. Sanhedrin* 10:1).

C. *Israel in the Mishnah and Companion Documents*

What does it mean to claim that a native category formation shows itself to be a systemic indicator, repeating in its small way the large message of the system viewed whole? The Mishnah, carried forward by the Tosefta, sets forth a system of hierarchical classification, and in that system, Israel serves as a taxic indicator in a labor of hierarchical classification. It therefore finds definition in transitive, antonymic relationships of two sorts, first, Israel as against "not-Israel," gentile, and second, "Israel" as a caste as against "priest," or "Levite." In both contexts Israel stands for a classification of persons in relationship to a counterpart classification in context. In the Mishnah's authorship's Israel, we confront an abstraction in a system of philosophy. Amplifying this matter, in *Abot*, "Israel[ites]" are shown to be beloved because the Torah was given to them and because that fact was made known to them. Then for the document at hand, the central issue is the Torah, not Israel. What is celebrated is the gift of the Torah. Thus "Israel" defined the frontiers on both the outer side of society and the social boundaries within, and this is, *Abot* adds, by reason of its having accepted the Torah and devoted itself to the study of the Torah.

To understand the meaning of "Israel" as the Mishnah and its associated documents of the second and third centuries sort matters out, we ask whether "the gentiles" also serve as a corresponding taxic indicator for gentile nations, in the way in which Israel does for Israelite castes? Specifically, does the authorship of the Mishnah differentiate when speaking of gentiles? The answer is no, for the gentiles represent an undifferentiated mass. In the system of the Mishnah, they cannot serve as taxic indicators corresponding to Israel. To the system of the Mishnah, whether or not a gentile is a Roman or an Aramean or a Syrian or a Briton does not matter. But to the Judaic system represented by the Yerushalmi and its associated writings, "gentile" may be Roman or other than Roman, for instance, and the world empires, Babylonia, Media, Greece, and Rome, are carefully differentiated. This act of further differentiation—we may call it "speciation"—makes a considerable difference in the appreciation of "gentile." It marks a different way of thinking about Israel in relationship to gentiles. The shift, later on, will carry us to an "Israel" that bears the socially vivid sense that the metaphor implicitly requires: a real social entity, with a story attached. Systemically, so too will the counterpart, Rome, gain the speciation that "the gentiles" lack.

In the first phase, just as gentile was an abstract category, so was

Israel. Kohen was a category, and so too Israel. When we see Israel as a classifier and taxonomic category, we confront an abstraction in a system of philosophy. The Israel we see in the second stratum of the literature of the dual Torah, by contrast, bears a socially vivid sense. The contrast is clear. "Israel," when viewed in the this-worldly framework of most of the Mishnah's discussions, emerges through a series of contrasts and comparisons, not of intrinsically important, systemically determinative facts. We know in that literature what Israel or an Israel is mainly when we can specify the antonym.

D. *Israel in the Second Phase in the Unfolding of Rabbinic Judaism: The Yerushalmi and Its Companions, the Rabbah-Midrash Compilations and the Bavli*

While Israel in the first phase of the formation of Judaism perpetually finds definition in relationship to its opposite and is thus transitive in its relationships, Israel in the second phase constituted an intransitive entity, defined in its own terms and not solely or mainly in relationship to other, comparable entities. This point registers through the enormous investment in the conception of Israel as sui generis. But Israel, represented as it is in the Yerushalmi and the Rabbah-Midrash compilations and the Bavli, as family bears that same trait of autonomy and self-evident definition. In that context too it is sui generis, there being no other family like that family.

Israel in the second phase of the canon of the Judaism of the dual Torah therefore stands for a real social group, not merely an abstraction, an entity in theory. Israel forms a family, and an encompassing theory of society, built upon that conception of Israel, permits us to describe the proportions and balances of the social entity at hand, showing how each component both is an Israel and contributes to the larger composite as well. Israel as sui generis carried in its wake a substantial doctrine of definition, a weighty collection of general laws of social history governing the particular traits and events of the social group. In comparing transitive to intransitive Israel, we move from Israel as not-gentile and Israel as not-priest to powerful statements of what Israel *is*.

Why has such a striking shift taken place? The amplified doctrine of Israel turns out to respond, point by point, to a competing view of Israel, that of Christianity—a view to which the recognition of

Christianity as religion of the Roman empire accorded prominence.
By claiming that Israel constituted "Israel after the flesh," the actual,
living, present family of Abraham and Sarah, Isaac and Rebecca,
Jacob and Leah and Rachel, sages met head-on the Christian claim
that there was—or could ever be—some other Israel, of a lineage
not defined by the family connection at all, so that the existing Jews
no longer constituted Israel. By representing Israel as sui generis,
sages moreover focused upon the systemic teleology, with its definition of salvation, in response to the Christian claim that salvation is
not of Israel but of the Church, now enthroned in this world as in
Heaven.

1. *Rome as Brother*
In response to the challenge of Christianity, sages' thought about
Israel centered, as it had not in the first phase of the Rabbinic canon,
on the issues of history and salvation, issues made not merely chronic
but acute by the political triumph. That accounts for what I believe
is an unprecedented reading of the outsider, contained in the two
propositions of Rome, first, as Esau or Edom or Ishmael, that is, as
part of the family, and, second, of Rome as the pig. Differentiating
Rome from other gentiles represented a striking concession indeed.
Rome is represented as only Christian Rome could have been represented: it looks kosher but it is unkosher. Pagan Rome never could
have looked kosher, but Christian Rome, with its appeal to ancient
Israel, could and did and moreover claimed to. It bore some traits
that validate, but lacked others that validate.

2. *Israel as Family*
The other metaphor—that of the family—proved equally pointed.
Sages framed their political ideas within the metaphor of genealogy
because, to begin with, they appealed to the fleshly connection, the
family, as the rationale for Israel's social existence. A family beginning with Abraham, Isaac, and Jacob, Israel today could best sort out
its relationships by drawing into the family other social entities with
which it found it had to relate. So Rome became the brother. That
affinity came to light only when Rome had turned Christian, and that
point marked the need for the extension of the genealogical net. But
the conversion to Christianity also justified sages' extending member-
ship in the family to Rome, for Christian Rome shared with Israel

the common patrimony of Scripture—and said so. The character of
sages' thought on Israel therefore proved remarkably congruent to the
conditions of public discourse that confronted them. But the substance of their doctrine—the rejection of metaphor in favor of the
claim that Israel formed an entity that was sui generis—derived from
within.

E. *A Social Metaphor and a Field Theory of Society: Israel and the Social Contract—Comparing the Mishnah's and the Yerushalmi's Israel*

The metaphor of Israel as family supplied an encompassing theory of
society, accounting for that sense of constituting a corporate social
entity that clearly infused the canonical writings from the very outset.
Such a theory explained not only who Israel as a whole was. It also
set forth the responsibilities of Israel's social entity, its society; it
defined the character of that entity; it explained who owes what to
whom and why; and it accounted for the inner structure and interplay of relationship within the community, here and now, constituted
by Jews in their villages and neighborhoods of towns. Accordingly,
Israel as family bridged the gap between an account of the entirety
of the social group Israel and a picture of the components of that
social group as they lived out their lives in their households and villages. An encompassing theory of society, covering all components
from least to greatest, holding the whole together in correct order and
proportion, derived from Israel viewed as extended family.

Can we say that the Mishnaic phase had presented an encompassing theory of society as a whole? In general terms, yes, But in
specifics, no. Invoking the metaphor Israel for a group identified with
the biblical Israel, the Mishnah accounted for the whole. And as to
the parts, the here and the now of household and village, the
Mishnah's Israel accomplished a suitable explanation. But that left a
considerable territory untouched; the space in between the large and
theoretical and the mundane was left vacant. To explain: the
Mishnah's system had explained by Israel the identification of that
large entity, the entirety of the social group, with biblical Israel, and
in their extraordinary exegesis of the everyday as modality of the
sacred, the Mishnah and its companions had also infused in the parts
the sense that the whole was meant to make. But the parts remained
just that: details of a larger whole that derive place and proportion

only in that whole. This abstraction of Israel as not not-Israel, holy and not gentile—holy people—left the middle-range components of society unaccounted for.

The Mishnah could explain village and "all Israel," just as its system used the word "Israel" for the individual and the entire social entity. But the region and its counterparts, the "we" composed of regions, the corporate society of the Jews of a given country, language-group, and the like, the real-life world of communities that transcended particular locations—these social facts of the middle distance did not constitute subdivisions of the Israel that knew all and each but nothing in between. The omitted entity was identified with the family itself, which played no important role in the Mishnah's system, except as one of the taxonomic indicators.

By contrast Israel as family imparted to the details an autonomy and a meaning of their own, so that each complex component of the whole formed a microcosm of the whole: family to village to Israel as one large family. The village then constituted Israel, as much as did the region, the neighborhood, the corporate society that people could empirically identify, the theoretical social entity that they could only imagine. All formed "all Israel," viewed under the aspect of Heaven, and of still greater consequence, each household—that is, each building block of the village community—constituted in itself a model of, the model for, Israel. The utter abstraction of the Mishnah had left Israel as individual or as "all Israel," and thus without articulated linkage to the concrete middle range of the Jews' everyday social life. Dealing with exquisite detail and the intangible whole, the Mishnah's system had left the realm of the society of Jews in the workaday household and village outside the metaphorical frame of Israel; and Israel, viewed in the image, after the likeness of, family, made up that omitted middle range.

The theory of Israel as a society made up of persons who, because they constituted a family, stood in a clear relationship of obligation and responsibility to one another corresponded to what people much later would call the social contract, a kind of compact that in palpable ways told families and households how in the aggregate they formed something larger and tangible. The web of interaction spun out of concrete interchange now was spun out of not the gossamer thread of abstraction and theory but the tough hemp of family ties. Israel formed a society because Israel was compared to an extended family. This, in sum and substance, supplied to the Jews in their households (themselves a made-up category that, in the end, transformed the relationship of the nuclear and extended family into an abstraction capable of holding together quite unrelated persons) an account of the tie from household to household, from village to village, encompassing ultimately "all Israel."

F. *Israel and the Social Rules of Judaisms*

Systems, by definition, speak for and to a social entity; otherwise, in a canonical document all we have is a book. And social groups—two or more persons sharing distinctive traits that distinguish them for other social entities—commonly perceive themselves to be something other, and more, than what they are. Concrete traits, then, stand for an abstract social entity, present even when not perceived, indeed imposing other traits besides those that are palpable. Accordingly, we have now to generalize and offer the beginnings of the generalizations promised by the labor of comparison and contrast to which I referred at the outset. Success in such an exercise will yield lessons for the description, analysis, and interpretation of other systems and their social entities. Thus, I have now to propose hypotheses for general discourse—three laws, to be exact—deriving from the particular case at hand. And to begin with, that requires comparison of the Judaism we have cursorily treated with other Judaisms, all to exemplify this other formulation of the question of religion addressed to Rabbinic Judaism in its formative age.

1. *The First Law: The Shape and Meaning Imputed to the Social Component Israel Will Conform to the Larger Interests of the System and in Detail Express the System's Main Point. The Case of Paul and Israel after the Spirit*

The constituent elements of a system will recapitulate the main message of the system, but in terms of particularities. Israel in the Mishnah embodied the method and message of the Mishnah's system, and the same is so of Israel in the Yerushalmi and its companions. We appeal, for proof that the law is not particular to the case of Rabbinic Judaism, to the Israel defined by Paul.

In his representation of his Israel, Paul presents us with a metaphor for which, in the documents of the Judaism of the dual Torah, I can find no counterpart in the Rabbinic context. They are (1) Israel compared to an olive tree, standing for Israel encompassing gentiles who believe but also Jews by birth who do not believe, and (2) Israel standing for the elect and those saved by faith and therefore by grace. These complex and somewhat disjoined metaphors and definitions form a coherent and simple picture when we see them not in detail but as part of the larger whole of Paul's entire system. For the issue of Israel for Paul forms a detail of a system centered upon a case in favor of salvation through Christ and faith in him alone, even without keeping the rules of the Torah as has "Israel after the flesh" kept the Torah. So does the consensus of the familiar and rich corpus of scholarship on Paul present matters, and I take the results as definitive.

The generative problematic that tells Paul what he wishes to know about Israel—how he proposes to utilize Israel as a building block of his larger system—derives from the larger concerns of the Christian system Paul proposes to work out. That problematic was framed in the need, in general, to explain the difference, as to salvific condition, between those who believed and those who did not believe in Christ. But it focused specifically upon the matter of Israel and how those who believed in Christ but did not derive from Israel related to both those who believed and also derived from Israel and those who did not believe but derived from Israel. Do the first-named have to keep the Torah? Are the nonbelieving Jews subject to justification? Since, had Paul been a gentile and not an Israel, the issue could not have proved critical in the working out of an individual system (but only in the address to the world at large), we may take for granted that Paul's own Jewish origin made the question at hand important, if not critical. What transformed the matter from a chronic into an acute question—the matter of salvation through keeping the Torah—encompassed also the matter of who is Israel.

For his part, Paul appeals, for his taxic indicator of Israel, to a consideration we have not found commonplace at all, namely, circumcision.[1] It is certainly implicit in the Torah, but the Mishnah's laws

---

[1] See Jonathan Z. Smith, "Fences and Neighbors," in *Approaches to Ancient Judaism*, ed. W. S. Green, 6 vols., Brown Judaic Studies (Missoula: Scholars Press, 1978) 2:1–25; and in Jonathan Z. Smith, *Imagining Religion: From Babylon to Jonestown* (Chicago: University of Chicago Press, 1982), 1–18.

explicitly accommodate as Israel persons who (for good and sufficient reasons) are not circumcised, and treat as not-Israel persons who are circumcised but otherwise do not qualify. So, for the Mishnah's system, circumcision forms a premise but not a presence, and a datum but not a decisive taxic indicator. Paul, by contrast, could have called Israel all those who are circumcised, and not-Israel all those who are not circumcised—pure and simple. It follows that for Paul, but not for the Mishnah, the matter of Israel and its definition forms part of a larger project of reclassifying Christians in terms not defined by the received categories—now a third race, a new race, a new man, in a new story. J. Z. Smith makes the matter entirely explicit to Paul's larger system: "Paul's theological arguments with respect to circumcision have their own internal logic and situation: that in the case of Abraham, it was posterior to faith (Rom. 4:9–12); that spiritual things are superior to physical things (Col. 3:11–14); that the Christian is the 'true circumcision' as opposed to the Jew (Phil. 3:3). . . . But these appear secondary to the fundamental taxonomic premise, the Christian is a member of a new taxon."[2]

Here we have an explicit definition of Israel, now not after the flesh but after the promise. Israel, then, is no longer a family in the concrete sense in that the Rabbinic documents represent it. "Israel after the flesh" who pursued righteousness that is based on law did not succeed in fulfilling that law because they did not pursue it through faith (Rom. 9:31), "and gentiles who did not pursue righteousness have attained it, that is, righteousness through faith" (Rom. 9:30). Now there is an Israel after the flesh but also "a remnant chosen by grace . . . the elect obtained it" (Rom. 11:5–6), with the consequence that the fleshly Israel remains but gentiles ("a wild olive shoot") have been grafted "to share the richness of the olive tree" (Rom. 11:17). Do these constitute Israel? Yes and no. They share in the promise. They are Israel in the earlier definition of the children of Abraham. There remains an Israel after the flesh, which has its place as well. And that place remains with God: "As regards election they are beloved for the sake of their forefathers. For the gifts and the call of God are irrevocable" (Rom. 11:28–29).

This very rapid and schematic account illustrates the law with

---

[2] Ibid.

which we began: the shape and meaning imputed to the social component Israel here conform to the larger interests of the system that is constructed by Paul, both episodically and also, in Romans, quite systematically. Israel as a detail expresses also the system's main point. For Paul's Judaic system, encompassing believing (former) gentiles but also retaining a systemic status for nonbelieving Jews, Israel forms an important component within a larger structure. In addition and more to the point, Israel finds definition on account of the logical requirements of that encompassing framework. Indeed, I cannot imagine making sense of the remarkably complex metaphor introduced by Paul—the metaphor of the olive tree—without understanding the problem of thought that confronted him and that he solved through, among other details, his thinking on Israel. The notion of entering Israel through belief but not behavior ("works") in one detail expresses the main point of Paul's system, which concerns not who is Israel but what faith in Christ means.

2. The Second Law: What an Israel Is Depends on Who Wants to Know:
Philosophers Imagine a Philosophical Israel, and Politicians Conceive a
Political Israel. The Cases of Philo and of the Library of Qumran
Not only does the category formation at hand—the social entity of a religious system of the social order—find its meaning in its systemic context. We shall now see that the very shaping of the category formation in its fundamental qualities, the identification of indicative traits, responds to the systemic context. By Israel as a category formation, different systems simply mean different things. They do not differ only on definition; they differ on what is defined to begin with. This we see when we contrast the fundamental category Israel as shaped, prior to specific definition, by philosophy and by politics.

By a philosopher in the present context, I mean an intellectual who attempts to state as a coherent whole, within a single system of thought and (implicit) explanation, diverse categories and classifications of data. By politician I mean a person of public parts, one who undertakes to shape a social polity, a person of standing in a social group, for example, a community, who proposes to explain in some theoretical framework the meaning and character of the life of that group or nation or society or community. In the context of Rabbinic Judaism, for example, I should classify the framers of the Mishnah as philosophers, those of the Yerushalmi and related writings (by their own word) as politicians. The related but distinct systems made by each group exhibit traits of philosophy and politics, respectively, for reasons I have now spelled out.

The generalization therefore is before us. Does it apply to more than our own case? For purposes of showing that the same phenomenon derives from other cases and therefore constitutes a law, not a mere generalization out of a case, I appeal to an individual and an authorship. Philo, the Jewish philosopher of Alexandria, serves as our example of the former; and the authorship of the more important writings of the community of Qumran, the latter. A brief exposition suffices.

For Philo, Israel forms a paradigmatic metaphor bearing three meanings. The first is ontological, which signifies the places of Israel in God's creation. The second is epistemological. This signifies the knowledge of God that Israel possesses. The third is political, referring to the polity that Israel possesses and projects in light of its ontological place and epistemological access to God.

Our point of interest is achieved when we perceive even from a distance the basic contours of Philo's vision of Israel. What we see is that, for Philo, Israel formed a category within a larger theory of how humanity knows divinity, an aspect of ontology and epistemology. True, Israel emerges as, if not unique, then sui generis. But that is only in the framework of a system of classification, so Israel is not really sui generis in the way in which, in the second phase of the Judaism of the dual Torah, Israel has no counterpart in kind, not merely in species. What makes an Israel into Israel for Philo is a set of essentially philosophical considerations concerning adherence to, or perception of, God. In the philosophical system of Philo, Israel constitutes a philosophical category, not a social entity in an everyday sense.

The library of Qumran (recording the theory of the community that valued those writings) serves as a test case for two distinct laws: first, that what matters, to begin with, is dictated by the traits of the one to whom the subject is important, not by the objective and indicative characteristics of the subject itself; and, second, that the importance of a topic derives from the character of the system that takes up that topic. We turn first to the systemic definition of Israel: what kind of social entity—precisely what classification of things—is at issue when I speak of Israel? And for what purpose?

By "Israel" the authorships of the documents of the library of

Qumran mean "us"—and no one else. Stated simply, what our authorships meant by "us" was simply Israel, or "the true Israel." That is why the group organized itself as a replication of "all Israel," as they read about Israel in those passages of Scripture that impressed them. They structured their group, in Geza Vermes's language, "so that it corresponded faithfully to that of Israel itself, dividing it into priests and laity, the priests being described as the 'sons of Zadok'— Zadok was High Priest in David's time—and the laity grouped after the biblical model into twelve tribes." This particular Israel then divided itself into units of thousands, hundreds, fifties, and tens—the new Israel that is the only Israel.

What an Israel is thus depends on who wants to know. Philo has given us a philosophical Israel. The authorships of the documents preserved by the Qumran library (and the community that valued those writings) viewed Israel not as a fictive entity possessing spiritual or intellectual—intangible—traits alone or mainly but as a concrete social group, an entity in the here and now, that may be defined by traits of persons subject to the same sanctions and norms, sharing the same values and ideals. Builders of a community, the authorships of the library of Qumran conceived and described in law a political Israel, one that exercised legitimate violence. Their Israel and Philo's bear nothing in common.

Note the contrast not only in the substance of the definition but in the very definition of what is defined. The one Israel—the Qumran one—constitutes a tangible, political entity. The Israel of the Qumran books is the Israel of history and eschatology and of Scripture, as much as the Israel of the authorship of the Yerushalmi, *Genesis Rabbah*, and *Leviticus Rabbah* refers back to the palpable Israel of Genesis and Leviticus. The other Israel—Philo's—comprises people of shared intellectual traits in Philo's larger picture of how God is known. This compares with how the Israel of the authorship of the Mishnah and related writings exhibits taxonomic traits and serves a function of classification.

Each set of politicians—the authors of the Qumran documents that pertain, those of the Yerushalmi and its companions—presents us with a political Israel, that is, an Israel that exhibits the traits of a community ("people," "nation"). Each set of philosophers—Philo and the Mishnah's framers—offers a philosophical Israel, with traits of a taxonomic character that carry out a larger systemic purpose of explanation and philosophical classification. We have, therefore, not a generalization of a particular case but a rule that can be tested in three cases, for three Judaisms.

3. *The Third Law: The Systemic Importance of the Category Israel Depends on the Generative Problematic—the Urgent Question—of the System Builders and Not on Their Social Circumstance. The Place of Israel within the Self-Evidently True Response Offered by the System Will Prove Congruent to the Logic of the System—That Alone. The Cases of Paul, Philo, the Library of Qumran, and the Rabbinic Sages of the Mishnah, Talmuds, and Midrash* The proposed law is that the system's generative question determines the importance of any category within the system. By "generative question," I mean the urgent question that a system answers in all its parts, the precipitating crisis (of thought, of action) that leads several generations of intellectuals to rethink the grounds of social being and to reconsider all fundamental questions in a new way. The negative version of the same law is obvious. The paramount character of a category in the social facts-*out-there*, in the streets and households (in the case of the social entity), has slight bearing upon the proportions and order of the system. Stated in the positive, the rule is that the systemic logic-*in-here* dictates all issues of proportion, balance, and order. We therefore ask ourselves how, on objective grounds and by appealing to data, not mere impressions, we may assess the relative importance of a given systemic structural category when we compare one system with another. So the systemic importance of "Israel" depends on the systemic question and its logic, not on the social facts of the times. Whether Israel takes an important place in a system is decided by the systemic logic, not by the circumstance of the Jews in the here and now. Systemopoeia—system building—is a symbolic transaction worked out in imagination, not a sifting and sorting of facts.

But how do we know whether any systemic component plays a more, or a less, important role? A judgment on the importance of a given entity or category in one system by comparison with the importance of that same entity or category in another need not rely upon subjective impressions. A reasonably objective measure of the matter lends hope to test the stated law. The criterion is this: does the system remain cogent without consideration of its Israel? Philo's does, the Mishnah's does, Paul's does not, the Qumran library's does not, and the Yerushalmi's does not.

The criterion of importance therefore does not derive from merely counting up a document's references to Israel. What we must do to assess the role and place of the social entity in a system is to ask a simple question: *were the entity or trait Israel to be removed from a given system, would that system radically change in character, or would it merely lose a detail?* What is required is a mental experiment, but not a very difficult one. What we do is simply present a reprise of our brief systemic descriptions. Let me state some bald facts.

FIRST, PAUL: Without an Israel, Paul would have had no system. The generative question of his system required him to focus attention on the definition of the social entity Israel. Paul originated among Jews but addressed both Jews and gentiles, seeking to form the lot into a single social entity "in Christ Jesus." The social dimension of his system formed the generative question with which he proposed to content.

SECOND, PHILO: Without an Israel, Philo, by contrast, could have done very well indeed. For even our brief and schematic survey of the Philo described by Wolfson and Goodenough has shown that, whatever mattered, Israel did not. It was a footnote, an illustration, a detail of a theory of knowledge of God, not the generative problematic even of the treatment of the knowledge of God, let alone of the system as a whole (which we scarcely approached and had no reason to approach!). We may therefore say that Israel formed an important category for Paul and not for Philo. Accordingly, the judgment of the matter rests on more than mere word counts, on the one side, or exercises of impression and taste, on the other. It forms part of a larger interpretation of the system as a whole and what constitutes the system's generative problematic.

THIRD, THE LIBRARY OF QUMRAN: If, moreover, we ask whether Israel is critical to the community at Qumran, a simple fact answers our question. Were we to remove Israel in general and in detail from the topical program at hand, we would lose, if not the entirety of the library, then nearly the whole of some documents and the larger part of many of them. The library of Qumran constitutes a vast collection of writings about Israel, its definition and conduct, history and destiny. We cannot make an equivalent statement about the entire corpus of Philo's writings, even though Philo obviously concerned himself with the life and welfare of the Israel of which, in Alexandria as well as the world over, he saw himself a part. The reason for the systemic importance of Israel among the faithful of Qumran, furthermore, derives from the meanings imputed to that category. The library stands for a social group that conceives of itself as Israel and that wishes, in these documents, to spell out what that Israel is and must do. The system as a whole forms an exercise in the definition of Israel as against that non-Israel composed not of gentiles but of erring (former) Israelites. The saving remnant is all that is left: Israel.

If, therefore, we wish to know whether Israel will constitute an important component in a Judaism, we ask about the categorical imperative and describe, as a matter of mere fact, the consequent categorical composition of that system, stated as a corpus of authoritative documents. A system in which Israel—the social entity to which the system's builders imagine they address themselves—plays an important role will treat Israel as part of its definitive structure, its generative system. The reason is that the system's categorical imperative will find important consequences in the definition of its Israel. A system (such as the Halakhic) in which the system's builders work on questions framed as entirely other than social category formations also will not yield tractates on Israel. If they explore the logic of issues different from those addressing a social entity, they will not accord to the topic of Israel the categorical and systemic importance that we have identified in some Judaisms but not in others. Discourse on Israel, in general (as in the Yerushalmi and its companions) or in acute detail concerning internal structure (as in the writings of Qumran), comes about because of the fundamental question addressed by the system viewed whole.

4. *The Hypothesis: The System Builders' Social (Including Political) Circumstance Defines the Generative Problematic That Imparts Self-Evidence to the Systemically Definitive Logic, Encompassing Its Social Component. The Cases of Paul, the Library of Qumran, and the Rabbinic Sages of the Mishnah, Talmuds, and Midrash*

What do I learn from the comparative study of Judaisms for the understanding of religion? These points:

(1) The systemically generative circumstance finds its definition in the out-there of the social, political world in which the system

builders—and their imagined audience—flourish. Extraordinary political crises, ongoing tensions of society, a religious crisis that challenges
long-held theological truth impose in time their definition upon
thought. They seize the attention and focus the concentration of the
systemopoieic thinkers, who propose to explain matters.

(2) Religions—in my language, religious systems of the social
order—propose an orderly response to a disorderly situation, and that
is their utility. Systems then come into existence at a point, and in a
context, in which thoughtful people identify questions that cannot be
avoided and must be solved. Such a circumstance, for the case at
hand, emerges in the realm of politics. That means it takes shape in
the context of persons in community, in the corporate society of
shared discourse. The acute, systemopoieic question, then, derives
from out-there; the system begins somewhere beyond the mind of the
thoughtful intellects who build systems. Having ruled out the systemopoieic power of authors' or authorships' circumstance, therefore, I
now invoke the systemopoieic power of the political setting of the
social group of which the system builders form a part (in their own
minds, the exemplification and realization).

(3) What, then, of self-evidence? Systemic logic enjoys self-
evidence. But it is circumstance that dictates the absolute given, the
sense of fittingness and irrefutable logic, that people find self-evident.
How does circumstance shape matters? System building forms a symbolic transaction and, by definition, represents symbol change for the
builders and their building. On the one hand, it is a social question
that sets the terms and also the limits of the symbolic transaction, so
that symbol change responds to social change (at least for some). On
the other hand, symbol change so endures that it imposes a new
shape upon a social world, as we can show was the case at Qumran
for the community that valued those writings and also was the case,
in the aftermath of Constantine, for the Jews who then constituted
the Israel for which the Rabbinic sages concerned themselves.

It follows that social change comes about through symbol change.
How shall we account for the origin of a system? We can show correlation between a system and its circumstance, and, it must follow,
between the internal logic of a system and the social givens in which
the system flourishes. But correlation is not explanation. And the
sources of explanation lie beyond the limits of cases, however many.
The question facing system builders carries with it one set of givens,

not some other—one urgent and ineluctable question, which, by definition, excludes others. The context of the system builders having framed the question before them, one set of issues, and not some other—issues of one type rather than some other—predominate. Now to make these general observations concrete through the cases at hand.

G. *Reprise of the Matter of Self-Evidence*

Matters concerning Paul's and Qumran's systems hardly require detailed specification. Paul's context told him that Israel constituted a categorical imperative, and it also told him what *about* Israel he had to discover in his thought on the encounter with Christ. The communards of Qumran by choice isolated themselves and in that context determined upon the generative issue of describing an Israel that, all by itself in the wilderness, would survive and form the saving remnant.

Paul—all scholarship concurs—faced a social entity ("Church" or "Christian community") made up of Jews but also gentiles, and some Jews expected people to obey the law—for example, to circumcise their sons. Given the natural course of lives, that was not a question to be long postponed; this imparts to it the acute, not merely chronic, character that it clearly displayed even in the earliest decade beyond Paul's vision. And that fact, in my judgment, explains why, for Paul, circumcision formed a critical taxic indicator in a way in which, for Philo, for the Mishnah, and other Judaic systems, it did not.

The circumstance of the library at Qumran is far better documented, since that community, through its rereading of Scripture, tells us that it originated in a break between its founder(s) and other officials. Consequently, my characterizing of the community of Qumran hardly moves beyond the evidence in hand. They responded to their own social circumstance, isolated and alone as it was, and formed a community unto itself, hence seeing their Israel, the social entity of their system, as what there was left of Scripture's Israel, that is, the remnant of Israel.

The Rabbinic sages made their documentary statements in reply to two critical questions—the one (the Mishnah and its companions) concerning sanctification, presented by the final failure of efforts to regain Jerusalem and restore the Temple cult, the other (the

Yerushalmi and its associates and continuators) concerning salvation, precipitated by the now unavoidable fact of Christianity's political triumph. Once each of the Judaisms for which a precipitating (in my jargon, systemopoieic) crisis can be identified passes before us, we readily see how the consequent program flowed from the particular politically generative crisis.

The case of the sages in both phases of the unfolding of the Rabbinic canon is the obvious example of the interplay of context and contents. There we see with great clarity both the precipitating event and the logic of self-evidence out of which a system spun its categorical program. That program, correlated with the systemopoieic event, would then define all else. If sanctification is the issue imposed by events, then the Mishnah will ask a range of questions of detail, at each point providing an exegesis of the everyday in terms of the hermeneutics of the sacred: Israel as different and holy within the terms specified by Scripture. If salvation proves the paramount claim of a now successful rival within Israel, then the authorship of *Genesis Rabbah* will ask the matriarchs and patriarchs to spell out the rules of salvation, insofar as they provide not merely precedents but paradigms of salvation. The authorship of *Leviticus Rabbah* will seek, in the picture of sanctification supplied by the book of Leviticus, the rules and laws that govern the salvation of Israel. The history of an Israel that is a political entity—family, sui generis, either, both (it hardly matters)—will dictate a paramount category for the authorship for which the Yerushalmi speaks.

And yet an element of a priori choice is obvious. And that matter of selectivity points toward symbol change as the prior, and social change as the consequent, fact. That is to say, social change forms a necessary but not sufficient explanation. There is a simple fact that seems to me to validate this judgment. It is that many Jews confronted the social change to which the system builders responded in the way they did. But—by definition—only the system builders reached the conclusions that they reached and composed the system that they created. There were other Jews who reached other conclusions (or none at all). Hence social crisis tells us the problem that engaged the system builders, but the character and structure of the crisis, viewed by itself, could not tell us the system that they would build.

The Rabbinic sages of the Mishnah and related documents formed

a group of Jews that identified the critical issue as that of sanctification, involving proper classification and ordering of all of the elements and components of Israel's reality. Not all Jews interpreted
events within that framework, however, and it follows that circumstances by themselves did not govern. The symbol change worked for
those for whom it worked, which, ultimately, changed the face of the
Jews' society. But in the second and fourth centuries were Jews who
found persuasive a different interpretation of events—whether the
defeat of Bar Kokhba or the conversion of Constantine—and became
Christian. Nor did all Christians concur with Paul that Jews and gentiles now formed a new social entity, an Israel other than the familiar one; the same social circumstance that required Paul to design his
system around Israel persuaded a later set of authorships in the
Gospels to tell the story of Jesus's life and teachings, a story in which
(as in the Mishnah's system) Israel formed a datum, a backdrop, but
hardly the main focus of discourse or the precipitating consideration.

What of the Qumran library? Diverse groups in the age in which
the writings of Qumran (and hence the system expressed in the books)
took shape formed within the larger society of the Jews in the Land
of Israel. And not all such smaller groups seized upon the option of
regarding themselves as the whole of (surviving) Israel. Many did not.
One such group, the Pharisees, presents an important structural parallel in its distinctive calculation of the holy calendar; in its provision
of stages for entry into the group; in its interest in the rules of purity
governing meals that realized, in a concrete communion, the social
existence of the group; and in diverse other ways. The Pharisees did
not regard themselves as coexistent with "all Israel," even while they
remained part of the everyday corporate community. They proposed
to exemplify their rules in the streets and marketplaces and to attain
influence in the people at large. So, merely forming what we now call
a sect did not require a group to identify itself as "all Israel," as did
the community of Qumran.

V. *The Question of Religion: What Is Now at Stake?*

The exposition, to this point, therefore leads us from interior questions of religious logic to the exterior ones of history and politics.
Stated in general terms, the issue is whether symbol change ("logic")
generates (for some) social change, or social change ("history")

precipitates symbol change. In the setting of this argument, it is whether society sets the issue, which the system then works out, or whether the inner logic of the system dictates the proportions and order and logic (this logic, as a matter of fact, serves very well where and when it serves). But this impasse in finding the reason need not impede our reaching one solid conclusion concerning systems and the symbolic transactions realized in them. It is the priority of the social entity in systemic formation, and this leads me back to my initial definition, for the present purpose and context, of religion and of what we study when we study religion—not history, not literature, not theology—but religion.

The religious system of the social order begins in the social entity, whether of two persons or of two hundred or of ten thousand—there and not in their canonical writings or even in their politics. The social group, however formed, frames the system; the system then defines its canon within and addresses the larger setting, the polis without. For our part, we describe systems from their end products, the writings that offer our sole entry. But we have then to work our way back from canon to system. We cannot be so deceived as to imagine either that the canon is the system or that the canon creates the system. Then the group's exegesis of the canon in terms of the everyday imparts to the system the power to sustain the community in a reciprocal and self-nourishing process. The community through its exegesis imposes continuity and unity on whatever it has chosen for its canon.

While, therefore, we cannot account for the origin of a system, we can explain its power to persist. That power derives from interchange and movement, like electricity from magnetism via a dynamo, specifically as a symbolic transaction. It is one in which social change comes to expression in symbol change. That symbolic transaction takes place in its exegesis of the systemic canon, which, in literary terms, constitutes the social entity's statement of itself. So, once more, the texts recapitulate the system. The system does not recapitulate the texts. The system comes before the texts and defines the canon. The exegesis of the canon then forms the ongoing social action that sustains the whole. A system selects and orders its documents, imputes to them as a whole, one to the next, a cogency that their original authorships have not expressed in and through the parts. A system expresses, through the composition formed of the documents, its deepest logic, and it also frames the just fit that joins system to circumstance. The whole works its way out through exegesis, and the history of any religious system—that is, the history of religion writ small—is the exegesis of its exegesis. And the first rule of the exegesis of systems is the simplest and the one with which I began and now conclude: the system does not recapitulate the canon; the canon recapitulates the system.

To conclude: the system forms a statement of a social entity, specifying its worldview and way of life in such a way that, to the participants in the system, the whole makes sound sense, beyond argument. So in the beginning are not words of inner and intrinsic affinity but (as Philo would want us to say) the "Word": the transitive logic, the system, all together, all at once, complete, whole, finished. Then the word awaits only the labor of exposition and articulation that the faithful, for centuries to come, will lavish at the altar of the faith.

When we ask that a religious composition speak to a society with a message of the "is" and the "ought" and with a meaning for the everyday, we focus on the power of that system to hold the whole together. It imparts coherence to the society that the system addresses, cogency to the lives of individuals who compose the society. And that system then forms a whole and well-composed structure. What of details—do they register in all their specificity? Yes, the structure stands somewhere, and indeed the place where it stands will secure for the system either an extended or an ephemeral span of life. But the system, for however long it lasts, serves. And that focus on the eternal present justifies my interest in analyzing why a system works (by which I mean that it successfully solves the urgent agenda of issues for the society) when it does, and why it ceases to work (by which I mean that it loses self-evidence—is bereft of its Israel, for example) when it no longer works. Granted, at no point does the canonical evidence contemplate the possibility of the system's not working, not now, not at the end of days; and at no point in the history of Rabbinic Judaism has it had to.

I cannot say that, had Erwin R. Goodenough or Harry A. Wolfson offered such advice when I asked them, on their death beds, for counsel, I would have proved worthy of it. I do not claim that at that time, decades ago, I would have possessed the wit to understand the advice that in the three chapters on history, literature, and religion I now offer. After all, here I stand, at age seventy, nearly five decades later, at the final period of a sustained and continuous scholarly career, and yet what have I to offer as a program for the future? It is no more than a sketch of questions of the most fundamental order imaginable. So, at the last, I find myself still a beginner, still puzzled by the basic questions.

BIBLIOGRAPHY

This bibliography is organized, as is this book, by the rubrics of history, literature, religion, and also theology, as well as by classifications that signify the intended audience and purpose of publications of mine. Within each category, the books are listed chronologically.

1. *The Precritical Stage*

A Life of Yohanan ben Zakkai. Leiden: Brill, 1962. Awarded the Abraham Berliner Prize in Jewish History, Jewish Theological Seminary of America, 1962. 2d ed., completely rev., 1970. Reprint: Classics in Judaic Studies. Binghamton: Global Publications, 2002.
  French translation: *Vie de Yohanan ben Zakkai.* Paris: Clio, 2000.
  Italian translation: Ferrara: Gallio Editori, 2002.
A History of the Jews in Babylonia. 5 vols. Leiden: Brill, 1965–1970. Reprint: South Florida Studies in the History of Judaism. Atlanta: Scholars Press, 1999.
  Vol. 1. *The Parthian Period.* 1965. 2d printing, rev., 1969. 3d printing: Brown Judaic Studies. Chico: Scholars Press, 1984.
    French: *Histoire des Juifs de Babylonie.* Tome 1. *L'epoque parthe.* Paris: Clio, 1997.
  Vol. 2. *The Early Sasanian Period.* 1966.
  Vol. 3. *From Shapur I to Shapur II.* 1968.
  Vol. 4. *The Age of Shapur II.* 1969.
  Vol. 5. *Later Sasanian Times.* 1970.
Aphrahat and Judaism: The Christian Jewish Argument in Fourth Century Iran. Leiden: Brill, 1971. Reprint: South Florida Studies in the History of Judaism. Atlanta: Scholars Press, 1999.

2. *The Beginning of the Critical Enterprise*

Development of a Legend: Studies on the Traditions Concerning Yohanan ben Zakkai. Leiden: Brill, 1970. Reprint: Classics of Judaic. Binghamton: Global Publications, 2002.
The Rabbinic Traditions about the Pharisees before 70. 3 vols. Leiden: Brill, 1971. 2d printing: South Florida Studies in the History of Judaism. Atlanta: Scholars Press, 1999.
  Vol. 1. *The Masters.*
  Vol. 2. *The Houses.*
  Vol. 3. *Conclusions.*
Eliezer ben Hyrcanus: The Tradition and the Man. 2 vols. Leiden: Brill, 1973.
  Vol. 1. *The Tradition.*
  Vol. 2. *The Man.*

3. *Literature*

Describing the Canon, Document by Document; the Stage of Translation,
Form Analysis, and Exegesis

A History of the Mishnaic Law of Purities. Vols. 1–20. Leiden: Brill, 1974–1977.
    Vol. 1. *Kelim: Chapters One through Eleven.* 1974.
    Vol. 2. *Kelim: Chapters Twelve through Thirty.* 1974.
    Vol. 3. *Kelim: Literary and Historical Problems.* 1974.
    Vol. 4. *Ohalot: Commentary.* 1975.
    Vol. 5. *Ohalot: Literary and Historical Problems.* 1975.
    Vol. 6. *Negaim: Mishnah-Tosefta.* 1975.
    Vol. 7. *Negaim: Sifra.* 1975.
    Vol. 8. *Negaim: Literary and Historical Problems.* 1975.
    Vol. 9. *Parah: Commentary.* 1976.
    Vol. 10. *Parah: Literary and Historical Problems.* 1976.
    Vol. 11. *Tohorot: Commentary.* 1976.
    Vol. 12. *Tohorot: Literary and Historical Problems.* 1976.
    Vol. 13. *Miqvaot: Commentary.* 1976.
    Vol. 14. *Miqvaot: Literary and Historical Problems.* 1976.
    Vol. 15. *Niddah: Commentary.* 1976.
    Vol. 16. *Niddah: Literary and Historical Problems.* 1976.
    Vol. 17. *Makhshirin.* 1977.
    Vol. 18. *Zabim.* 1977.
    Vol. 19. *Tebul Yom: Yadayim.* 1977.
    Vol. 20. *Uqsin: Cumulative Index, Parts I–XX.* 1977.
    2d printing of *A History of the Mishnaic Law of Purities,* vols. 13–14: *The Judaic Law*
    of Baptism: Tractate Miqvaot in the Mishnah and the Tosefta—a Form-Analytical Translation
    and Commentary, and a Legal and Religious History. South Florida Studies in the History
    of Judaism. Atlanta: Scholars Press, 1995.
The Tosefta: Translated from the Hebrew. Vols. 2–6. New York: Ktav, 1977–1980. 2d
    printing: South Florida Academic Commentary Series. Atlanta: Scholars Press,
    1990–1999.
    Vol. 2. *Second Division: Moed.*
    Vol. 3. *Third Division: Nashim.*
    Vol. 4. *Fourth Division: Neziqin.*
    Vol. 5. *Fifth Division: Qodoshim.*
    Vol. 6. *Sixth Division: Tohorot.* 2d printing with a new preface.
The Tosefta in English. 2 vols. Peabody: Hendrickson, 2001.
    Vol. 1. *Zeraim, Moed, and Nashim.* With a new introduction.
    Vol. 2. *Neziqin, Qodoshim, and Toharot.* With a new introduction.
A History of the Mishnaic Law of Holy Things. Vols. 1–5. Leiden: Brill, 1979.
    Vol. 1. *Zebahim: Translation and Explanation.*
    Vol. 2. *Menahot: Translation and Explanation.*
    Vol. 3. *Hullin, Bekhorot: Translation and Explanation.*
    Vol. 4. *Arakhin, Temurah: Translation and Explanation.*
    Vol. 5. *Keritot, Meilah, Tamid, Middot, Qinnim: Translation and Explanation.*
A History of the Mishnaic Law of Women. Vols. 1–4. Leiden: Brill, 1979–1980.
    Vol. 1. *Yebamot: Translation and Explanation.*
    Vol. 2. *Ketubot: Translation and Explanation.*
    Vol. 3. *Nedarim, Nazir: Translation and Explanation.*
    Vol. 4. *Sotah, Gittin, Qiddushin: Translation and Explanation.*

Form Analysis and Exegesis: A Fresh Approach to the Interpretation of Mishnah. Minneapolis: University of Minnesota Press, 1980.
A History of the Mishnaic Law of Appointed Times. Vols. 1–4. Leiden: Brill, 1981–1983.
    Vol. 1. *Shabbat: Translation and Explanation.*
    Vol. 2. *Erubin, Pesahim: Translation and Explanation.*
    Vol. 3. *Sheqalim, Yoma, Sukkah: Translation and Explanation.*
    Vol. 4. *Besah, Rosh Hashanah, Taanit, Megillah, Moed Qatan, Hagigah: Translation and Explanation.*
The Talmud of the Land of Israel: A Preliminary Translation and Explanation. Vols. 9–12, 14–15, 17–34. Chicago: Univeristy of Chicago Press, 1982–1991.
    Vol. 9. *Hallah.* 1991.
    Vol. 10. *Orlah, Bikkurim.* 1991.
    Vol. 11. *Shabbat.* 1991.
    Vol. 12. *Erubin.* 1990.
    Vol. 14. *Yoma.* 1990.
    Vol. 15. *Sheqalim.* 1990.
    Vol. 17. *Sukkah.* 1988.
    Vol. 18. *Besah, Taanit.* 1987.
    Vol. 19. *Megillah.* 1987.
    Vol. 20. *Hagigah, Moed Qatan.* 1986.
    Vol. 21. *Yebamot.* 1986.
    Vol. 22. *Ketubot.* 1985.
    Vol. 23. *Nedarim.* 1985.
    Vol. 24. *Nazir.* 1985.
    Vol. 25. *Gittin.* 1985
    Vol. 26. *Qiddushin.* 1984.
    Vol. 27. *Sotah.* 1984.
    Vol. 28. *Baba Qamma.* 1984.
    Vol. 29. *Baba Mesia.* 1984.
    Vol. 30. *Baba Batra.* 1984.
    Vol. 31. *Sanhedrin, Makkot.* 1984.
    Vol. 32. *Shebuot.* 1983.
    Vol. 33. *Abodah Zarah.* 1982.
    Vol. 34. *Horayot, Niddah.* 1982.
Editor: *In the Margins of the Yerushalmi: Notes on the English Translation.* Brown Judaic Studies. Chico: Scholars Press, 1983.
Torah from Our Sages: Pirke Avot—a New American Translation and Explanation. Chappaqua: Rossel, 1983. Paperback ed., 1987.
Editor: *Law as Literature.* With William Scott Green. Semeia Studies. Chico: Scholars Press, 1983.
A History of the Mishnaic Law of Damages. Vols. 1–4. Leiden: Brill, 1983–1985.
    Vol. 1. *Baba Qamma: Translation and Explanation.*
    Vol. 2. *Baba Mesia: Translation and Explanation.*
    Vol. 3. *Baba Batra, Sanhedrin, Makkot: Translation and Explanation.*
    Vol. 4. *Shebuot, Eduyyot, Abodah Zarah, Abot, Horayyot: Translation and Explanation.*
The Talmud of Babylonia: An American Translation. Brown Judaic Studies. Vols. 1–6, 11–15, 17–25, 27–29, 31–34, 36. Chico, then Atlanta: Scholars Press, 1984–1995.
    Vol. 1. *Tractate Berakhot.*
    Vol. 2. *Tractate Shabbat.*
      A. *Chapters One and Two.*
      B. *Chapters Three through Six.*
      C. *Chapters Seven through Ten.*

D. *Chapters Eleven through Seventeen.*
E. *Chapters Eighteen through Twenty-Four.*
Vol. 3. *Tractate Erubin.*
   A. *Chapters One and Two.*
   B. *Chapters Three and Four.*
   C. *Chapters Five and Six.*
   D. *Chapters Seven through Ten.*
Vol. 4. *Tractate Pesahim.*
   A. *Chapter One.*
   B. *Chapters Two and Three.*
   C. *Chapters Four through Six.*
   D. *Chapters Seven and Eight.*
   E. *Chapters Nine and Ten.*
Vol. 5. *Tractate Yoma.*
   A. *Chapters One and Two.*
   B. *Chapters Three through Five.*
   C. *Chapters Six through Eight.*
Vol. 6. *Tractate Sukkah.*
Vol. 11. *Tractate Moed Qatan.*
Vol. 12. *Tractate Hagigah.*
Vol. 13. *Tractate Yebamot.*
   A. *Chapters One through Three.*
   B. *Chapters Four through Six.*
   C. *Chapters Seven through Nine.*
   D. *Chapters Ten through Sixteen.*
Vol. 14. *Tractate Ketubot.*
   A. *Chapters One through Three.*
   B. *Chapters Four through Seven.*
   C. *Chapters Eight through Thirteen.*
Vol. 15. *Tractate Nedarim.*
   A. *Chapters One through Four.*
   B. *Chapters Five through Eleven.*
Vol. 17. *Tractate Sotah.*
Vol. 18. *Tractate Gittin.*
   A. *Chapters One through Three.*
   B. *Chapters Four and Five.*
   C. *Chapters Six through Nine.*
Vol. 19. *Tractate Qiddushin.*
   A. *Chapter One.*
   B. *Chapters Two through Four.*
Vol. 20. *Tractate Baba Qamma.*
   A. *Chapters One through Three.*
   B. *Chapters Four through Seven.*
   C. *Chapters Eight through Ten.*
Vol. 21. *Tractate Baba Mesia.*
   A. *Introduction, Chapters One and Two.*
   B. *Chapters Three and Four.*
   C. *Chapters Five and Six.*
   D. *Chapters Seven through Ten.*
Vol. 22. *Tractate Baba Batra.*
   A. *Chapters One and Two.*
   B. *Chapter Three.*

    C. *Chapters Four through Six.*
    D. *Chapters Seven and Eight.*
    E. *Chapters Nine and Ten.*
Vol. 23. *Tractate Sanhedrin.*
    A. *Chapters One through Three.*
    B. *Chapters Four through Eight.*
    C. *Chapters Nine through Eleven.*
Vol. 24. *Tractate Makkot.*
Vol. 25. *Tractate Abodah Zarah.*
    A. *Chapters One and Two.*
    B. *Chapters Three, Four, and Five.*
Vol. 27. *Tractate Shebuot.*
    A. *Chapters One through Three.*
    B. *Chapters Four through Eight.*
Vol. 28. *Tractate Zebahim.*
    A. *Chapters One through Three.*
    B. *Chapters Four through Eight.*
    C. *Chapters Nine through Fourteen.*
Vol. 29. *Tractate Menahot.*
    A. *Chapters One through Three.*
    B. *Chapters Four through Seven.*
    C. *Chapters Eight through Thirteen.*
Vol. 31. *Tractate Bekhorot.*
    A. *Chapters One through Four.*
    B. *Chapters Five through Nine.*
Vol. 32. *Tractate Arakhin.*
Vol. 33. *Tractate Temurah.*
Vol. 34. *Tractate Keritot.*
Vol. 36. *Tractate Niddah.*
    A. *Chapters One through Three.*
    B. *Chapters Four through Ten.*
For *Leviticus Rabbah,* see *Judaism and Scripture: The Evidence of Leviticus Rabbah,* in section 5, below.
Genesis Rabbah, The Judaic Commentary on Genesis: A New American Translation. 3 vols. Brown Judaic Studies. Atlanta: Scholars Press, 1985.
    Vol. 1. *Parashiyyot One through Thirty-Three: Genesis 1:1–8:14.*
    Vol. 2. *Parashiyyot Thirty-Four through Sixty-Seven: Genesis 8:15–28:9.*
    Vol. 3. *Parashiyyot Sixty-Eight through One Hundred: Genesis 28:10–50:26.*
Sifra, The Judaic Commentary on Leviticus: A New Translation—the Leper, Leviticus 13:1–14:57. With a section by Roger Brooks. Brown Judaic Studies. Chico: Scholars Press, 1985. Based on *Negaim, Sifra,* vol. 6 of *A History of the Mishnaic Law of Purities.*
Editor: *The Tosefta: Translated from the Hebrew.* Vol. 1. *The First Division (Zeraim).* New York: Ktav, 1985.
The Tosefta: Its Structure and Its Sources. Brown Judaic Studies. Atlanta: Scholars Press, 1986. Reprise of pertinent results in *A History of the Mishnaic Law of Purities.*
Sifré to Numbers: An American Translation. 2 vols. Brown Judaic Studies. Atlanta: Scholars Press, 1986.
    Vol. 1. *1–58.*
    Vol. 2. *59–115.* The translation of *Parashiyyot* 116–161 is given in *Sifré to Numbers,* vol. 12 of *The Components of the Rabbinic Documents: From the Whole to the Parts* (see section 6, below).

The Fathers according to Rabbi Nathan: An Analytical Translation and Explanation. Brown Judaic Studies. Atlanta: Scholars Press, 1986.
The Mishnah: A New Translation. New Haven and London: Yale University Press, 1987. Choice, Outstanding Academic Book List, 1989. 2d printing, 1990. Paperbound ed., 1991. CD Rom ed.: Logos, 1996. CD Rom/Web ed.: OakTree Software, Inc. Altamonte Springs, Fla.
Pesiqta deRab Kahana. An Analytical Translation and Explanation. 2 vols. Brown Judaic Studies. Atlanta: Scholars Press, 1987.
　Vol. 1. *1–14.*
　Vol. 2. *15–28, with an Introduction to Pesiqta deRab Kahana.*
For *Pesiqta Rabbati,* see *From Tradition to Imitation: The Plan and Program of Pesiqta deRab Kahana and Pesiqta Rabbati,* in section 4, below.
Sifré to Deuteronomy: An Analytical Translation. 2 vols. Brown Judaic Studies. Atlanta: Scholars Press, 1987.
　Vol. 1. *Pisqaot One through One Hundred Forty-Three: Debarim, Waethanan, Eqeb, Re'eh.*
　Vol. 2. *Pisqaot One Hundred Forty-Four through Three Hundred Fifty-Seven: Shofetim, Ki Tese, Ki Tabo, Nesabim, Ha'azinu, Zot Habberakhah.*
Sifra: An Analytical Translation. 3 vols. Brown Judaic Studies. Atlanta: Scholars Press, 1988.
　Vol. 1. *Introduction and Vayyiqra Dibura Denedabah and Vayiqqra Dibura Dehobah.*
　Vol. 2. *Sav, Shemini, Tazria, Negaim, Mesora, and Zabim.*
　Vol. 3. *Aharé Mot, Qedoshim, Emor, Behar, and Behuqotai.*
Mekhilta Attributed to R. Ishmael: An Analytical Translation. 2 vols. Brown Judaic Studies. Atlanta: Scholars Press, 1988.
　Vol. 1. *Pisha, Beshallah, Shirata, and Vayassa.*
　Vol. 2. *Amalek, Bahodesh, Neziqin, Kaspa, and Shabbata*
Translating the Classics of Judaism: In Theory and in Practice. Brown Judaic Studies. Atlanta: Scholars Press, 1989.
Lamentations Rabbah: An Analytical Translation. Brown Judaic Studies. Atlanta: Scholars Press, 1989.
Esther Rabbah I: An Analytical Translation. Brown Judaic Studies. Atlanta: Scholars Press, 1989.
Ruth Rabbah: An Analytical Translation. Brown Judaic Studies. Atlanta: Scholars Press, 1989.
Song of Songs Rabbah: An Analytical Translation. 2 vols. Brown Judaic Studies. Atlanta: Scholars Press, 1990.
　Vol. 1. *Song of Songs Rabbah to Song Chapters One through Three.*
　Vol. 2. *Song of Songs Rabbah to Song Chapters Four through Eight.*

4. History of Ideas, Law, and Literature

Introducing the Documents, Comparing and Contrasting the Documentary Components of the Canon of Formative Judaism

Invitation to the Talmud: A Teaching Book. New York: Harper & Row, 1973. 2d printing, 1974. Paperback ed., 1975. Reprint, 1982. 2d ed., completely rev.: San Francisco: Harper & Row, 1984. Paperback ed., 1988. 2d printing, in paperback, of the second ed.: South Florida Studies in the History of Judaism. Atlanta: Scholars Press, 1998. 3d printing: Classics in Judaic Studies. Binghamton: Global Publications, 2000.
A History of the Mishnaic Law of Purities. Vols. 21–22. Leiden: Brill, 1977.
　Vol. 21. *The Redaction and Formulation of the Order of Purities in the Mishnah and Tosefta.*
　Vol. 22. *The Mishnaic System of Uncleanness: Its Context and History.*

The Mishnah before 70. Brown Judaic Studies. Atlanta: Scholars Press, 1987. Reprise of pertinent results of *A History of the Mishnah Law of Purities*, vols. 3, 5, 8, 10, 12, 14, 16, 17, 18.

A History of the Mishnaic Law of Holy Things. Vol. 6. *The Mishnaic System of Sacrifice and Sanctuary.* Leiden: Brill, 1979.

A History of the Mishnaic Law of Women. Vol. 5. *The Mishnaic System of Women.* Leiden: Brill, 1980.

A History of the Mishnaic Law of Appointed Times. Vol. 5. *The Mishnaic System of Appointed Times.* Leiden: Brill, 1981.

The Talmud of the Land of Israel: A Preliminary Translation and Explanation. Vol. 35. *Introduction, Taxonomy.* Chicago: University of Chicago Press, 1983.

A History of the Mishnaic Law of Damages. Vol. 5. *The Mishnaic System of Damages.* Leiden: Brill, 1985.

The Integrity of Leviticus Rabbah: The Problem of the Autonomy of a Rabbinic Document. Brown Judaic Studies. Chico: Scholars Press, 1985.

Comparative Midrash: The Plan and Program of Genesis Rabbah and Leviticus Rabbah. Brown Judaic Studies. Atlanta: Scholars Press, 1986.

Canon and Connection: Intertextuality in Judaism. Studies in Judaism. Lanham: University Press of America, 1986.

From Tradition to Imitation: The Plan and Program of Pesiqta deRab Kahana and Pesiqta Rabbati. Brown Judaic Studies. Atlanta: Scholars Press, 1987. With a fresh translation of *Pesiqta Rabbati Pisqaot* 1–5, 15.

Midrash as Literature: The Primacy of Documentary Discourse. Studies in Judaism. Lanham: University Press of America, 1987.

The Bavli and Its Sources: The Question of Tradition in the Case of Tractate Sukkah. Brown Judaic Studies. Atlanta: Scholars Press, 1987.

What Is Midrash? Philadelphia: Fortress Press, 1987. 2d printing: Atlanta: Scholars Press, 1994.

Sifré to Deuteronomy: An Introduction to the Rhetorical, Logical, and Topical Program. Brown Judaic Studies. Atlanta: Scholars Press, 1987.

Invitation to Midrash: The Working of Rabbinic Bible Interpretation. A Teaching Book. San Francisco: Harper & Row, 1988. 2d printing, in paperback: South Florida Studies in the History of Judaism. Atlanta: Scholars Press, 1998.

Sifra in Perspective: The Documentary Comparison of the Midrashim of Ancient Judaism. Brown Judaic Studies. Atlanta: Scholars Press, 1988.

Mekhilta Attributed to R. Ishmael: An Introduction to Judaism's First Scriptural Encyclopaedia. Brown Judaic Studies. Atlanta: Scholars Press, 1988.

Uniting the Dual Torah: Sifra and the Problem of the Mishnah. Cambridge and New York: Cambridge University Press, 1989.

The Midrash Compilations of the Sixth and Seventh Centuries. An Introduction to the Rhetorical, Logical, and Topical Program. 4 vols. Brown Judaic Studies. Atlanta: Scholars Press, 1990.
Vol. 1. *Lamentations Rabbah.*
Vol. 2. *Esther Rabbah I.*
Vol. 3. *Ruth Rabbah.*
Vol. 4. *Song of Songs Rabbah.*

A Midrash Reader. Minneapolis: Augsburg-Fortress, 1990. 2d printing: Atlanta: Scholars Press, 1994.

Making the Classics in Judaism: The Three Stages of Literary Formation. Brown Judaic Studies. Atlanta: Scholars Press, 1990.

The Mishnah: An Introduction. Northvale, N.J.: Jason Aronson, 1989. Paperback ed., 1994.

The Midrash: An Introduction. Northvale, N.J.: Jason Aronson, 1990. Paperback ed., 1994.

The Canonical History of Ideas: The Place of the So-Called Tannaite Midrashim—Mekhilta Attributed to R. Ishmael, Sifra, Sifré to Numbers, and Sifré to Deuteronomy. South Florida Studies in the History of Judaism. Atlanta: Scholars Press, 1990.

Tradition as Selectivity: Scripture, Mishnah, Tosefta, and Midrash in the Talmud of Babylonia—the Case of Tractate Arakhin. South Florida Studies in the History of Judaism. Atlanta: Scholars Press, 1990.

Language as Taxonomy: The Rules for Using Hebrew and Aramaic in the Babylonian Talmud. South Florida Studies in the History of Judaism. Atlanta: Scholars Press, 1990.

The Bavli That Might Have Been: The Tosefta's Theory of Mishnah-Commentary Compared with That of the Babylonian Talmud. South Florida Studies in the History of Judaism. Atlanta: Scholars Press, 1990.

The Talmud: Close Encounters. Minneapolis: Fortress Press, 1991. 2d printing, 1996.

The Rules of Composition of the Talmud of Babylonia: The Cogency of the Bavli's Composite. South Florida Studies in the History of Judaism. Atlanta: Scholars Press, 1991.

The Bavli's One Voice: Types and Forms of Analytical Discourse and Their Fixed Order of Appearance. South Florida Studies in the History of Judaism. Atlanta: Scholars Press, 1991.

The Bavli's One Statement. The Metapropositional Program of Babylonian Talmud Tractate Zebahim Chapters One and Five. South Florida Studies in the History of Judaism. Atlanta: Scholars Press, 1991.

How the Bavli Shaped Rabbinic Discourse. South Florida Studies in the History of Judaism. Atlanta: Scholars Press, 1991.

The Discourse of the Bavli: Language, Literature, and Symbolism—Five Recent Findings. South Florida Studies in the History of Judaism. Atlanta: Scholars Press, 1991.

The Yerushalmi, the Talmud of the Land of Israel: An Introduction. Northvale, N.J.: Jason Aronson, 1992.

The Tosefta: An Introduction. South Florida Studies in the History of Judaism. Atlanta: Scholars Press, 1992.

The Bavli, the Talmud of Babylonia: An Introduction. South Florida Studies in the History of Judaism. Atlanta: Scholars Press, 1992.

The Bavli's Massive Miscellanies: The Problem of Agglutinative Discourse in the Talmud of Babylonia. South Florida Studies in the History of Judaism. Atlanta: Scholars Press, 1992.

Sources and Traditions: Types of Composition in the Talmud of Babylonia. South Florida Studies in the History of Judaism. Atlanta: Scholars Press, 1992.

The Law behind the Laws: The Bavli's Essential Discourse. South Florida Studies in the History of Judaism. Atlanta: Scholars Press, 1992.

The Bavli's Primary Discourse: Mishnah Commentary, Its Rhetorical Paradigms, and Their Theological Implications in the Talmud of Babylonia Tractate Moed Qatan. South Florida Studies in the History of Judaism. Atlanta: Scholars Press, 1992.

How to Study the Bavli: The Languages, Literatures, and Lessons of the Talmud of Babylonia. South Florida Studies in the History of Judaism. Atlanta: Scholars Press, 1992.

Form-Analytical Comparison in Rabbinic Judaism: Structure and Form in The Fathers and The Fathers according to Rabbi Nathan. South Florida Studies in the History of Judaism. Atlanta: Scholars Press, 1992.

The Bavli's Intellectual Character: The Generative Problematic in Bavli Baba Qamma Chapter One and Bavli Shabbat Chapter One. South Florida Studies in the History of Judaism. Atlanta: Scholars Press, 1992.

Decoding the Talmud's Exegetical Program: From Detail to Principle in the Bavli's Quest for Generalization—Tractate Shabbat. South Florida Studies in the History of Judaism. Atlanta: Scholars Press, 1992.

The Principal Parts of the Bavli's Discourse: A Final Taxonomy—Mishnah-Commentary, Sources, Traditions, and Agglutinative Miscellanies. South Florida Studies in the History of Judaism. Atlanta: Scholars Press, 1992.

The Torah in the Talmud: A Taxonomy of the Uses of Scripture in the Talmuds—Tractate Qiddushin in the Talmud of Babylonia and the Talmud of the Land of Israel. 2 vols. South Florida Studies in the History of Judaism. Atlanta: Scholars Press, 1993.
Vol. 1. *Bavli Qiddushin Chapter One.*
Vol. 2. *Yerushalmi Qiddushin Chapter One, and a Comparison of the Uses of Scripture by the Two Talmuds.*
The Bavli's Unique Voice: A Systematic Comparison of the Talmud of Babylonia and the Talmud of the Land of Israel. 7 vols. South Florida Studies in the History of Judaism. Atlanta: Scholars Press, 1993.
Vol. 1. *Bavli and Yerushalmi Qiddushin Chapter One Compared and Contrasted.*
Vol. 2. *Yerushalmi's, Bavli's, and Other Canonical Documents' Treatment of the Program of Mishnah-Tractate Sukkah Chapters One, Two, and Four Compared and Contrasted: A Reprise and Revision of The Bavli and Its Sources.*
Vol. 3. *Bavli and Yerushalmi to Selected Mishnah-Chapters in the Division of Moed: Erubin Chapter One and Moed Qatan Chapter Three.*
Vol. 4. *Bavli and Yerushalmi to Selected Mishnah-Chapters in the Division of Nashim: Gittin Chapter Five and Nedarim Chapter One, and Niddah Chapter One.*
Vol. 5. *Bavli and Yerushalmi to Selected Mishnah-Chapters in the Division of Neziqin: Baba Mesia Chapter One and Makkot Chapters One and Two.*
Vol. 6. *Bavli and Yerushalmi to a Miscellany of Mishnah-Chapters: Gittin Chapter One, Qiddushin Chapter Two, and Hagigah Chapter Three.*
Vol. 7. *What Is Unique about the Bavli in Context? An Answer Based on Inductive Description, Analysis, and Comparison.*
From Text to Historical Context in Rabbinic Judaism: Historical Facts in Systemic Documents. 3 vols. South Florida Studies in the History of Judaism. Atlanta: Scholars Press, 1993–1994.
Vol. 1. *The Mishnah, Tosefta, Abot, Sifra, Sifré to Numbers, and Sifré to Deuteronomy.* 1993.
Vol. 2. *The Later Midrash-Compilations: Genesis Rabbah, Leviticus Rabbah, Pesiqta deRab Kahana.* 1994.
Vol. 3. *The Latest Midrash-Compilations: Song of Songs Rabbah, Ruth Rabbah, Esther Rabbah I, and Lamentations Rabbah.* 1994.
Introduction to Rabbinic Literature. Doubleday Anchor Reference Library. New York: Doubleday, 1994. Religious Book Club Selection, 1994. Paperback ed., 1999. Italian translation: Bologna: Edizioni Piemme, 2003.
Where the Talmud Comes From: A Talmudic Phenomenology—Identifying the Free-Standing Building Blocks of Talmudic Discourse. South Florida Studies in the History of Judaism. Atlanta: Scholars Press, 1995.
The Initial Phases of the Talmud's Judaism. 4 vols. South Florida Studies in the History of Judaism. Atlanta: Scholars Press, 1995.
Vol. 1. *Exegesis of Scripture.*
Vol. 2. *Exemplary Virtue.*
Vol. 3. *Social Ethics.*
Vol. 4. *Theology.*
Talmudic Dialectics: Types and Forms. 2 vols. South Florida Studies in the History of Judaism. Atlanta: Scholars Press, 1995.
Vol. 1. *Introduction: Tractate Berakhot and the Divisions of Appointed Times and Women.*
Vol. 2. *The Divisions of Damages and Holy Things and Tractate Niddah.*
Rationality and Structure: The Bavli's Anomalous Juxtapositions. South Florida Studies in the History of Judaism. Atlanta: Scholars Press, 1997.
The Modes of Thought of Rabbinic Judaism. 2 vols. Academic Studies in the History of Judaism. Binghamton: Global Publications, 2000.
Vol. 1. *Types of Analysis.*
Vol. 2. *Types of Argumentation.*

Extra- and Non-documentary Writing in the Canon of Formative Judaism. 3 vols. Academic Studies in the History of Judaism. Binghamton: Global Publications, 2001.
Vol. 1. *The Pointless Parallel: Hans-Jürgen Becker and the Myth of the Autonomous Tradition in Rabbinic Documents.*
Vol. 2. *Paltry Parallels: The Negligible Proportion and Peripheral Role of Free-Standing Compositions in Rabbinic Documents.*
Vol. 3. *Peripatetic Parallels.* Brown Judaic Studies. Chico: Scholars Press, 1985. 2d ed., rev., of *The Peripatetic Saying: The Problem of the Thrice-Told Tale in Talmudic Literature.*

5. Religion

Reconstructing and Interpreting the History of the Formation of Judaism

From Politics to Piety: The Emergence of Pharisaic Judaism. Englewood Cliffs: Prentice-Hall, 1973. 2d printing: New York: Ktav, 1978.
Japanese translation: *Parisai Ha towa Nanika. Seifi Kara Keiken e.* Tokyo: Kyo Bun Kwan, 1988.
The Idea of Purity in Ancient Judaism: The Haskell Lectures, 1972–1973. Leiden: E. J. Brill, 1973.
Judaism. The Evidence of the Mishnah. Chicago: University of Chicago Press, 1981. Choice, Outstanding Academic Book List, 1982–1983. Paperback ed., 1984. 2d printing, 1985. 3d printing, 1986. 2d ed., augmented: Brown Judaic Studies. Atlanta: Scholars Press, 1987.
Hebrew translation: *Hayyahadut le'edut hammishnah.* Tel Aviv: Sifriat Poalim, 1987.
Italian translation: *Il Giudaismo nella testimonianza della Mishnah.* Translated by Giorgio Volpe. Bologna: Centro Editoriale Dehoniane, 1995.
Judaism without Christianity: An Introduction to the Religious System of the Mishnah in Historical Context. Hoboken: Ktav Publishing House, 1991. Abbreviated version of *Judaism: The Evidence of the Mishnah.*
Judaism in Society: The Evidence of the Yerushalmi—toward the Natural History of a Religion. Chicago: University of Chicago Press, 1983. Choice, Outstanding Academic Book List, 1984–1985. 2d printing, with a new preface: South Florida Studies in the History of Judaism. Atlanta: Scholars Press, 1991.
Ancient Israel after Catastrophe: The Religious World-View of the Mishnah—the Richard Lectures for 1982. Charlottesville: University Press of Virginia, 1983.
Judaism in the Beginning of Christianity. Philadelphia: Fortress Press, 1983. 2d printing, 1988. 3d printing, 1990. 5th printing,1994. British ed.: London: SPCK, 1984.
French translation: *Le judaisme à l'aube du christianisme.* Paris: Editions du Cerf, 1986.
Dutch translation: *De Joodse wieg van het Christendom.* Kampen: J. H. Kok, 1987.
Norwegian translation: *Jødedommen i den første kristne tid.* Translated by Johan B. Hygen. Trondheim: Tapir Publishers, University of Trondheim, 1987.
German translation: *Judentum in frühchristlicher Zeit.* Stuttgart: Calwerverlag, 1988.
Italian translation: *Il Giudaismo nei primi secoli del Christianismo.* Brescia: Morcelliano, 1989.
Japanese translation: *Iesu Jidai No Yudayakyo.* Tokyo: Kyo Bun Kwan, 1992.
The Foundations of Judaism: Method, Teleology, Doctrine. 3 vols. Philadelphia: Fortress Press, 1983–1985.
Vol. 1. *Midrash in Context: Exegesis in Formative Judaism.* 2d printing: Brown Judaic Studies. Atlanta: Scholars Press, 1988.
Vol. 2. *Messiah in Context: Israel's History and Destiny in Formative Judaism.* 2d printing: Studies in Judaism. Lanham: University Press of America, 1988.

Vol. 3. *Torah: From Scroll to Symbol in Formative Judaism.* 2d printing: Brown Judaic Studies. Atlanta: Scholars Press, 1988.

The Foundations of Judaism. Philadelphia: Fortress Press, 1988. Abridged ed. of the trilogy. 2d printing: South Florida Studies in the History of Judaism. Atlanta: Scholars Press, 1994.

Dutch translation: *Grondslagen van het Jodendom: Tora, Misjna, Messias.* Translated by Liesbeth Mok and Klaas A. D. Smelik. Boxtel and Leuven: Katholieke Bijbelstichting and Vlaamse Bijbelstichting, 1991.

Italian translation: *I fondamenti del giudaismo.* Translated by Piero Stefani. Florence: Editrice la Giuntina, 1992.

Editor: *"To See Ourselves as Others See Us": Jews, Christians, "Others" in Late Antiquity.* Studies in the Humanities. Chico: Scholars Press, 1985.

The Oral Torah—the Sacred Books of Judaism: An Introduction. San Francisco: Harper & Row, 1985. Paperback ed., 1987. Bnai Brith Jewish Book Club Selection, 1986. 2d printing: South Florida Studies in the History of Judaism. Atlanta: Scholars Press, 1991.

Judaism and Scripture: The Evidence of Leviticus Rabbah. Chicago: University of Chicago Press, 1986. Fresh translation of Margulies's text and systematic analysis of problems of composition and redaction. Jewish Book Club Selection, 1986.

Judaism: The Classical Statement—the Evidence of the Bavli. Chicago: University of Chicago Press, 1986. Choice, Outstanding Academic Book List, 1987.

Judaism in the Matrix of Christianity. Philadelphia: Fortress Press, 1986. British ed.: Edinburgh, T. & T. Collins, 1988. 2d printing, with a new introduction: South Florida Studies in the History of Judaism. Atlanta: Scholars Press, 1990.

Editor: *Goodenough on History of Religion and on Judaism.* Brown Judaic Studies. Atlanta: Scholars Press, 1986.

From Description to Conviction: Essays on the History and Theology of Judaism. Brown Judaic Studies. Atlanta: Scholars Press, 1987.

Editor: *Scriptures of the Oral Torah: Sanctification and Salvation in the Sacred Books of Judaism.* San Francisco: Harper & Row, 1987. Jewish Book Club Selection, 1988. 2d printing: Brown Judaic Studies. Atlanta: Scholars Press, 1990.

Vanquished Nation, Broken Spirit: The Virtues of the Heart in Formative Judaism. New York: Cambridge University Press, 1987. Jewish Book Club Selection, 1987.

Editor: *Judaic Perspectives on Ancient Israel.* Philadelphia: Fortress Press, 1987.

Editor: *Judaisms and Their Messiahs in the Beginning of Christianity.* With William Scott Green. New York: Cambridge University Press, 1987.

Judaism and Christianity in the Age of Constantine: Issues of the Initial Confrontation. Chicago: University of Chicago Press, 1987.

Death and Birth of Judaism: The Impact of Christianity, Secularism, and the Holocaust on Jewish Faith. New York: Basic Books, 1987. 2d printing: South Florida Studies in the History of Judaism. Atlanta: Scholars Press, 1993.

Self-Fulfilling Prophecy: Exile and Return in the History of Judaism. Boston: Beacon Press, 1987. 2d printing, with a new introduction: South Florida Studies in the History of Judaism. Atlanta: Scholars Press, 1990.

The Enchantments of Judaism: Rites of Transformation from Birth through Death. New York: Basic Books, 1987. Judaic Book Club Selection, September 1987. Jewish Book Club Selection, October 1987. 2d printing: Atlanta: South Florida Studies in the History of Judaism. Scholars Press, 1991. Edition on tape: Princeton: Recording for the Blind, 1992.

The Making of the Mind of Judaism. Brown Judaic Studies. Atlanta: Scholars Press, 1987.

Editor: *Goodenough's Jewish Symbols: An Abridged Edition.* Princeton: Princeton University Press, 1988. Paperback ed., 1992.

Editor: *Science, Magic, and Religion in Concert and in Conflict: Judaic, Christian, Philosophical, and Social Scientific Perspectives.* New York: Oxford University Press, 1988. Paperback ed., 1993.

Judaism and Its Social Metaphors: Israel in the History of Jewish Thought. New York: Cambridge University Press, 1988.

The Incarnation of God: The Character of Divinity in Formative Judaism. Philadelphia: Fortress Press, 1988. Reprint: South Florida Studies in the History of Judaism. Atlanta: Scholars Press, 1992. Reprint: Classics of Judaic. Binghamton: Global Publications, 2000.

The Formation of the Jewish Intellect: Making Connections and Drawing Conclusions in the Traditional System of Judaism. Brown Judaic Studies. Atlanta: Scholars Press, 1988.

Writing with Scripture: The Authority and Uses of the Hebrew Bible in the Torah of Formative Judaism. Philadelphia: Fortress Press, 1989. 2d printing: South Florida Studies in the History of Judaism. Atlanta: Scholars Press, 1994.

The Economics of the Mishnah. Chicago: University of Chicago Press, 1989. Reprint: South Florida Studies in the History of Judaism. Atlanta: Scholars Press, 1998.

The Philosophical Mishnah. 4 vols. Brown Judaic Studies. Atlanta: Scholars Press, 1989.
Vol. 1. *The Initial Probe.*
Vol. 2. *The Tractates' Agenda: From Abodah Zarah to Moed Qatan.*
Vol. 3. *The Tractates' Agenda: From Nazir to Zebahim.*
Vol. 4. *The Repertoire.*

From Literature to Theology in Formative Judaism: Three Preliminary Studies. Brown Judaic Studies. Atlanta: Scholars Press, 1989.

Editor: *The Christian and Judaic Invention of History.* Studies in Religion. Atlanta: Scholars Press for American Academy of Religion, 1990.

Torah through the Ages: A Short History of Judaism. New York and London: Trinity Press International and SCM, 1990.

Rabbinic Political Theory: Religion and Politics in the Mishnah. Chicago: University of Chicago Press, 1991.

Judaism as Philosophy: The Method and Message of the Mishnah. Columbia: University of South Carolina Press, 1991. Paperback ed.: Baltimore: Johns Hopkins University Press, 1999.

Editor: *Essays in Jewish Historiography.* South Florida Studies in the History of Judaism. Atlanta: Scholars Press, 1991. Reprint of essays in *History and Theory* 27 (1988), ed. Ada Rapoport-Albert, with a new introduction and an appendix.

Symbol and Theology in Early Judaism. Minneapolis: Fortress Press, 1991. Reprint: South Florida Studies in the History of Judaism. Atlanta: Scholars Press, 1999.

Judaismo Rabinico. Documentacion y estudios para el dialogo entre Judios y Cristianos. Madrid: El Olivo, 1991. Five lectures in Spanish, given in Madrid in 1991.

Judaism and Story: The Evidence of The Fathers according to Rabbi Nathan. Chicago: University of Chicago Press, 1992.

The Transformation of Judaism: From Philosophy to Religion. Champaign: University of Illinois Press, 1992. Paperback ed.: Baltimore: Johns Hopkins University Press, 1999.

Talmudic Thinking: Language, Logic, and Law. Columbia: University of South Carolina Press, 1992.

Judaism and Zoroastrianism at the Dusk of Late Antiquity: How Two Ancient Faiths Wrote Down Their Great Traditions. South Florida Studies in the History of Judaism. Atlanta: Scholars Press, 1993.

Purity in Rabbinic Judaism: A Systematic Account of the Sources, Media, Effects, and Removal of Uncleanness. South Florida Studies in the History of Judaism. Atlanta: Scholars Press, 1993.

Rabbinic Literature and the New Testament: What We Cannot Show, We Do Not Know. Philadelphia: Trinity Press International, 1993.

Androgynous Judaism: Masculine and Feminine in the Dual Torah. Macon: Mercer University Press, 1993. Jewish Book Club Selection.

Judaism States Its Theology: The Talmudic Re-presentation. South Florida Studies in the History of Judaism. Atlanta: Scholars Press, 1993.

The Judaism behind the Texts: The Generative Premises of Rabbinic Literature. 5 vols. in 7. South Florida Studies in the History of Judaism. Atlanta: Scholars Press, 1993–1994.

    Vol. 1. *The Mishnah.*

        A. *The Division of Agriculture.* 1993.

        B. *The Divisions of Appointed Times, Women, and Damages (through Sanhedrin).* 1993.

        C. *The Divisions of Damages (from Makkot), Holy Things, and Purities.* 1993.

    Vol. 2. *The Tosefta, Tractate Abot, and the Earlier Midrash-Compilations: Sifra, Sifré to Numbers, and Sifré to Deuteronomy.* 1993.

    Vol. 3. *The Later Midrash-Compilations: Genesis Rabbah, Leviticus Rabbah, and Pesiqta de Rab Kahana.* 1994.

    Vol. 4. *The Latest Midrash-Compilations: Song of Songs Rabbah, Ruth Rabbah, Esther Rabbah I, and Lamentations Rabbati, and The Fathers according to Rabbi Nathan.* 1994.

    Vol. 5. *The Talmuds of the Land of Israel and Babylonia.* 1994.

Rabbinic Judaism: The Documentary History of the Formative Age. Bethesda: CDL Press, 1994.

The Judaism the Rabbis Take for Granted. South Florida Studies in the History of Judaism. Atlanta: Scholars Press, 1995.

Judaism's Theological Voice: The Melody of the Talmud. Chicago: University of Chicago Press, 1995.

Rabbinic Judaism: Structure and System. Minneapolis: Fortress Press, 1996. Reprint: South Florida Studies in the History of Judaism. Atlanta: Scholars Press, 1999.

The Presence of the Past, the Pastness of the Present: History, Time, and Paradigm in Rabbinic Judaism. Bethesda: CDL Press, 1996.

Jerusalem and Athens: The Congruity of Talmudic and Classical Philosophy. Supplements to the Journal for the Study of Judaism. Leiden: Brill, 1997.

    Italian translation: Ferrara: Gallio Editori, 2003.

The Theology of Rabbinic Judaism: A Prolegomenon. South Florida Studies on the History of Judaism. Atlanta: Scholars Press, 1997.

The Halakhah of the Oral Torah: A Religious Commentary, Introduction. Vol. 1. Part 1. *Between Israel and God: Faith, Thanksgiving—Tractate Berakhot; Enlandisement; Tractates Kilayim, Shebi'it, and 'Orlah.* South Florida Studies in the History of Judaism. Atlanta: Scholars Press, 1997. The remainder of this project, originally planned for 24 vols., was recast as *The Halakhah: An Encyclopaedia of the Law of Judaism,* below.

The Theological Grammar of the Oral Torah. 3 vols. Binghamton: Dowling College Press/Global Publications of Binghamton University [SUNY], 1999.

    Vol. 1. *Vocabulary: Native Categories.*

    Vol. 2. *Syntax: Connections and Constructions.*

    Vol. 3. *Semantics: Models of Analysis, Explanation and Anticipation.*

The Theology of the Oral Torah: Revealing the Justice of God. Kingston and Montreal: McGill-Queens University Press, and Ithaca: Cornell University Press, 1999.

Rabbinic Judaism: The Theological System. Leiden, Boston, and Cologne: Brill, forthcoming (est.). Condensation, in paperback, of *The Theology of the Oral Torah.*

The Halakhah: An Encyclopaedia of the Law of Judaism. 5 vols. Brill Reference Library of Ancient Judaism. Leiden: Brill, 1999.

    Vol. 1. *Between Israel and God.* Part A. *Faith, Thanksgiving, Enlandisement: Possession and Partnership.*

    Vol. 2. *Between Israel and God.* Part B. *Transcendent Transactions: Where Heaven and Earth Intersect.*

    Vol. 3. *Within Israel's Social Order.*

Vol. 4. *Inside the Walls of the Israelite Household*. Part A. *At the Meeting of Time and Space; Sanctification in the Here and Now—the Table and the Bed; Sanctification and the Marital Bond; the Desacralization of the Household—the Bed.*

Vol. 5. *Inside the Walls of the Israelite Household*. Part B. *The Desacralization of the Household—the Table; Foci, Sources, and Dissemination of Uncleanness; Purification from the Pollution of Death.*

How the Rabbis Liberated Women. South Florida Studies in the History of Judaism. Atlanta: Scholars Press, 1999.

From Scripture to 70: The Pre-rabbinic Beginnings of the Halakhah. South Florida Studies in the History of Judaism. Atlanta: Scholars Press, 1999.

What, Exactly, Did the Rabbinic Sages Mean by "the Oral Torah"? An Inductive Answer to the Question of Rabbinic Judaism. South Florida Studies in the History of Judaism. Atlanta: Scholars Press, 1999.

The Mishnah: Social Perspectives. Leiden: Brill, 1999.

The Mishnah: Religious Perspectives. Leiden: Brill, 1999.

How Judaism Reads the Bible. Baltimore: Chizuk Amuno Congregation, 1999. Published lecture.

The Emergence of Judaism: Jewish Religion in Response to the Critical Issues of the First Six Centuries. Studies in Judaism. Lanham: University Press of America, 2000.

German translation: *Die Gestaltwerdung des Judentums: Die jüdische Religion als Antwort auf die kritischen Herausforderungen der ersten sechs Jahrhunderte der christlichen Åra*. Translated and edited by Johann Maier. Judentum und Umwelt. Frankfurt, Bern, and New York: Peter Lang, 1994.

The Four Stages of Rabbinic Judaism. London: Routledge, 2000.

The Halakhah and the Aggadah: Theological Perspectives. South Florida Studies in the History of Judaism. Atlanta: Scholars Press, 2000.

Recovering Judaism: The Universal Dimension of Jewish Religion. Minneapolis: Fortress Press, 2000.

Scripture and the Generative Premises of the Halakhah: A Systematic Inquiry. 4 vols. Academic Studies in the History of Judaism. Binghamton: Global Publications, 2000.

Vol. 1. *Halakhah Based Principally on Scripture and Halakhic Categories Autonomous of Scripture.*

Vol. 2. *Scripture's Topics Derivatively Amplified in the Halakhah.*

Vol. 3. *Scripture's Topics Independently Developed in the Halakhah: From the Babas through Miqvaot.*

Vol. 4. *Scripture's Topics Independently Developed in the Halakhah: From Moed Qatan through Zebahim.*

The Unity of Rabbinic Discourse. 3 vols. Studies in Judaism. Lanham: University Press of America, 2000.

Vol. 1. *Aggadah in the Halakhah.*

Vol. 2. *Halakhah in the Aggadah.*

Vol. 3. *Halakhah and Aggadah in Concert.*

Dual Discourse, Single Judaism: The Category-Formations of the Halakhah and of the Aggadah Defined, Compared, and Contrasted. Studies in Judaism. Lanham: University Press of America, 2000.

Judaism's Story of Creation: Scripture, Halakhah, Aggadah. Brill Reference Library of Ancient Judaism. Leiden: Brill, 2000.

The Aggadic Role in Halakhic Discourse. 3 vols. Studies in Judaism. Lanham: University Press of America, 2000.

Vol. 1. *An Initial Probe: Three Tractates—Moed Qatan, Nazir, and Horayot; the Mishnah and the Tosefta—the Division of Purities; the Mishnah, the Tosefta, and the Yerushalmi—the Division of Agriculture; the Mishnah-Tosefta-Bavli—the Division of Holy Things.*

Vol. 2. *The Mishnah, Tosefta, Yerushalmi, and Bavli to Tractate Berakhot—the Division of Appointed Times and the Division of Women.*
Vol. 3. *The Mishnah, Tosefta, Yerushalmi, and Bavli to the Division of Damages and Tractate Niddah; Sifra and the two Sifrés.*
The Messiah in Ancient Judaism. With William Scott Green. Brill Reference Library of Ancient Judaism. Leiden: Brill, 2001.
The Theology of the Halakhah. Brill Reference Library of Ancient Judaism. Leiden: E. J. Brill, 2001.
The Social Teaching of Rabbinic Judaism. 3 vols. Brill Reference Library of Ancient Judaism. Leiden: Brill, 2001.
Vol. 1. *Corporate Israel and the Individual Israelite.*
Vol. 2. *Between Israelites.*
Vol. 3. *God's Presence in Israel.*
A Theological Commentary to the Midrash. 9 vols. Studies in Judaism. Lanham: University Press of America, 2001.
Vol. 1. *Pesiqta deRab Kahana.*
Vol. 2. *Genesis Rabbah.*
Vol. 3. *Song of Songs Rabbah.*
Vol. 4. *Leviticus Rabbah.*
Vol. 5. *Lamentations Rabbati.*
Vol. 6. *Ruth Rabbah and Esther Rabbah I.*
Vol. 7. *Sifra.*
Vol. 8. *Sifré to Numbers and Sifré to Deuteronomy.*
Vol. 9. *Mekhilta Attributed to R. Ishmael.*
The Theological Foundations of Rabbinic Midrash. Brill Reference Library of Formative Judaism. Leiden. Brill, 2002. Paperback ed., 2002.

Planned

Editor: *The Mishnah in Contemporary Study.* With Alan Avery-Peck. Leiden: Brill, 2002.
Editor: *The Midrash: An Encyclopaedia of Bible-Interpretation in Formative Judaism.* With Alan J. Avery-Peck. Brill Reference Library of Ancient Judaism. Leiden: Brill, 2003.

6. *Talmudic Hermeneutics*

The Talmud of Babylonia: An Academic Commentary. 36 vols. in 46. South Florida Academic Commentary Series. Atlanta: Scholars Press, 1994–1999.
Vol. 1. *Bavli Tractate Berakhot.*
Vol. 2. *Bavli Tractate Shabbat.*
  A. *Chapters One through Twelve.*
  B. *Chapters Thirteen through Twenty-Four.*
Vol. 3. *Bavli Tractate Erubin.*
  A. *Chapters One through Five.*
  B. *Chapters Six through Eleven.*
Vol. 4. *Bavli Tractate Pesahim.*
  A. *Chapters One through Seven.*
  B. *Bavli Tractate Pesahim: Chapters Eight through Eleven.*
Vol. 5. *Bavli Tractate Yoma.*
Vol. 6. *Bavli Tractate Sukkah.*

Vol. 7. *Bavli Tractate Besah.*
Vol. 8. *Bavli Tractate Rosh Hashanah.*
Vol. 9. *Bavli Tractate Taanit.* 1999.
Vol. 10. *Bavli Tractate Megillah.*
Vol. 11. *Bavli Tractate Moed Qatan.*
Vol. 12. *Bavli Tractate Hagigah.*
Vol. 13. *Bavli Tractate Yebamot.*
   A. *Chapters One through Eight.*
   B. *Chapters Nine through Seventeen.*
Vol. 14. *Bavli Tractate Ketubot.*
   A. *Chapters One through Six.*
   B. *Chapters Seven through Fourteen.*
Vol. 15. *Bavli Tractate Nedarim.*
Vol. 16. *Bavli Tractate Nazir.* 1999.
Vol. 17. *Bavli Tractate Sotah.*
Vol. 18. *Bavli Tractate Gittin.*
Vol. 19. *Bavli Tractate Qiddushin.*
Vol. 20. *Bavli Tractate Baba Qamma.*
Vol. 21. *Bavli Tractate Baba Mesia.*
   A. *Chapters One through Six.*
   B. *Chapters Seven through Eleven.*
Vol. 22. *Bavli Tractate Baba Batra.*
   A. *Chapters One through Six.*
   B. *Chapters Seven through Eleven.*
Vol. 23. *Bavli Tractate Sanhedrin.*
   A. *Chapters One through Seven.*
   B. *Chapters Eight through Twelve.*
Vol. 24. *Bavli Tractate Makkot.*
Vol. 25. *Bavli Tractate Abodah Zarah.*
Vol. 26. *Bavli Tractate Horayot.*
Vol. 27. *Bavli Tractate Shebuot.*
Vol. 28. *Bavli Tractate Zebahim.*
   A. *Chapters One through Seven.*
   B. *Chapters Eight through Fifteen.*
Vol. 29. *Bavli Tractate Menahot.*
   A. *Chapters One through Six.*
   B. *Chapters Seven through Fourteen.*
Vol. 30. *Bavli Tractate Hullin.*
Vol. 31. *Bavli Tractate Bekhorot.*
Vol. 32. *Bavli Tractate Arakhin.*
Vol. 33. *Bavli Tractate Temurah.*
Vol. 34. *Bavli Tractate Keritot.*
Vol. 35. *Bavli Tractate Meilah and Tamid.*
Vol. 36. *Bavli Tractate Niddah.*
The Talmud of Babylonia: A Complete Outline. 4 vols. in 8. South Florida Academic
   Commentary Series. Atlanta: Scholars Press, 1995–1996.
   Vol. 1. *Tractate Berakhot and the Division of Appointed Times.*
      A. *Berakhot, Shabbat, and Erubin.*
      B. *Pesahim through Hagigah.*
   Vol. 2. *The Division of Women.*
      A. *Yebamot through Ketubot.*
      B. *Nedarim through Qiddushin.*
   Vol. 3. *The Division of Damages.*

A. *Baba Qamma through Baba Batra.*
B. *Sanhedrin through Horayot.*
Vol. 4. *The Division of Holy Things and Tractate Niddah.*
A. *Zebahim through Hullin.*
B. *Bekhorot through Niddah.*
The Talmud of the Land of Israel: An Outline of the Second, Third, and Fourth Divisions. 3 vols. in 8. South Florida Academic Commentary Series. Atlanta: Scholars Press, 1995–1996.
Vol. 1. *Tractate Berakhot and the Division of Appointed Times.*
A. *Berakhot and Shabbat.*
B. *Erubin, Yoma, and Besah.*
C. *Pesahim and Sukkah.*
D. *Taanit, Megillah, Rosh Hashanah, Hagigah, and Moed Qatan.*
Vol. 2. *The Division of Women.*
A. *Yebamot to Nedarim.*
B. *Nazir to Sotah.*
Vol. 3. *The Division of Damages and Tractate Niddah.*
A. *Baba Qamma, Baba Mesia, Baba Batra, Horayot, and Niddah.*
B. *Sanhedrin, Makkot, Shebuot, and Abodah Zarah.*
The Two Talmuds Compared. 3 vols. in 14. South Florida Academic Commentary Series. Atlanta: Scholars Press, 1995–1996.
Vol. 1. *Tractate Berakhot and the Division of Appointed Times in the Talmud of the Land of Israel and the Talmud of Babylonia.*
A. *Yerushalmi Tractate Berakhot.*
B. *Tractate Shabbat.*
C. *Tractate Erubin.*
D. *Tractates Yoma and Sukkah.*
E. *Tractate Pesahim.*
F. *Tractates Besah, Taanit, and Megillah.*
G. *Tractates Rosh Hashanah, Hagigah, and Moed Qatan.*
Vol. 2. *The Division of Women in the Talmud of the Land of Israel and the Talmud of Babylonia.*
A. *Tractates Yebamot and Ketubot.*
B. *Tractates Nedarim, Nazir, and Sotah.*
C. *Tractates Qiddushin and Gittin.*
Vol. 3. *The Division of Damages and Tractate Niddah in the Talmud of the Land of Israel and the Talmud of Babylonia.*
A. *Tractates Baba Qamma and Baba Mesia.*
B. *Baba Batra and Niddah.*
C. *Sanhedrin and Makkot.*
D. *Shebuot, Abodah Zarah, and Horayot.*
The Components of the Rabbinic Documents: From the Whole to the Parts. 12 vols. in 32. South Florida Academic Commentary Series. Atlanta: Scholars Press, 1997–1998. 2d printing, in 12 vols., with a new introduction: see *The Midrash: A Form-Analytical Translation and Outline*, below.
Vol. 1. *Sifra.* 1997.
Part i. *Introduction and Parts One through Three, Chapters One through Ninety-Eight.*
Part ii. *Parts Four through Nine, Chapters Ninety-Nine through One Hundred Ninety-Four.*
Part iii. *Parts Ten through Thirteen, Chapters One Hundred Ninety-Five through Two Hundred Seventy-Seven.*
Part iv. *A Topical and Methodical Outline of Sifra.*
Vol. 2. *Esther Rabbah I.* 1997.
Vol. 3. *Ruth Rabbah.* 1997.

Vol. 4. *Lamentations Rabbati.* 1997.
Vol. 5. *Song of Songs Rabbah.* 1997.
  Part i. *Introduction and Parashiyyot One through Four.*
  Part ii. *Parashiyyot Five through Eight and a Topical and Methodical Outline of Song of Songs Rabbah.*
Vol. 6. *The Fathers Attributed to Rabbi Nathan.* 1997.
Vol. 7. *Sifré to Deuteronomy.* 1997.
  Part i. *Introduction and Parts One through Four.*
  Part ii. *Parts Five through Ten.*
  Part iii. *A Topical and Methodical Outline of Sifré to Deuteronomy.*
Vol. 8. *Mekhilta Attributed to R. Ishmael.* 1997.
  Part i. *Introduction; Pisha, Beshallah, and Shirata.*
  Part ii. *Vayassa, Amalek, Bahodesh, Neziqin, Kaspa, and Shabbata.*
  Part iii. *A Topical and Methodical Outline of Mekhilta Attributed to R. Ishmael.*
Vol. 9. *Genesis Rabbah.* 1998.
  Part i. *Introduction; Genesis Rabbah Chapters One through Twenty-One.*
  Part ii. *Genesis Rabbah Chapters Twenty-Two through Forty-Eight.*
  Part iii. *Genesis Rabbah Chapters Forty-Nine through Seventy-Three.*
  Part iv. *Genesis Rabbah Chapters Seventy-Four through One Hundred.*
  Part v. *A Topical and Methodical Outline of Genesis Rabbah: Bereshit through Vaere, Chapters One through Fifty-Seven.*
  Part vi. *A Topical and Methodical Outline of Genesis Rabbah: Hayye Sarah through Miqqes, Chapters Fifty-Eight through One Hundred.*
Vol. 10. *Leviticus Rabbah.* 1998.
  Part i. *Introduction; Leviticus Rabbah Parashiyyot One through Seventeen.*
  Part ii. *Leviticus Rabbah Parashiyyot Eighteen through Thirty-Seven.*
  Part iii. *Leviticus Rabbah: A Topical and Methodical Outline.*
Vol. 11. *Pesiqta deRab Kahana.* 1998.
  Part i. *Introduction; Pesiqta deRab Kahana Pisqaot One through Eleven.*
  Part ii. *Pesiqta deRab Kahana Pisqaot Twelve through Twenty-Eight.*
  Part iii. *Pesiqta deRab Kahana: A Topical and Methodical Outline.*
Vol. 12. *Sifré to Numbers.* 1998.
  Part i. *Introduction; Pisqaot One through Eighty-Four.*
  Part ii. *Pisqaot Eighty-Five through One Hundred Twenty-Two.*
  Part iii. *Pisqaot One Hundred Twenty-Three through One Hundred Sixty-One.*
  Part iv. *Sifré to Numbers: A Topical and Methodical Outline.*
The Midrash: A Form-Analytical Translation and Outline. 12 vols. Peabody: Hendrickson, 2001. Reprint, with a new introduction, of *The Components of the Rabbinic Documents.*
Vol. 1. *Mekhilta Attributed to R. Ishmael.*
Vol. 2. *Sifra.*
Vol. 3. *Sifré to Numbers.*
Vol. 4. *Sifré to Deuteronomy.*
Vol. 5. *Genesis Rabbah.*
Vol. 6. *Leviticus Rabbah.*
Vol. 7. *Pesiqta deRab Kahana.*
Vol. 8. *Song of Songs Rabbah.*
Vol. 9. *Lamentations Rabbati.*
Vol. 10. *Esther Rabbah I.*
Vol. 11. *Ruth Rabbah.*
Vol. 12. *The Fathers according to Rabbi Nathan.*
The Documentary Form-History of Rabbinic Literature. 7 vols. in 14. South Florida Academic Commentary Series. Atlanta: Scholars Press, 1998.
Vol. 1. *The Documentary Forms of the Mishnah.*

Vol. 2. *The Aggadic Sector: Tractate Abot, Abot deRabbi Natan, Sifra, Sifré to Numbers, and Sifré to Deuteronomy.*
Vol. 3. *The Aggadic Sector: Mekhilta Attributed to R. Ishmael and Genesis Rabbah.*
Vol. 4. *The Aggadic Sector: Leviticus Rabbah, and Pesiqta deRab Kahana.*
Vol. 5. *The Aggadic Sector: Song of Songs Rabbah, Ruth Rabbah, Lamentations Rabbati, and Esther Rabbah I.*
Vol. 6. *The Halakhic Sector: The Talmud of the Land of Israel.*
  A. *Berakhot and Shabbat through Taanit.*
  B. *Megillah through Qiddushin.*
  C. *Sotah through Horayot and Niddah.*
Vol. 7. *The Halakhic Sector: The Talmud of Babylonia.*
  A. *Tractates Berakhot and Shabbat through Pesahim.*
  B. *Tractates Yoma through Ketubot.*
  C. *Tractates Nedarim through Baba Mesia.*
  D. *Tractates Baba Batra through Horayot.*
  E. *Tractates Zebahim through Bekhorot.*
  F. *Tractates Arakhin through Niddah, and Conclusions.*
The Talmud of the Land of Israel: An Academic Commentary to the Second, Third, and Fourth Divisions. 28 vols. in 31. South Florida Academic Commentary Series. Atlanta: Scholars Press, 1998–1999.
Vol. 1. *Yerushalmi Tractate Berakhot.*
Vol. 2. *Yerushalmi Tractate Shabbat.*
  A. *Chapters One through Ten.*
  B. *Chapters Eleven through Twenty-Four, and the Structure of Yerushalmi Shabbat.*
Vol. 3. *Yerushalmi Tractate Erubin.*
Vol. 4. *Yerushalmi Tractate Yoma.*
Vol. 5. *Yerushalmi Tractate Pesahim.*
  A. *Chapters One through Six.*
  B. *Chapters Seven through Ten, and the Structure of Yerushalmi Pesahim.*
Vol. 6. *Yerushalmi Tractate Sukkah.*
Vol. 7. *Yerushalmi Tractate Besah.*
Vol. 8. *Yerushalmi Tractate Taanit.*
Vol. 9. *Yerushalmi Tractate Megillah.*
Vol. 10. *Yerushalmi Tractate Rosh Hashanah.*
Vol. 11. *Yerushalmi Tractate Hagigah.*
Vol. 12. *Yerushalmi Tractate Moed Qatan.*
Vol. 13. *Yerushalmi Tractate Yebamot.*
  A. *Chapters One through Ten.*
  B. *Yerushalmi Tractate Yebamot: Chapters Eleven through Seventeen, and the Structure of Yerushalmi Yebamot.*
Vol. 14. *Yerushalmi Tractate Ketubot.*
Vol. 15. *Yerushalmi Tractate Nedarim.*
Vol. 16. *Yerushalmi Tractate Nazir.*
Vol. 17. *Yerushalmi Tractate Gittin.*
Vol. 18. *Yerushalmi Tractate Qiddushin.*
Vol. 19. *Yerushalmi Tractate Sotah.*
Vol. 20. *Yerushalmi Tractate Baba Qamma.*
Vol. 21. *Yerushalmi Tractate Baba Mesia.*
Vol. 22. *Yerushalmi Tractate Baba Batra.*
Vol. 23. *Yerushalmi Tractate Sanhedrin.*
Vol. 24. *Yerushalmi Tractate Makkot.*
Vol. 25. *Yerushalmi Tractate Shebuot.*
Vol. 26. *Yerushalmi Tractate Abodah Zarah.*

Vol. 27. *Yerushalmi Tractate Horayot.*
Vol. 28. *Yerushalmi Tractate Niddah.*
The Native Category-Formations of the Aggadah. 2 vols. Studies in Judaism. Lanham: University Press of America, 2000.
Vol. 1. *The Later Midrash-Compilations.*
Vol. 2. *The Earlier Midrash-Compilations.*
The Hermeneutics of the Rabbinic Category-Formations: An Introduction. Studies in Judaism. Lanham: University Press of America, 2000.
The Comparative Hermeneutics of Rabbinic Judaism. 8 vols. Academic Studies in Ancient Judaism. Binghamton: Global Publications, 2000.
Vol. 1. *Introduction; Berakhot and Seder Mo'ed.*
Vol. 2. *Seder Nashim.*
Vol. 3. *Seder Neziqin.*
Vol. 4. *Seder Qodoshim.*
Vol. 5. *Seder Tohorot: Part Kelim through Parah.*
Vol. 6. *Seder Tohorot: Tohorot through Uqsin.*
Vol. 7. *The Generic Hermeneutics of the Halakhah: A Handbook.*
Vol. 8. *Why This, Not That? Ways Not Taken in the Halakhic Category-Formations of the Mishnah-Tosefta-Yerushalmi-Bavli.*

7. Constructive and Comparative Theology

From Description to Conviction

Fellowship in Judaism: The First Century and Today. London: Valentine, Mitchell, 1963.
History and Torah: Essays on Jewish Learning. New York: Schocken Books, 1964. Paperback ed., 1967. London: Valentine, Mitchell, 1965.
Judaism in the Secular Age: Essays on Fellowship, Community, and Freedom. London: Valentine Mitchell, and New York: Ktav, 1970.
Editor: *Contemporary Judaic Fellowship: In Theory and in Practice.* New York: Ktav, 1972.
Editor: *Understanding Jewish Theology: Classical Themes and Modern Perspectives.* New York: Ktav, 1973. 5th printing: 1992. Reprint: Classics in Judaic Studies. Binghamton: Global Publications/SUNY, 2001.
The Glory of God Is Intelligence: Four Lectures on the Role of Intellect in Judaism. Introduction by S. Kent Brown. Religious Studies Monograph Series 3. Provo: Religious Studies Center, Brigham Young University, 1978.
Stranger at Home: Zionism, "The Holocaust," and American Judaism. Chicago: University of Chicago Press, 1980. Paperback ed., 1985. 2d printing, 1985. 3d printing, 1988. Paperback reprint: South Florida – Rochester – St. Louis Studies on Religion and the Social Order. Atlanta: Scholars Press, 1997.
Tzedakah: Can Jewish Philanthropy Buy Jewish Survival? Chappaqua: Rossel, 1982. 2d printing, 1983. 4th printing, 1988. 5th printing: Brown Judaic Studies. Atlanta: Scholars Press, 1990. 6th printing, New York: Union of American Hebrew Congregations, 1997.
The Jewish War against the Jews: Reflections on Golah, Shoah, and Torah. New York: Ktav, 1984.
Israel in America: A Too-Comfortable Exile? Boston: Beacon, 1985. Paperback ed., 1986. 2d printing: Studies in Judaism. Lanham: University Press of America, 1990. 3d printing, 1994.
Editor: *To Grow in Wisdom: An Anthology of Abraham Joshua Heschel.* With Noam M. M. Neusner. New York: Madison Books, 1989.

Who, Where, and What Is "Israel"? Zionist Perspectives on Israeli and American Judaism. Studies in Judaism. Lanham: University Press of America, 1989.

The Religious World of Contemporary Judaism: Observations and Convictions. Brown Judaic Studies. Atlanta: Scholars Press, 1989.

The Bible and Us: A Priest and a Rabbi Read the Scriptures Together. With Andrew M. Greeley. New York: Warner Books, 1990. Trade paperback ed., 1991. Jewish Book Club Alternative Selection.

   Portuguese translation: *A Bíblia e Nós: Um padre e um rabino interpretam as Sagradas Escrituras.* São Paulo: Editora Siciliano, 1994.

   Spanish translation: *La Biblia y Nosotros.* Madrid: Editora Planeta, 1995.

   2d ed., rev.: *Common Ground: A Priest and a Rabbi Read the Scriptures Together.* Cleveland: Pilgrim Press, 1996.

Jews and Christians: The Myth of a Common Tradition. New York and London: Trinity Press International and SCM Press, 1990. Reprint: Classics in Judaic Studies. Binghamton: Global Publications, 2000.

The Foundations of the Theology of Judaism: An Anthology. 3 vols. 1990–1992.

   Vol. 1. *God.* Northvale, N.J.: Jason Aronson, 1990. Jewish Book Club Main Selection.

   Vol. 2. *Torah.* South Florida Studies in the History of Judaism. Atlanta: Scholars Press, 1992.

   Vol. 3. *Israel.* South Florida Studies in the History of Judaism. Atlanta: Scholars Press, 1992.

Telling Tales: Making Sense of Christian and Judaic Nonsense—the Urgency and Basis for Judaeo-Christian Dialogue. Louisville: Westminster/John Knox Press, 1993.

A Rabbi Talks with Jesus: An Intermillennial, Interfaith Exchange. New York: Doubleday, 1993. Jewish Book Club Main Selection, February 1993. Paperback ed.: New York: Image Books, 1994.

   Italian translation: *Disputa immaginaria tra un rabbino e Gesù: Quale maestro seguire?* Casale Monferrato: Redizioni Piemme, 1996.

   Swedish translation: *En rabbin medtalar med Jesus.* Stockholm: Verbum, 1996.

   German translation: *Ein Rabbi Spricht mit Jesus: Ein jüdisch-christlicher Dialogue.* Munich: Claudius, 1997.

   Polish translation under contract.

   2d ed.: *A Rabbi Talks with Jesus.* Montreal and Kingston: McGill-Queens University Press, and Ithaca: Cornell University Press, 2000. 2d printing, 2001.

Editor: *Judaism Transcends Catastrophe: God, Torah, and Israel Beyond the Holocaust.* 5 vols. Macon, Ga.: Mercer University Press, 1994–1997.

   Vol. 1. *Faith Renewed: The Judaic Affirmation Beyond the Holocaust.* 1994.

   Vol. 2. *God Commands.* 1995.

   Vol. 3. *The Torah Teaches.* 1996.

   Vol. 4. *Eternal Israel Endures.* 1997.

   Vol. 5. *Faith Seeking Understanding: The Tasks of Theology in Twenty-First Century Judaism.* 1997.

Judaism in the New Testament: Practices and Beliefs. With Bruce D. Chilton. London: Routledge, 1995.

Children of the Flesh, Children of the Promise: An Argument with Paul about Judaism as an Ethnic Religion. Cleveland: Pilgrim Press, 1995.

Christianity and Judaism: The Formative Categories. With Bruce D. Chilton. 3 vols. Philadelphia: Trinity Press International, 1995–1997.

   Vol. 1. *Revelation: The Torah and the Bible.* 1995.

   Vol. 2. *The Body of Faith: Israel and Church.* 1997.

   Vol. 3. *God in the World.* 1997.

The Intellectual Foundations of Christian and Jewish Discourse: The Philosophy of Religious Argument. With Bruce D. Chilton. London: Routledge, 1997.

Editor: *Forging a Common Future: Catholic, Judaic, and Protestant Relations for a New Millennium.* Cleveland: Pilgrim Press, 1997.

Judaeo-Christian Debates: God, Kingdom, Messiah. With Bruce D. Chilton. Minneapolis: Fortress Press, 1998. Choice, List of Fifty Best Academic Books of 1998.

Types of Authority in Formative Christianity and Judaism: Institutional, Charismatic, and Intellectual. With Bruce D. Chilton. London: Routledge, 1999.

Jewish and Christian Doctrines: The Classics Compared. With Bruce D. Chilton. London: Routledge, 1999.

Virtues and Vices: Stories of the Moral Life. With Andrew M. Greeley and Mary G. Durkin. Louisville: Westminster/John Knox Press, 1999. Catholic Book Club Selection, 1999.

Talmud Torah: Ways to God's Presence through Learning. New York and Jerusalem: Gefen, 2000.

Comparing Spiritualities: Formative Christianity and Judaism on Finding Life and Meeting Death. With Bruce D. Chilton. Harrisburg: Trinity Press International, 2000.

Editor: *The Missing Jesus: Rabbinic Judaism and the New Testament.* With Craig Evans and Bruce D. Chilton. Binghamton: Global Publications for International Studies in Formative Christianity and Judaism, 2000.

Editor: *His Brother's Keeper: James the Just and His Mission.* With Bruce D. Chilton. Louisville: Westminster/John Knox Press, 2001.

Planned

Comparative Theology: Judaism and Christianity. With Bruce D. Chilton.

Comparative Theology: Judaism and Christianity—a Sourcebook. With Bruce D. Chilton.

8. Exposition of Problems of Method and Auseinandersetzungen *with Other Viewpoints*

Editor: *The Formation of the Babylonian Talmud: Studies on the Achievements of Late Nineteenth and Twentieth Century Historical and Literary-Critical Research.* Leiden: Brill, 1970. Reprint: Classics in Judaic Studies. Binghamton: Global Publications, 2002.

Editor: *The Modern Study of the Mishnah.* Leiden: Brill, 1973. Reprint: Classics in Judaic Studies. Binghamton: Global Publications, 2002.

Editor: *Soviet Views of Talmudic Judaism: Five Papers by Yu. A. Solodukho.* Leiden: Brill, 1973.

Method and Meaning in Ancient Judaism. Brown Judaic Studies. Missoula: Scholars Press, 1979. 2d printing, 1983.

Second Series. Brown Judaic Studies. Chico: Scholars Press, 1980.

Third Series. Brown Judaic Studies. Chico: Scholars Press, 1980.

Fourth Series. Brown Judaic Studies. Atlanta: Scholars Press, 1989.

Editor: *The Study of Ancient Judaism.* 2 vols. New York: Ktav, 1981. 2d printing: South Florida Studies in the History of Judaism. Atlanta: Scholars Press, 1992.

Vol. 1. *Mishnah, Midrash, Siddur.*

Vol. 2. *The Palestinian and Babylonian Talmuds.*

Editor: *Take Judaism, for Example: Studies toward the Comparison of Religions.* Chicago: University of Chicago Press, 1983. 2d printing: South Florida Studies in the History of Judaism. Atlanta: Scholars Press, 1992. Reprint: Classics in Judaic Studies. Binghamton: Global Publications, 2001.

From Mishnah to Scripture: The Problem of the Unattributed Saying. Brown Judaic Studies. Chico: Scholars Press, 1984. Reprise and reworking of materials in *A History of the Mishnaic Law of Purities.*

In Search of Talmudic Biography: The Problem of the Attributed Saying. Brown Judaic Studies. Chico: Scholars Press, 1984. Reprise and reworking of materials in *Eliezer ben Hyrcanus: The Tradition and the Man.*

Ancient Judaism: Debates and Disputes. Brown Judaic Studies. Chico: Scholars Press, 1984.

Second Series. South Florida Studies in the History of Judaism. Atlanta: Scholars Press, 1990.

Third Series. *Essays on the Formation of Judaism, Dating Sayings, Method in the History of Judaism, the Historical Jesus, Publishing Too Much, and Other Current Issues.* South Florida Studies in the History of Judaism. Atlanta: Scholars Press, 1993.

Fourth Series. *Historical, Literary, Theological, and Religious Issues.* South Florida Studies in the History of Judaism. Atlanta: Scholars Press, 1996.

The Peripatetic Saying: The Problem of the Thrice-Told Tale in Talmudic Literature. Brown Judaic Studies. Chico: Scholars Press, 1985. Reprise and reworking of materials in *Development of a Legend* and *Rabbinic Traditions about the Pharisees before 70.* For the 2d ed., see *Peripatetic Parallels,* in section 3, above.

The Memorized Torah: The Mnemonic System of the Mishnah. Brown Judaic Studies. Chico: Scholars Press, 1985. Reprise and reworking of materials in *Rabbinic Traditions about the Pharisees before 70,* vols. 1 and 3, and *A History of the Mishnaic Law of Purities,* vol. 21.

The Public Side of Learning: The Political Consequences of Scholarship in the Context of Judaism. Studies in Religion. Chico: Scholars Press for the American Academy of Religion, 1985.

Reading and Believing: Ancient Judaism and Contemporary Gullibility. Brown Judaic Studies. Atlanta: Scholars Press, 1986.

Ancient Judaism and Modern Category-Formation: "Judaism," "Midrash," "Messianism," and Canon in the Past Quarter-Century. Studies in Judaism. Lanham: University Press of America, 1986.

Oral Tradition in Judaism: The Case of the Mishnah. Albert Bates Lord Monograph Studies in Oral Tradition. New York: Garland, 1987. Restatement of results in various works on the Mishnah together with a fresh account of the problem.

Struggle for the Jewish Mind: Debates and Disputes on Judaism Then and Now. Studies in Judaism. Lanham: University Press of America, 1987.

First Principles of Systemic Analysis: The Case of Judaism in the History of Religion. Studies in Judaism. Lanham: University Press of America, 1988.

The Systemic Analysis of Judaism. Brown Judaic Studies. Atlanta: Scholars Press, 1988.

Why No Gospels in Talmudic Judaism? Brown Judaic Studies. Atlanta: Scholars Press, 1988.

Paradigms in Passage: Patterns of Change in the Contemporary Study of Judaism. Studies in Judaism. Lanham: University Press of America, 1988.

Wrong Ways and Right Ways in the Study of Formative Judaism: Critical Method and Literature, History, and the History of Religion. Brown Judaic Studies. Atlanta: Scholars Press, 1988.

The Ecology of Religion: From Writing to Religion in the Study of Judaism. Nashville: Abingdon, 1989. Paperback ed.: South Florida Studies in the History of Judaism. Atlanta: Scholars Press, 1997.

The Social Study of Judaism: Essays and Reflections. 2 vols. Brown Judaic Studies. Atlanta: Scholars Press, 1989.

Editor: *The Social Foundations of Judaism.* With Calvin Goldscheider. Englewood Cliffs: Prentice Hall, 1989.

Editor: *Religious Writings and Religious Systems: Systemic Analysis of Holy Books in Christianity, Islam, Buddhism, Greco-Roman Religions, Ancient Israel, and Judaism.* 2 vols. Brown Studies in Religion. Atlanta: Scholars Press, 1989.

Vol. 1. *Islam, Buddhism, Greco-Roman Religions, Ancient Israel, and Judaism.*
Vol. 2. *Christianity.*
Studying Classical Judaism: A Primer. Louisville: Westminster/John Knox Press, 1991.
Judaic Law from Jesus to the Mishnah: A Systematic Reply to Professor E. P. Sanders. South Florida Studies in the History of Judaism. Atlanta: Scholars Press, 1993.
Are There Really Tannaitic Parallels to the Gospels? A Refutation of Morton Smith. South Florida Studies in the History of Judaism. Atlanta: Scholars Press, 1993.
Why There Never Was a "Talmud of Caesarea": Saul Lieberman's Mistakes. South Florida Studies in the History of Judaism. Atlanta: Scholars Press, 1994.
The Documentary Foundation of Rabbinic Culture: Mopping Up after Debates with Gerald L. Bruns, S. J. D. Cohen, Arnold Maria Goldberg, Susan Handelman, Christine Hayes, James Kugel, Peter Schaefer, Eliezer Segal, E. P. Sanders, and Lawrence H. Schiffman. South Florida Studies in the History of Judaism. Atlanta: Scholars Press, 1995.
Editor: *Religion and the Social Order: What Kinds of Lessons Does History Teach? Papers at the Conference on the Historical Study of Religion and Society.* South Florida – St. Louis – Rochester Studies in Religion and the Social Order. Atlanta: Scholars Press, 1995.
Editor: *Judaism in Late Antiquity.* 5 vols. in 9. Handbuch der Orientalistik. Judaistik. Leiden: E. J. Brill, 1995–2000. Paperback ed.: Boston: E. J. Brill, 2002.
Vol. 1. *Literary and Archaeological Sources.* 1995.
Vol. 2. *Historical Syntheses.* 1995.
Vol. 3. *Where We Stand: Issues and Debates.*
    Part 1. With Alan J. Avery-Peck. 1999.
    Part 2. 1999.
    Part 3. 2000.
    Part 4. 2000.
Vol. 4. *Death, Life-after-Death, Resurrection, and the World to Come in the Judaisms of Antiquity.* 1999.
Vol. 5. *Judaism at Qumran.*
    Part 1. *Theory of Israel, Way of Life.* With Alan J. Avery-Peck. 1999.
    Part 2. *World View.* With Alan J. Avery-Peck. 1999.
Editor: *Religion and the Political Order: The Ideal Politics of Christianity, Islam, and Judaism.* South Florida – St. Louis – Rochester Studies in Religion and the Social Order. Atlanta: Scholars Press, 1996.
Are the Talmuds Interchangeable? Christine Hayes's Blunder. South Florida Studies in the History of Judaism. Atlanta: Scholars Press, 1996.
The Place of the Tosefta in the Halakhah of Formative Judaism: What Alberdina Houtman Didn't Notice. South Florida Studies in the History of Judaism. Atlanta: Scholars Press, 1998.
How Adin Steinsaltz Misrepresents the Talmud: Four False Propositions from His "Reference Guide." South Florida Studies in the History of Judaism. Atlanta: Scholars Press, 1998.
Editor: *Religious Belief and Economic Behavior: Judaism, Christianity, Islam.* South Florida Studies in the History of Judaism. Atlanta: Scholars Press, 1999.
Editor: *Religion and Economics: New Perspectives.* With Bruce D. Chilton. Academic Studies of Religion and the Social Order. Binghamton: Global Publications, 2000.
Editor: *Judaism in Late Antiquity.* Part 5. *The Judaism of Qumran:. A Systemic Reading of the Dead Sea Scrolls.* Handbuch der Orientalistik. Leiden: Brill, 2000.
Vol. 1. *Way of Life.*
Vol. 2. *World View and Theory of Israel.* With Alan J. Avery-Peck and Bruce D. Chilton.
Contemporary Views of Ancient Judaism: Disputes and Debates. Academic Studies in the History of Judaism. Binghamton: Global Publications, 2001.

Editor: *Religious Texts and Material Contexts*. With James F. Strange. Studies in Ancient Judaism. Lanham: University Press of America, 2001.
The Three Questions of Formative Judaism: History, Literature, and Religion. Brill Reference Library of Judaism. Leiden: Brill, 2002.

9. *Restatement of Results*

Systematic Haute Vulgarisation *for the Wider Scholarly World*

Early Rabbinic Judaism: Historical Studies in Religion, Literature, and Art. Leiden: Brill, 1975. Reprint: Classics in Judaic Studies. Binghamton: Global Publications, 2002.
The Academic Study of Judaism: Essays and Reflections. New York: Ktav Publishing House, 1975. 2d printing: Brown Judaic Studies. Chico: Scholars Press, 1982.
Second Series. New York: Ktav Publishing House, 1977.
Third Series. *Three Contexts of Jewish Learning*. New York: Ktav Publishing House, 1980.
Talmudic Judaism in Sasanian Babylonia: Essays and Studies. Leiden: Brill, 1976.
Judaism in the American Humanities. Brown Judaic Studies. Chico: Scholars Press, 1981.
Second Series. *Jewish Learning and the New Humanities*. Brown Judaic Studies. Chico: Scholars Press, 1983.
Das pharisäische und talmudische Judentum. Edited by Hermann Lichtenberger. Foreword by Martin Hengel. Tübingen: J. C. B. Mohr (Paul Siebeck), 1984.
Formative Judaism: Religious, Historical, and Literary Studies. 1982–1993.
First Series. Brown Judaic Studies. Chico: Scholars Press, 1982.
Second Series. Brown Judaic Studies. Chico: Scholars Press, 1983.
Third Series. *Torah, Pharisees, and Rabbis*. Brown Judaic Studies. Chico: Scholars Press, 1983.
Fourth Series. *Problems of Classification and Composition*. Brown Judaic Studies. Chico: Scholars Press, 1984.
Fifth Series. *Revisioning the Written Records of a Nascent Religion*. Brown Judaic Studies. Chico: Scholars Press, 1985.
Sixth Series. Brown Judaic Studies. Atlanta: Scholars Press, 1989.
Seventh Series. *The Formation of Judaism, Intentionality, Feminization of Judaism, and Other Current Results*. South Florida Studies in the History of Judaism. Atlanta: Scholars Press, 1993.
Major Trends in Formative Judaism. Brown Judaic Studies. Chico: Scholars Press, 1983–1985.
First Series. *Society and Symbol in Political Crisis*. 1983.
Second Series. *Texts, Contents, and Contexts*. 1984.
Third Series. *The Three Stages in the Formation of Judaism*. 1985.
The Pharisees: Rabbinic Perspectives. New York: Ktav Publishing House, 1985. Reprise of *Rabbinic Traditions about the Pharisees before 70*.
Israel and Iran in Talmudic Times: A Political History. Studies in Judaism. Lanham: University Press of America, 1986. Reprise of materials in *A History of the Jews in Babylonia*, parts of ch. 1 of each volume of vols. 2–5. Jewish Book Club Selection, 1988.
Judaism, Christianity, and Zoroastrianism in Talmudic Babylonia. Studies in Judaism. Lanham: University Press of America, 1986. Reprise of materials in *A History of the Jews in Babylonia*, parts of ch. 1 of each volume of vols. 2–5, and of *Aphrahat and Judaism*. Reprint: Brown Judaic Studies. Atlanta: Scholars Press, 1990.
Israel's Politics in Sasanian Iran: Jewish Self-Government in Talmudic Times. Studies in

Judaism. Lanham: University Press of America, 1986. Reprise of materials in *A History of the Jews in Babylonia*, parts of ch. 2 of each volume of vols. 2–5.
The Religious Study of Judaism. 4 vols. Studies in Judaism. Lanham: University Press of America, 1986–1988.
    Vol. 1. *Description, Analysis, Interpretation.* 1986.
    Vol. 2. *The Centrality of Context.* 1986.
    Vol. 3. *Context, Text, and Circumstance.* 1987.
    Vol. 4. *Ideas of History, Ethics, Ontology, and Religion in Formative Judaism.* 1988.
Understanding Seeking Faith. Essays on the Case of Judaism. Vols. 1–3: Brown Judaic Studies. Atlanta: Scholars Press, 1986–1989. Vol. 4: South Florida Studies in the History of Judaism. Atlanta: Scholars Press, 1995.
    Vol. 1. *Debates on Method, Reports of Results.* 1986.
    Vol. 2. *Literature, Religion, and the Social Study of Judaism.* 1987.
    Vol. 3. *Society, History, and the Political and Philosophical Uses of Judaism.* 1989.
    Vol. 4. *Judaism Then and Now.* 1995.
The Wonder-Working Lawyers of Talmudic Babylonia: The Theory and Practice of Judaism in Its Formative Age. Studies in Judaism. Lanham: University Press of America, 1987. Reprise of materials in *A History of the Jews in Babylonia*, vols. 2–5.
School, Court, Public Administration: Judaism and Its Institutions in Talmudic Babylonia. Brown Judaic Studies. Atlanta: Scholars Press, 1987. Reprise of materials in *A History of the Jews in Babylonia*, vols. 3–5.
A Religion of Pots and Pans? Modes of Philosophical and Theological Discourse in Ancient Judaism—Essays and a Program. Brown Judaic Studies. Atlanta: Scholars Press, 1988.
Medium and Message in Judaism. First Series. Brown Judaic Studies. Atlanta: Scholars Press, 1989.
Lectures on Judaism in the Academy and in the Humanities. South Florida Studies in the History of Judaism. Atlanta: Scholars Press, 1990.
Lectures on Judaism in the History of Religion. South Florida Studies in the History of Judaism. Atlanta: Scholars Press, 1990.
The Formation of Judaism in Retrospect and Prospect. South Florida Studies in the History of Judaism. Atlanta: Scholars Press, 1991.
The Twentieth-Century Construction of "Judaism": Essays on the Religion of Torah in the History of Religion. South Florida Studies in the History of Judaism. Atlanta: Scholars Press, 1991.
The City of God in Judaism, and Other Methodological and Comparative Studies. South Florida Studies in the History of Judaism. Atlanta: Scholars Press, 1991.
Åbo Addresses and Other Recent Essays on Judaism in Time and Eternity. South Florida Studies in the History of Judaism. Atlanta: Scholars Press, 1994.
Rabbinic Judaism in the Formative Age: Disputes and Debates. South Florida Studies in the History of Judaism. Atlanta: Scholars Press, 1994.
Judaism after the Death of "the Death of God": The Canterbury Addresses and Other Essays on the Renaissance of Judaism in Contemporary Jewry. South Florida Studies in the History of Judaism. Atlanta: Scholars Press, 1994.
Formative Judaism. New Series. 2 vols. South Florida Studies in the History of Judaism. Atlanta: Scholars Press, 1996–1997.
    Vol. 1. 1996. *Current Issues and Arguments.*
    Vol. 2. *Chapters on Form-History, Documentary Description, and the Social, Religious, and Theological Study of Judaism.* 1997.
Religion and Law: How through Halakhah Judaism Sets Forth Its Theology and Philosophy. South Florida Studies in the History of Judaism. Atlanta: Scholars Press, 1996.
Uppsala Addresses and Other Recent Essays and Reviews on Judaism Then and Now. South Florida Studies in the History of Judaism. Atlanta: Scholars Press, 1996.

The Mind of Classical Judaism. 4 vols. South Florida Studies in the History of Judaism. Atlanta: Scholars Press, 1997.

Vol. 1. *The Philosophy and Political Economy of Formative Judaism: The Mishnah's System of the Social Order.*

Vol. 2. *Modes of Thought: Making Connections and Drawing Conclusions.*

Vol. 3. *From Philosophy to Religion.*

Vol. 4. *What Is "Israel"? Social Thought in the Formative Age.*

Messages to Moscow, and Other Current Lectures on Learning and Community in Judaism. South Florida Studies in the History of Judaism. Atlanta: Scholars Press, 1998.

Jewish Law from Moses to the Mishnah: The Hiram College Lectures on Religion for 1999 and Other Papers. South Florida Studies in the History of Judaism. Atlanta: Scholars Press, 1998.

Formative Judaism: History, Hermeneutics, Law, and Religion—Ten Recent Essays. Academic Studies in the History of Judaism. Binghamton: Global Publications, 2000.

A Reader's Guide to the Talmud. Leiden: Brill, 2001.

How the Talmud Works. 2 vols. Leiden: Brill, 2001.

Vol. 1. *The Bavli's Coherent Intellectual Program.*

Vol. 2. *The Bavli's Formal Cogency.*

The Halakhah: Religious and Historical Perspectives. Leiden: E. J. Brill, 2001.

10. Toward the Creation of the New Academy:
i. Scholarly Books Organized and Edited

Editor: *Report of the 1965–1966 Seminar on Religions in Antiquity.* Hanover: Dartmouth College Comparative Studies Center, 1966. Reprint, 1984.

Editor: *Religions in Antiquity: Essays in Memory of Erwin Ramsdell Goodenough.* Supplements to Numen 14. Leiden: Brill, 1968. 2d printing, 1970; third printing, 1972.

Editor: *Christianity, Judaism, and Other Greco-Roman Cults: Studies for Morton Smith at Sixty.* 4 vols. Leiden: Brill, 1975.

Vol. 1. *New Testament.*

Vol. 2. *Early Christianity.*

Vol. 3. *Judaism before 70.*

Vol. 4. *Judaism after 70, Other Greco-Roman Cults.*

Editor: *Essays in Honor of Yigael Yadin.* With Geza Vermes. Special issue of *Journal of Jewish Studies,* 1982.

Editor: *The New Humanities and Academic Disciplines: The Case of Jewish Studies.* Madison: University of Wisconsin Press, 1984. On graduate education in Judaic studies.

Editor: *New Perspectives on Ancient Judaism.* 3 vols. Studies in Judaism. Lanham: University Press, 1987.

Vol. 1. *Contents and Contexts in Judaic and Christian Interpretation: Formative Judaism.* Essays in honor of Howard Clark Kee. 2d printing: Brown Judaic Studies. Atlanta: Scholars Press, 1990.

Vol. 2. *Contents and Contexts in Judaic and Christian Interpretation: Ancient Israel, Formative Christianity.* Essays in honor of Howard Clark Kee.

Vol. 3. *Judaic and Christian Interpretation of Texts: Contents and Contexts.*

Editor: *Religion and Society in Ancient Times: Essays in Honor of Howard Clark Kee.* Philadelphia: Fortress Press, 1988.

Editor: *From Ancient Israel to Modern Judaism: Intellect in Quest of Understanding—Essays in Honor of Marvin Fox.* 4 vols. Brown Judaic Studies. Atlanta: Scholars Press, 1989.

Vol. 1. *What Is at Stake in the Judaic Quest for Understanding? Judaic Learning and the*

Locus of Education; Ancient Israel; Formative Christianity; Judaism in the Formative Age—Religion.

Vol. 2. *Judaism in the Formative Age—Theology and Literature; Judaism in the Middle Ages—the Encounter with Christianity, the Encounter with Scripture; Philosophy and Theology.*

Vol. 3. *Judaism in the Middle Ages—Philosophers; Hasidism; Messianism in Modern Times; the Modern Age—Philosophy.*

Vol. 4. *The Modern Age—Theology, Literature, History.*

Editor: *Approaches to Ancient Judaism.* Vol. 6. *Studies in the Ethnography and Literature of Judaism.* Brown Judaic Studies. Atlanta: Scholars Press, 1989.

Editor: *Approaches to Ancient Judaism.* New Series. Vols. 1–4, 7, 9–16. South Florida Studies in the History of Judaism. Atlanta: Scholars Press, 1991–1999.

Vol. 1. 1991.

Vol. 2. 1991.

Vol. 3. *Historical and Literary Studies.* 1993.

Vol. 4. *Religious and Theological Studies.* 1993.

Vol. 7. 1995.

Vol. 9. 1996.

Vol. 10. 1997.

Vol. 11. 1997.

Vol. 12. 1997.

Vol. 13. 1998.

Vol. 14. 1998.

Vol. 15. 1999.

Vol. 16. 1999.

Editor: *The Origins of Judaism: Religion, History, and Literature in Late Antiquity.* With William Scott Green. 13 vols. in 20. New York: Garland Press, 1991. Reprinted scholarly essays, with introductions.

Vol. 1. *Normative Judaism.* 3 vols.

Vol. 2. *The Pharisees and Other Sects.* 2 vols.

Vol. 3. *Judaism and Christianity in the First Century.* 2 vols.

Vol. 4. *Controversies in the Study of Judaic Religion and Theology.*

Vol. 5. *History of the Jews in the Second and First Centuries B.C.* 2 vols.

Vol. 6. *History of the Jews in the First Century of the Common Era.*

Vol. 7. *History of the Jews in the Second Century of the Common Era.*

Vol. 8. *History of the Jews in the Second through Seventh Centuries of the Common Era.* 2 vols.

Vol. 9. *The Literature of Formative Judaism: The Mishnah and the Tosefta.*

Vol. 10. *The Literature of Formative Judaism: The Talmuds.*

Vol. 11. *The Literature of Formative Judaism: The Midrash-Compilations.* 2 vols.

Vol. 12. *The Literature of Formative Judaism: The Targumim and Other Jewish Writings in Late Antiquity.*

Vol. 13. *The Literature of Formative Judaism: Controversies on the Literature of Formative Judaism.*

Editor: *Judaism in Cold War America, 1945–1990.* 10 vols. New York: Garland Press, 1993. Reprinted scholarly essays, with introductions.

Vol. 1. *The Challenge of America: Can Judaism Survive in Freedom?*

Vol. 2. *In the Aftermath of the Holocaust.*

Vol. 3. *Israel and Zion in American Judaism: The Zionist Fulfillment.*

Vol. 4. *Judaism and Christianity: The New Relationship.*

Vol. 5. *The Religious Renewal of Jewry.*

Vol. 6. *The Reformation of Reform Judaism.*

Vol. 7. *Conserving Conservative Judaism.*

Vol. 8. *The Alteration of Orthodoxy.*

Vol. 9. *The Academy and Traditions of Jewish Learning.*
Vol. 10. *The Rabbinate in America: Reshaping an Ancient Calling.*
Ancient Judaism: Religious and Theological Perspectives. First Series. South Florida Studies in the History of Judaism. Atlanta: Scholars Press, 1996.
Chairman of the Editorial Board: *The Annual of Rabbinic Judaism: Ancient, Medieval, and Modern.* 3 vols. Leiden: Brill, 1998–2000.
Vol. 1. 1998.
Vol. 2. 1999.
Vol. 3. 2000.
Editor: *Marvin Fox: Collected Essays on Philosophy and on Judaism.* 3 vols. Academic Studies in the History of Judaism. Binghamton: Global Publications, 2001.
Vol. 1. *Greek Philosophy, Maimonides.*
Vol. 2. *Some Philosophers.*
Vol. 3. *Ethics, Reflections.*

Now Under Way

Chairman of the Editorial Board: *The Review of Rabbinic Judaism: Ancient, Medieval, and Modern.* Vols. 4–5. Leiden: Brill, 2001–2002.
Vol. 4, nos. 1–2. 2001.
Vol. 5, nos. 1–3. 2002.
Editor: *George H. E. Nickelsburg in Perspective: An On-going Dialogue of Learning.* Leiden and Boston: Brill, 2003.

Planned

Chairman of the Editorial Board: *The Review of Rabbinic Judaism: Ancient, Medieval, and Modern.* Vol. 5, nos. 1–3. Leiden: Brill, 2003.

11. *Toward the Creation of the New Academy: ii. Providing Textbooks for Undergraduate Instruction and Trade Books for the Public at Large*

The Way of Torah: An Introduction to Judaism. Religious Life of Man, ed. Frederick Streng. Encino: Dickenson, 1970. 2d printing, 1971. 3d printing, 1971. 2d ed., rev., 1973. 3d printing, 1976. 3d ed., thoroughly rev.: Belmont: Wadsworth, 1979. 3d printing, 1980. 4th printing, 1982. 5th printing, 1983. 6th printing, 1985. 7th printing, 1986. 4th ed., completely rev. and rewritten, 1988. 2d printing, 1988. 3d printing, 1990. 4th printing, 1991. 5th ed., rev. and augmented, 1992. 6th ed.: Living Religion of Man, ed. Charles Hallisey. Belmont: Wadsworth/Thompson International, 1997. 7th ed.: rev., and augmented, 2003.
There We Sat Down: Talmudic Judaism in the Making. Nashville: Abingdon, 1972. 2d printing: New York: Ktav, 1978.
American Judaism: Adventure in Modernity. Englewood Cliffs: Prentice-Hall, 1972. 2d printing, 1973. 3d printing, 1976. 4th printing: New York: Ktav, 1978.
Editor: *Life of Torah: Readings in the Jewish Religious Experience.* Encino: Dickenson, 1974. 3d printing: Belmont: Wadsworth, l980. 6th printing, 1984. 7th printing, 1987.
Editor: *Understanding Rabbinic Judaism: From Talmudic to Modern Times.* New York: Ktav, 1974. 2d printing, 1977. 4th printing, 1985. Reprint: Classics in Judaic Studies. Binghamton: Global Publications/SUNY, 2001.
First Century Judaism in Crisis: Yohanan ben Zakkai and the Renaissance of Torah. Nashville: Abingdon, 1975. 2d printing: New York: Ktav, 1981.

Editor: *Understanding American Judaism: Toward the Description of a Modern Religion.* 2 vols.
New York: Ktav, 1975. Reprint: Classics in Judaic Studies. Binghamton: Global
Publications/SUNY, 2001.
Vol. 1. *The Synagogue and the Rabbi.*
Vol. 2. *The Sectors of American Judaism: Reform, Orthodoxy, Conservatism, and Recon-
structionism.*
Between Time and Eternity: The Essentials of Judaism. Encino: Dickenson, 1976. 5th print-
ing: Belmont: Wadsworth, 1983. 6th printing, 1987.
Our Sages, God, and Israel: An Anthology of the Yerushalmi. Chappaqua: Rossel, 1984.
Jewish Book Club Selection, 1985.
How to Grade Your Professors and Other Unexpected Advice. Boston: Beacon, 1984. 2d print-
ing, 1984.
Genesis and Judaism: The Perspective of Genesis Rabbah—an Analytical Anthology. Brown
Judaic Studies. Atlanta: Scholars Press, 1986.
From Testament to Torah: An Introduction to Judaism in Its Formative Age. Englewood Cliffs:
Prentice Hall, 1987.
Christian Faith and the Bible of Judaism. Grand Rapids: Wm. B. Eerdmans, 1987. 2d
printing: Brown Judaic Studies. Atlanta: Scholars Press, 1990.
Confronting Creation: How Judaism Reads Genesis—an Anthology of Genesis Rabbah.
Columbia: University of South Carolina Press, 1991.
An Introduction to Judaism: Textbook and Anthology. Louisville: Westminster/John Knox
Press, 1992. 2d printing, 1999.
A Short History of Judaism: Three Meals, Three Epochs. Minneapolis: Fortress Press, 1992.
*Sources of the Transformation of Judaism: From Philosophy to Religion in the Classics of
Judaism—a Reader.* South Florida Studies in the History of Judaism. Atlanta:
Scholars Press, 1992.
The Mishnah: Introduction and Reader—an Anthology. Library of Rabbinic Literature.
Philadelphia: Trinity Press International, 1992.
Fortress Introduction to American Judaism: What the Books Say, What the People Do.
Minneapolis: Fortress Press, 1993.
Israel's Love Affair with God: Song of Songs. Bible of Judaism Library. Philadelphia:
Trinity Press International, 1993.
*Classical Judaism: Torah, Learning, Virtue—an Anthology of the Mishnah, Talmud, and
Midrash.* 3 vols. Essen and New York: Peter Lang, 1993.
Vol. 1. *Torah.*
Vol. 2. *Learning.*
Vol. 3. *Virtue.*
Conservative, American, and Jewish—I Wouldn't Want It Any Other Way. Lafayette:
Huntington House, 1993. Jewish Book Club Selection, March 1994.
Editor: *World Religions in America: An Introduction.* Louisville: Westminster/John Knox
Press, 1994. Library Guild Selection, Methodist Church Libraries, 1994. Jewish
Book Club Selection, July 1995. 3d printing, 1996. 4th printing, 1998. 2d ed.,
1999. Reprinted annually. 3d ed., 2002.
*"Your People Will Be My People": The Mother of the Messiah in Judaism; How the Rabbis
Read the Book of Ruth—an Anthology of Ruth Rabbah.* Bible of Judaism Library.
Philadelphia: Trinity Press International, 1994.
*The Woman Who Saved Israel: How the Rabbis Read the Book of Esther—an Anthology of Esther
Rabbah.* Bible of Judaism Library. Philadelphia: Trinity Press International, 1994.
How Judaism Reads the Torah. 4 vols. Essen and New York: Peter Lang, 1994.
Vol. 1. *How Judaism Reads the Ten Commandments: An Anthology of the Mekhilta Attributed
to R. Ishmael.*
Vol. 2. *"You Shall Love Your Neighbor as Yourself": How Judaism Defines the Covenant to
Be a Holy People—an Anthology of Sifra to Leviticus.*

Vol. 3. *Wayward Women in the Wilderness: An Anthology of Sifré to Numbers.*
Vol. 4. *"I Deal Death and I Give Life": How Classical Judaism Confronts Holocaust—an Anthology of Sifré to Deuteronomy.*
Scripture and Midrash in Judaism. 3 vols. Frankfurt and New York: Peter Lang, 1994.
   Vol. 1 *Exegesis: An Anthology of Sifra and the two Sifrés.*
   Vol. 2. *Proposition: An Anthology of Genesis Rabbah, Leviticus Rabbah, Pesiqta deRab Kahana.*
   Vol. 3. *Theology: An Anthology of Lamentations Rabbati, Song of Songs Rabbah, Esther Rabbah, Ruth Rabbah.*
The Classics of Judaism: An Introduction to Mishnah, Talmud, and Midrash. Louisville: Westminster/John Knox Press, 1995.
The Talmudic Anthology. 3 vols. Frankfurt and New York: Peter Lang, 1995.
   Vol. 1. *Torah: Issues of Ethics.*
   Vol. 2. *God: Issues of Theology.*
   Vol. 3. *Israel: Issues of Public Policy.*
Judaism in Modern Times: An Introduction and Reader. Oxford: Blackwell, 1995. Romanian translation: Bucharest: Editura Hasefer, 2002.
The Price of Excellence: Universities in Conflict during the Cold War Era. With Noam M. M. Neusner. New York: Continuum, 1995.
The Talmud: Introduction and Reader. South Florida Studies in the History of Judaism. Atlanta: Scholars Press, 1995.
Understanding the Talmud: A Dialogic Approach. Hoboken: Ktav Publishing House, 2000. Reissue of *The Talmud: Introduction and Reader,* with Hebrew texts.
Editor: *Dictionary of Judaism in the Biblical Period, from 450 B.C. to 600 A.D.* 2 vols. New York: MacMillan, 1995. Reprint in 1 vol.: Peabody: Hendrickson, 1999.
Editor: *The Religion Factor: An Introduction to How Religion Matters.* With William Scott Green. Louisville: Westminster/John Knox Press, 1996.
Beyond Catastrophe: The Rabbis' Reading of Isaiah's Vision, Israelite Messiah-Prophecies in Formative Judaism, an Anthology of Pesiqta deRab Kahana for the Seven Sabbaths after the Ninth of Ab. South Florida Studies in the History of Judaism. Atlanta: Scholars Press, 1996.
The Book of Jewish Wisdom: The Talmud of the Well-Considered Life. With Noam M. M. Neusner. New York: Continuum, 1996. Reprint: Classics in Judaic Studies. Binghamton: Global Publications, 2001.
Trading Places: The Intersecting Histories of Christianity and Rabbinic Judaism. With Bruce D. Chilton. Cleveland: Pilgrim Press, 1997.
Trading Places: A Reader and Sourcebook on the Intersecting Histories of Christianity and Rabbinic Judaism. With Bruce D. Chilton. Cleveland: Pilgrim Press, 1997.
Editor: *The Pilgrim Library of World Religions.* 5 vols. Cleveland: Pilgrim Press, 1997–2000.
   Vol. 1. *Christianity, Judaism, Islam, Buddhism, and Hinduism on God.* 1997.
   Vol. 2. *Judaism, Islam, Buddhism, Hinduism and Christianity on Sacred Texts and Authority.* 1998.
   Vol. 3. *Buddhism, Hinduism Christianity, Judaism, and Islam, on Evil and Suffering.* 1999.
   Vol. 4. *Islam, Buddhism, Hinduism, Christianity, and Judaism on Woman and the Family.* 1999.
   Vol. 5. *Hinduism, Christianity, Judaism, Islam, and Buddhism on the Afterlife.* 2000.
Editor: *Signposts on the Way of Torah: A Reader for The Way of Torah.* Living Religion of Man, ed. Charles Hallisey. Belmont: Wadsworth/Thompson International, 1998.
Comparing Religions through Law: Judaism and Islam. With Tamara Sonn. London: Routledge, 1999. Listed in Best books on Law and Religion, 1990–2000, *Journal of Law and Religion,* 2001.
Editor-in-Chief: *The Encyclopaedia of Judaism.* With William Scott Green and Alan J. Avery-Peck. 3 vols. Leiden: E. J. Brill, 1999, and New York: Continuum, 1999.

Under the Auspices of the Museum of Jewish Heritage. Awards: "Book of the Year" Citation, Choice, 2000; American Libraries (American Library Association): Outstanding Reference Sources 2001, selected by Reference Users' Service Association of ALA.

Reaffirming Higher Education. With Noam M. M. Neusner. New Brunswick: Transaction Publishers, 2000.

Judaism and Islam in Practice: A Source Book of the Classical Age. With Tamara Sonn and Jonathan Brockopp. London: Routledge, 2000.

Editor: *Comparing Religious Traditions.* 3 vols. Belmont: Wadsworth, 2000.

Vol. 1. *Judaism, Christianity, Islam, Hinduism, and Buddhism on the Ethics of Family Life: What Do We Owe One Another?*

Vol. 2. *Judaism, Christianity, Islam, Hinduism, and Buddhism on Making an Honest Living: What Do We Owe the Community?*

Vol. 3. *Judaism, Christianity, Islam, Hinduism, and Buddhism on Virtue: What Do We Owe Ourselves?*

Editor: *The Companion to Judaism.* With Alan J. Avery-Peck. Oxford: Blackwells, 2000.

Editor: *The Blackwell Reader in Judaism.* With Alan J. Avery-Peck. Oxford: Blackwells, 2000.

A Handbook of Formative Judaism. Louisville: Westminster/John Knox Press, 2002.

Turning Points: Transformations in the Formation of Judaism. Peabody: Hendrickson, 2002.

Judaism: An Introduction. London and New York: Penguin, 2002.

Under Way

Editor: *The Three Religions of One God: Islam, Christianity, and Judaism.* With Bruce D. Chilton and William Graham. Leiden: Brill, 2002.

Editor: *Encyclopaedia of Judaism.* Supplements 1–3. Leiden: Brill, 2002.

Editor: *Judaism from Moses to Muhammad: An Interpretation—Turning Points and Focal Points.* With Alan Avery-Peck and William Scott Green. Leiden: Brill, 2003.

Editor: *God's Rule: The Politics of World Religions.* Washington: Georgetown University Press, 2003.

12. Toward the Creation of the New Academy: iii. Facing the Future—Children's Textbooks

Learn Mishnah. New York: Behrman, 1978. Reprinted many times since.

Italian translation: *Come si studia la Mishna.* Rome: Unione delle Communità Israelitiche Italiane, 1983.

Learn Talmud. New York: Behrman, 1979. Reprinted many times since.

Meet Our Sages. New York: Behrman, 1980. Reprinted many times since.

Mitzvah. Chappaqua: Rossel, 1981. Reprint, 1983. 3d printing, 1985. Reprinted many times since.